Life Among the Paiutes

Life Among the Paiutes

THEIR WRONGS AND CLAIMS

Sarah Winnemucca Hopkins

PRACTICAL FOX

PORTLAND, OREGON

Harcover ISBN: 978-1-7320603-2-6
Paperback ISBN: 978-1-7320306-3-3
Ebook ISBN: 978-1-7320306-4-0

CONTENTS

I. FIRST MEETING OF PAIUTES AND WHITES

II. DOMESTIC AND SOCIAL MORALITIES

III. WARS AND THEIR CAUSES

IV. CAPTAIN TRUCKEE'S DEATH

V. RESERVATION OF PYRAMID AND MUDDY LAKES

VI. THE MALHEUR AGENCY

VII. THE BANNOCK WAR

VIII. THE YAKIMA AFFAIR

Appendix A

Appendix B

Appendix C

PUBLISHER'S NOTE, 2020

Life Among the Paiutes was first published in 1883, and the words of Sarah Winnemucca Hopkins still stand among the most important and most compelling books on western Native Americans. It's one of the earliest books written by a Native woman, and it details her own life and interactions as an interpreter with settlers and soldiers that came west. It's a story that resonates today and is worth being presented for modern readers in accessible formats.

That meant updating a few things using twenty-first-century publishing conventions and technology without changing the author's words. My goal was to make her book as readable and modern as possible while making very few editorial changes. These include:

· Changing Piutes to the modern spelling used by the tribes today, Paiutes.

· Making spellings, especially of names and places, consistent throughout the text.

· Using consistent capitalization for terms like Spirit Father.

· Using consistent hyphenation of terms like soldier-father.

· Changing terms that used to be two words, such as any one, to the modern spelling: anyone.

· Creating new lines for new speakers in dialog.

· Inserting paragraph breaks when a new topic was introduced.

· Inserting section breaks when a completely new story begins or when a significant amount of time has passed between one scene and the next.

· Clarifying the subject of sentences that used unclear pronouns.

· Using commas in longer sentences to group clauses together for clarity.

· Using em dashes sparingly to set off or emphasize phrases for clarity.

There are many things that are particular to the author's style and so were left as they were in the original, including:

· All italics in the text are the author's.

· Run-on sentences were retained unless they became confusing, in which case a comma or em dash was used.

· Family titles are lowercase, even when used in place of a name, such as father or brother.

· The author's usage of that and which were retained, though style conventions for these terms have changed over the past century.

I chose to delete the footnotes provided by the original editor, Mary Mann, for the same of space and readability. But the letters supporting Winnemucca Hopkins's observations and positions, along with her Notes of appreciation for their support, are included in the appendices.

KRISTEN HALL-GEISLER
PUBLISHER, PRACTICAL FOX

EDITOR'S PREFACE, 1883

My editing has consisted in copying the original manuscript in correct orthography and punctuation, with occasional emendations by the author, of a book which is an heroic act on the part of the writer. Mrs. Hopkins came to the East from the Pacific coast with the courageous purpose of telling in detail to the mass of our people, "extenuating nothing and setting down naught in malice," the story of her people's trials. Finding that in extemporaneous speech she could only speak at one time of a few points, she determined to write out the most important part of what she wished to say. In fighting with her literary deficiencies she loses some of the fervid eloquence which her extraordinary colloquial command of the English language enables her to utter, but I am confident that no one would desire that her own original words should be altered. It is the first outbreak of the American Indian in human literature, and has a single aim, to tell the truth as it lies in the heart and mind of a true patriot, and one whose knowledge of the two races gives her an opportunity of comparing them justly. At this moment, when the United States seem waking up to their duty to the original possessors of our immense territory, it is of the first importance to hear what only an Indian and an Indian woman can tell. To tell it was her own deep impulse, and the dying charge given her by her father, the truly parental chief of his beloved tribe.

MARY MANN

CHAPTER I

FIRST MEETING OF PAIUTES AND WHITES

I WAS BORN somewhere near 1844 but am not sure of the precise time. I was a very small child when the first white people came into our country. They came like a lion—yes, like a roaring lion—and have continued so ever since, and I have never forgotten their first coming. My people were scattered at that time over nearly all the territory now known as Nevada. My grandfather was chief of the entire Paiute nation and was camped near Humboldt Lake with a small portion of his tribe when a party traveling eastward from California was seen coming. When the news was brought to my grandfather, he asked what they looked like. When told that they had hair on their faces and were white, he jumped up and clasped his hands together, and cried aloud, "My white brothers, my long-looked for white brothers, have come at last!"

He immediately gathered some of his leading men and went to the place where the party had gone into camp. Arriving near them, he was commanded to halt in a manner that was readily

1

understood without an interpreter.

Grandpa at once made signs of friendship by throwing down his robe and throwing up his arms to show them he had no weapons, but in vain. They kept him at a distance. He knew not what to do. He had expected so much pleasure in welcoming his white brothers to the best in the land that, after looking at them sorrowfully for a little while, he came away quite unhappy. But he would not give them up so easily. He took some of his most trustworthy men and followed them day after day, camping near them at night and traveling in sight of them by day, hoping in this way to gain their confidence. But he was disappointed, poor dear old soul!

I can imagine his feelings, for I have drunk deeply from the same cup. When I think of my past life and the bitter trials I have endured, I can scarcely believe I live, and yet I do. And with the help of Him who notes the sparrow's fall, I mean to fight for my downtrodden race while life lasts.

Seeing they would not trust him, my grandfather left them, saying, "Perhaps they will come again next year."

Then he summoned his whole people and told them this tradition: "In the beginning of the world there were only four, two girls and two boys. Our forefather and mother were only two, and we are their children. You all know that a great while ago, there was a happy family in this world. One girl and one boy were dark, and the others were white. For a time they got along together without quarrelling, but soon they disagreed, and there was trouble. They were cross to one another and fought, and our parents were very much grieved. They prayed that their children might learn better, but it did not do any good. And afterward the whole household was made so unhappy that the father and mother saw that they must separate their children.

"And then our father took the dark boy and girl, and the white boy and girl, and asked them, 'Why are you so cruel to each other?' They hung down their heads and would not speak. They were ashamed. He said to them, 'Have I not been kind to you all and given you everything your hearts wished for? You do not have to hunt and kill your own game to live upon. You see, my dear children, I have power to call whatsoever kind of game we want to eat, and I also have the power to separate my dear children if they are not good to each other.' So he separated his children by a word. He said, 'Depart from each other, you cruel children. Go across the mighty ocean and do not seek each other's lives.'

"So the light girl and boy disappeared by that one word. And their parents saw them no more, and they were grieved, although they knew their children were happy. And by and by the dark children grew into a large nation, and we believe it is the one we belong to, and that the nation that sprung from the white children will sometime send someone to meet us and heal all the old trouble.

"Now the white people we saw a few days ago must certainly be our white brothers, and I want to welcome them. I want to love them as I love all of you. But they would not let me; they were afraid. But they will come again, and I want you one and all to promise that, should I not live to welcome them myself, you will not hurt a hair on their heads but welcome them as I tried to do."

How good of him to try and heal the wound, and how vain were his efforts! My people had never seen a white man, and yet they existed and were a strong race. The people promised as he wished, and they all went back to their work.

The next year came a great emigration and camped near Humboldt Lake. The name of the man in charge of the trains was Captain Johnson, and they stayed three days to rest their horses, as they had a long journey before them without water. During their stay my grandfather and some of his people called upon them, and they all shook hands, and when our white brothers were going away,

they gave my grandfather a white tin plate. Oh, what a time they
had over that beautiful gift; it was so bright! They say that after
they left, my grandfather called for all his people to come together,
and he then showed them the beautiful gift which he had received
from his white brothers. Everybody was so pleased; nothing like
it was ever seen in our country before. My grandfather thought
so much of it that he bored holes in it and fastened it on his head
and wore it as his hat. He held it in as much admiration as my
white sisters hold their diamond rings or a sealskin jacket. So that
winter they talked of nothing but their white brothers.

The following spring there came great news down the
Humboldt River saying that there were some more of the white
brothers coming, and there was something among them that was
burning all in a blaze. My grandfather asked them what it was like.
They told him it looked like a man; it had legs and hands and a
head, but the head had quit burning, and it was left quite black.
There was the greatest excitement among my people everywhere
about the men in a blazing fire. They were excited because they did
not know there were any people in the world but the two—that is,
the Indians and the whites. They thought that was all of us in the
beginning of the world, and of course we did not know where the
others had come from, and we don't know yet. Ha! Ha! Oh, what
a laughable thing that was! It was two negroes wearing red shirts!

The third year more emigrants came, and that summer
Captain Fremont, who is now General Fremont. My grandfather
met him, and they were soon friends. They met just where the
railroad crosses Truckee River, now called Wadsworth, Nevada.
Captain Fremont gave my grandfather the name of Captain Truckee,
and he also called the river after him. Truckee is an Indian word;
it means *all right* or *very well*. A party of twelve of my people went to
California with Captain Fremont. I do not know just how long
they were gone.

During the time my grandfather was away in California, where he stayed till after the Mexican war, there was a girl baby born in our family. I can just remember it. It must have been in spring, because everything was green. I was away playing with some other children when my mother called me to come to her, so I ran to her. She then asked me to sit down, which I did. She then handed me some beautiful beads and asked me if I would like to buy something with them.

I said, "Yes, mother, some pine nuts."

My mother said, "Would you like something else you can love and play with? Would you like to have a little sister?"

I said, "Yes, dear mother, a little, little sister; not like my sister Mary, for she won't let me play with her. She leaves me and goes with big girls to play."

And then my mother wanted to know if I would give my pretty beads for the little sister. Just then the baby let out such a cry it frightened me, and I jumped up and cried so that my mother took me in her arms and said it was a little sister for me, and not to be afraid. This is all I can remember about it.

WHEN MY grandfather went to California, he helped Captain Fremont fight the Mexicans. When he came back, he told the people what a beautiful country California was. Only eleven returned home, one having died on the way back.

They spoke to their people in the English language, which was very strange to them all. Captain Truckee, my grandfather, was very proud of it indeed. They all brought guns with them. My grandfather would sit down with us for hours and would say over and over again, "Goodee gun, goodee, goodee gun, heap shoot." They also brought some of the soldiers' clothes with all their brass buttons, and my people were very much astonished to see the clothes, and all that time they were peaceable toward their white brothers. They had learned to love them, and they hoped more of them would come. Then my people were less barbarous than they are nowadays.

That same fall, after my grandfather came home, he told my father to take charge of his people and hold the tribe, as he was going back to California with as many of his people as he could get to go with him. So my father took his place as chief of the Paiutes and had it as long as he lived. Then my grandfather started back to California again with about thirty families.

That same fall, very late, the emigrants kept coming. It was this time that our white brothers first came amongst us. They could not get over the mountains, so they had to live with us. It was on Carson River, where the great Carson City stands now. You call my people blood-seeking. My people did not seek to kill them, nor did they steal their horses—no, no, far from it. During the winter my people helped them. They gave them such as they had to eat. They did not hold out their hands and say, "You can't have anything to eat unless you pay me." No, no such word was used by us savages at that time, and the persons I am speaking of are living yet; they could speak for us if they choose to do so.

The following spring, before my grandfather returned home, there was a great excitement among my people on account of fearful news coming from different tribes that the people whom they called their white brothers were killing everybody that came in their way, and all the Indian tribes had gone into the mountains to save their lives. So my father told all his people to go into the mountains and hunt and lay up food for the coming winter. Then we all went into the mountains.

There was a fearful story they told us children. Our mothers told us that the whites were killing everybody and eating them. So we were all afraid of them. Every dust that we could see blowing in the valleys, we would say it was the white people.

In the late fall, my father told his people to go to the rivers and fish, and we all went to the Humboldt River. The women went to work gathering wild seed, which they grind between the rocks. The stones are round, big enough to hold in the hands. The women did this when they got back, and when they had gathered all they could, they put it in one place and covered it with grass, and then over the grass mud. After it is covered, it looks like an Indian wigwam.

Oh, what a fright we all got one morning to hear some white people were coming. Everyone ran as best they could. My poor mother was left with my little sister and me. Oh, I never can forget it. My poor mother was carrying my little sister on her back and trying to make me run, but I was so frightened I could not move my feet. While my poor mother was trying to get me along, my aunt overtook us, and she said to my mother, "Let us bury our girls, or we shall all be killed and eaten up." So they went to work and buried us, and told us if we heard any noise not to cry out, for if we did they would surely kill us and eat us. So our mothers buried me and my cousin, planted sage bushes over our faces to keep the sun from burning them, and there we were left all day.

Oh, can anyone imagine my feelings *buried alive*, thinking every minute that I was to be unburied and eaten up by the people that my grandfather loved so much? With my heart throbbing and not daring to breathe, we lay there all day. It seemed that the night would never come.

Thanks be to God! The night came at last. Oh, how I cried and said, "Oh, father, have you forgotten me? Are you never coming for me?" I cried so I thought my very heartstrings would break.

At last we heard some whispering. We did not dare to whisper to each other, so we lay still. I could hear their footsteps coming nearer and nearer. I thought my heart was coming right out of my mouth. Then I heard my mother say, "It is right here!" Oh, can anyone in this world ever imagine what were my feelings when I was dug up by my poor mother and father? My cousin and I were once more happy in our mothers' and fathers' care, and we were taken to where all the rest were.

I was once buried alive; but my second burial shall be forever, where no father or mother will come and dig me up. It shall not be with throbbing heart that I shall listen for coming footsteps. I shall be in the sweet rest of peace, I, the chieftain's weary daughter.

Well, while we were in the mountains hiding, the people that my grandfather called our white brothers came along to where our winter supplies were. They set everything we had left on fire. It was a fearful sight. It was all we had for the winter, and it was all burnt during that night. My father took some of his men during the night to try and save some of it, but they could not; it had burnt down before they got there.

These were the last white men that came along that fall. My people talked fearfully that winter about those they called our white brothers. My people said they had something like awful thunder and lightning, and with that they killed everything that came in their way.

This whole band of white people perished in the mountains, for it was too late to cross them. We could have saved them, only my people were afraid of them. We never knew who they were or where they came from. So, poor things, they must have suffered fearfully, for they all starved there. The snow was too deep.

EARLY IN the following spring, my father told all his people to go to the mountains, for there would be a great emigration that

summer. He told them he had had a wonderful dream and wanted
to tell them all about it. He said, "Within ten days come together
at the sink of Carson, and I will tell you my dream." The subchiefs
went everywhere to tell their people what my father had told them
to say, and when the time came, we all went to the sink of Carson.

Just about noon, while we were on the way, a great many of
our men came to meet us, all on their horses. Oh, what a beautiful
song they sang for my father as they came near us! We passed them,
and they followed us, and as we came near to the encampment,
every man, woman, and child were out looking for us. They had
a place all ready for us. Oh, how happy everybody was! One could
hear laughter everywhere, and songs were sung by happy women
and children.

My father stood up and told his people to be merry and happy
for five days. It is a rule among our people always to have five days
to settle anything. My father told them to dance at night and that
the men should hunt rabbits and fish, and some were to have
games of football or any kind of sport or playthings they wished,
and the women could do the same, as they had nothing else to do.
My people were so happy during the five days. The women ran
races, and the men ran races on foot and on horses.

My father got up very early one morning and told his people
the time had come, that we could no longer be happy as of old,
as the white people we called our brothers had brought a great
trouble and sorrow among us already.

He went on and said, "These white people must be a great
nation, as they have houses that move. It is wonderful to see them
move along. I fear we will suffer greatly by their coming to our
country. They come for no good to us, although my father said
they were our brothers, but they do not seem to think we are like
them. What do you all think about it? Maybe I am wrong. My
dear children, there is something telling me that I am not wrong,

because I am sure they have minds like us and think as we do, and I know that they were doing wrong when they set fire to our winter supplies. They surely knew it was our food."

And this was the first wrong done to us by our white brothers. Now comes the end of our merrymaking.

Then my father told his people his fearful dream, as he called it. He said, "I dreamt this same thing three nights, the very same. I saw the greatest emigration that has yet been through our country. I looked north and south and east and west, and saw nothing but dust, and I heard a great weeping. I saw women crying, and I also saw my men shot down by the white people. They were killing my people with something that made a great noise like thunder and lightning, and I saw the blood streaming from the mouths of my men that lay all around me. I saw it as if it was real. Oh, my dear children! You may all think it is only a dream; nevertheless, I feel that it will come to pass. And to avoid bloodshed, we must all go to the mountains during the summer, or till my father comes back from California. He will then tell us what to do. Let us keep away from the emigrant roads and stay in the mountains all summer. There are to be a great many pine nuts this summer, and we can lay up great supplies for the coming winter, and if the emigrants don't come too early, we can take a run down and fish for a month, and lay up dried fish. I know we can dry a great many in a month, and young men can go into the valleys on hunting excursions and kill as many rabbits as they can. In that way we can live in the mountains all summer and all winter too." So ended my father's dream.

During that day one could see old women getting together talking over what they had heard my father say. They said, "It is true what our great chief has said, for it was shown to him by a higher power. It is not a dream. Oh, it surely will come to pass. We shall no longer be a happy people, as we now are; we shall no longer go here and there as of old; we shall no longer build our big fires as a signal to our friends, for we shall always be afraid of being seen by those bad people."

"Surely they don't eat people?"

"Yes, they do eat people, because they ate each other up in the mountains last winter."

This was the talk among the old women during the day. "Oh, how grieved we are! Oh, where will it end?"

That evening one of our doctors called for a council, and all the men gathered together in the council tent to hear what their medicine man had to say, for we all believe our doctor is greater than any human being living. We do not call him a medicine man because he gives medicine to the sick, as your doctors do. Our medicine man cures the sick by the laying on of hands, and we have doctresses as well as doctors. We believe that our doctors can communicate with holy spirits from heaven. We call heaven the Spirit Land.

Well, when all the men get together, of course there must be smoking the first thing. After the pipe has passed round five times to the right, it stops, and then he tells them to sing five songs. He is the leader in the song singing. He sings heavenly songs, and he says he is singing with the angels. It is hard to describe these songs. They are all different, and he says the angels sing them to him. Our doctors never sing war-songs, except at a war dance, as they never go themselves on the warpath.

While they were singing the last song, he said, "Now I am going into a trance. While I am in the trance, you must smoke just as you did before. Not a word must be spoken while I am in the trance."

About fifteen minutes after the smoking was over, he began to make a noise as if he was crying a great way off. The noise came nearer and nearer, until he breathed, and after he came to, he kept on crying. And then he prophesied and told the people that my father's dream was true in one sense of the word, that is, "Our people will not all die at the hands of our white brothers. They will kill a great many with their guns, but they will bring among us a fearful disease that will cause us to die by hundreds."

We all wept, for we believed this word came from heaven.

So ended our feast, and every family went to its own home in the pine nut mountains and remained there till the pine nuts were ripe. They ripen about the last of June.

LATE IN that fall, there came news that my grandfather was on his way home. Then my father took a great many of his men and went to meet his father, and there came back a runner saying that all our people must come together. It was said that my grandfather was bringing bad news. All our people came to receive their chieftain; all the old and young men and their wives went to meet him.

One evening there came a man saying that all the women who had little children should go to a high mountain. They wanted them to go because they brought white men's guns, and they made such a fearful noise, it might even kill some of the little children. My grandfather had lost one of his men while he was away. So all the women that had little children went. My mother was among the rest; and every time the guns were heard by us, the children would scream. I thought, for one, that my heart would surely break. So some of the women went down from the mountain and told them not to shoot anymore or their children would die with fright. When our mothers brought us down to our homes, the nearer we came to the camp, the more I cried.

"Oh, mother, mother, don't take us there!" I fought my mother; I bit her. Then my father came and took me in his arms and carried me to the camp. I put my head in his bosom and would not look up for a long time.

I heard my grandfather say, "So the young lady is ashamed because her sweetheart has come to see her. Come, dearest, that won't do, after I have had such a hard time to come to see my sweetheart, that she should be ashamed to look at me."

Then he called my two brothers to him and said to them, "Are you glad to see me?" And my brothers both told him that they were glad to see him. Then my grandfather said to them, "See that young lady? She does not love her sweetheart any more, does she? Well, I shall not live if she does not come and tell me she loves me. I shall take that gun, and I shall kill myself."

That made me worse than ever, and I screamed and cried so hard that my mother had to take me away. So they kept weeping for the little one three or four days. I did not make up with my grandfather for a long time. He sat day after day and night after night telling his people about his white brothers. He told them that the whites were really their brothers, that they were very kind to everybody, especially to children, that they were always ready to give something to children. He told them what beautiful things their white brothers had, what beautiful clothes they wore, and about the big houses that go on the mighty ocean and travel faster than any horse in the world. His people asked him how big they were.

"Well, as big as that hill you see there, and as high as the mountain over us."

"Oh, that is not possible. It would sink surely."

"It is every word truth, and that is nothing to what I am going to tell you. Our white brothers are a mighty nation and have more wonderful things than that. They have a gun that can shoot a ball bigger than my head and that can go as far off as that mountain you see over there."

The mountain he spoke of at that time was about twenty miles across from where we were. People opened their eyes when my grandfather told of the many battles they had with the Mexicans, and about their killing so many of the Mexicans, and taking their big city away from them, and how mighty they were. These wonderful things were talked about all winter long. The funniest thing was that he would sing some of the soldier's roll-calls, and the air to "The Star Spangled Banner," which everybody learned during the winter.

He then showed us a more wonderful thing than all the others that he had brought. It was a paper, which he said could talk to him. He took it out, and he would talk to it and talk with it.

He said, "This can talk to all our white brothers, and our white sisters, and their children. Our white brothers are beautiful, and our white sisters are beautiful, and their children are beautiful!" He also said the paper can travel like the wind, and it can go and talk with their fathers and brothers and sisters, and come back to tell what they are doing and whether they are well or sick.

After my grandfather told us this, our doctors and doctresses said, "If they can do this wonderful thing, they are not truly human but pure spirits. None but heavenly spirits can do such wonderful things. We can communicate with the spirits, yet we cannot do wonderful things like them. Oh, our great chieftain, we are afraid your white brothers will yet make your people's hearts bleed. You see if they don't; for we can see it. Their blood is all around us, and the dead are lying all about us, and we cannot escape it. It will come. Then you will say our doctors and doctresses did know. Dance, sing, play—it will do no good; we cannot drive it away. They have already done the mischief while you were away."

But this did not go far with my grandfather. He kept talking to his people about the good white people and told them all to get ready to go with him to California the following spring.

VERY LATE that fall, my grandfather and my father and a great many more went down to the Humboldt River to fish. They brought back a great many fish, which we were very glad to get, for none of our people had been down to fish the whole summer.

When they came back, they brought us more news. They said there were some white people living at the Humboldt sink. They were the first ones my father had seen face to face. He said they were not like "humans." They were more like owls than anything else. They had hair on their faces, and had white eyes, and looked beautiful! I tell you we children had to be very good indeed during the winter, for we were told that if we were not good they would come and eat us up. We remained there all winter.

The next spring the emigrants came as usual, and my father and grandfather and uncles, and many more, went down on the Humboldt River on fishing excursions. While they were thus fish-ing, their white brothers came upon them and fired on them, and killed one of my uncles, and wounded another. Nine more were wounded, and five died afterward. My other uncle got well again and is living yet. Oh, that was a fearful thing indeed!

After all these things had happened, my grandfather still stood up for his white brothers.

Our people had council after council to get my grandfather to give his consent that they should go and kill those white men who were at the sink of Humboldt. No, they could do nothing of the kind while he lived. He told his people that his word was more to him than his son's life—or anyone else's life either.

"Dear children," he said, "think of your own words to me; you promised. You want me to say to you, 'Go and kill those that are at the sink of Humboldt.' After your promise, how dare you to ask me to let your hearts be stained with the blood of those who are innocent of the deed that has been done to us by others? Is not my dear beloved son laid alongside of your dead, and you say

I stand up for their lives. Yes, it is very hard indeed; but nevertheless, I know and you know that those men who live at the sink are not the ones that killed our men."

While my grandfather was talking, he wept, and men, women, and children were all weeping. One could hardly hear him talking.

After he was through talking came the saddest part. The widow of my uncle who was killed and my mother and father all had long hair. They cut off their hair and also cut long gashes in their arms and legs, and they were all bleeding as if they would die with the loss of blood. This continued for several days, for this is the way we mourn for our dead. When the woman's husband dies, she is first to cut off her hair, and then she braids it and puts it across his breast; then his mother and sisters, his father and brothers, and all his kinsfolk cut their hair. The widow is to remain unmarried until her hair is the same length as before, and her face is not to be washed all that time, and she is to use no kind of paint nor to make any merriment with other women until the day is set for her to do so by her father-in-law, or if she has no father-in-law, by her mother-in-law, and then she is at liberty to go where she pleases. The widower is at liberty when his wife dies, but he mourns for her in the same way, by cutting his hair off.

IT WAS late that fall when my grandfather prevailed with his people to go with him to California. It was this time that my mother accompanied him. Everything had been got ready to start on our journey. My dear father was to be left behind. How my poor mother begged to stay with her husband! But my grandfather told her that she could come back in the spring to see her husband, so we started for California leaving my poor papa behind. All my kinsfolk went with us but one aunt and her children.

The first night found us camped at the sink of Carson, and

the second night we camped on Carson River. The third day, as we were traveling along the river, some of our men who were ahead came back and said there were some of our white brothers' houses ahead of us. So my grandfather told us all to stop where we were while he went to see them. He was not gone long, and when he came back, he brought some hard bread which they gave him. He told us that was their food, and he gave us all some to taste. That was the first I ever tasted.

Then my grandfather once more told his people that his paper talked for him, and he said, "Just as long as I live and have that paper which my white brothers' great chieftain has given me, I shall stand by them, come what will." He held the paper up toward heaven and kissed it as if it was really a person. "Oh, if I should lose this," he said, "we shall all be lost. So, children, get your horses ready, and we will go on, and we will camp with them tonight, or by them, for I have a sweetheart along who is dying for fear of my white brothers." He meant me, for I was always crying and hiding under somebody's robes, for we had no blankets then.

Well, we went on, but we did not camp with them, because my poor mother and brothers and sisters told my grandfather that I was sick with crying for fright and for him not to camp too close to them. The women were speaking two words for themselves and one for me, for they were just as afraid as I was. I had seen my brother Natchez crying when the men came back and said there were white men ahead of us. So my grandfather did as my mother wished him to do, and we went on by them but I did not know it, as I had my head covered while we were passing their camp. I was riding behind my older brother, and we went on and camped quite a long way from them that night.

So we traveled on to California but did not see any more of our white brothers till we got to the head of Carson River, about fifteen miles above where great Carson City now stands.

"Now give me the baby." It was my baby sister that grandpa took from my mother. I peeped from under my mother's fur, and I saw someone take my little sister.

Then I cried out, "Oh, my sister! Don't let them take her away."

And once more my poor grandfather told his people that his white brothers and sisters were very kind to children. I stopped crying and looked at them again. Then I saw them give my brother and sister something white. My mother asked her father what it was, and he said it was *pe-har-be*, which means "sugar."

Just then one of the women came to my mother with some in her hand, and grandpa said, "Take it, my child."

Then I held out my hand without looking. That was the first gift I ever got from a white person, which made my heart very glad.

When they went away, my grandfather called me to him and said I must not be afraid of the white people for they are very good. I told him that they looked so very bad I could not help it.

We traveled with them at that time two days, and the third day we all camped together where some white people were living in large white houses. My grandpa went to one of the houses, and when he came back, he said his white brothers wanted him to come and get some beef and hard bread. So he took four men with him to get it, and they gave him four boxes of hard bread and a whole side of beef. The next morning we got our horses ready to go on again.

There was some kind of a fight; that is, the captain of the train was whipping negroes who were driving his team. That made my poor grandfather feel very badly. He went to the captain and told him he would not travel with him. He came back and said to his people that he would not travel with his white brothers any farther. We traveled two days without seeing any more of my grandfather's white brothers.

At last we came to a very large encampment of white people, and they ran out of their wagons—or wood-houses, as we called them—and gathered round us. I was riding behind my brother. I was so afraid, I told him to put his robe over me, but he didn't do so. I scratched him and bit him on his back, and then my poor grandfather rode up to the tents where they were, and he was asked to stay there all night with them.

After grandpa had talked awhile, he said to his people that he would camp with his brothers. So he did. Oh, what nice things we all got from my grandpa's white brothers! Our men got red shirts, and our women got calico for dresses. Oh, what a pretty dress my sister got! I did not get anything, because I hid all the time. I was hiding under some robes. No one knew where I was.

After all the white people were gone, I heard my poor mother cry out, "Oh, where is my little girl? Oh, father, can it be that the white people have carried her away? Oh, father, go and find her, go, go, and find her!"

And I also heard my brothers and sister cry. Yet I said nothing, because they had not called me to get some of the pretty things. When they began to cry, I began crawling out, and then my grandfather scolded me and told me that his brothers loved good children but not bad ones like me. How I did cry and wished that I had stayed at home with my father! I went to sleep crying. I did not forget what had happened.

There was a house near where we camped. My grandfather went down to the house with some of his men, and pretty soon we saw them coming back. They were carrying large boxes, and we were all looking at them. My mother said there were two white men coming with them.

"Oh, mother, what shall I do? Hide me!" I just danced round like a wild one, which I was. I was behind my mother.

When they were coming nearer, I heard my grandpa say, "Make a place for them to sit down."

Just then, I peeped round my mother to see them. I gave

one scream, and said, "Oh, mother, the owls!" I only saw their big white eyes, and I thought their faces were all hair.

My mother said, "I wish you would send your brothers away, for my child will die."

I imagined I could see their big white eyes all night long. They were the first ones I had ever seen in my life.

We went on the next day and passed some more of our white brothers' houses, as we called their wagons at that time. We camped on the Sanvada [Sierra] mountains and spent the night. My grandfather said everything that was good about the white people to me. At last we were camped upon the summit, and it snowed very hard all night, and in the morning my grandfather told his people to hurry and get their horses and travel on for fear we might get snowed into the mountains.

That night we overtook some emigrants who were camped there to rest their oxen. This time I watched my grandfather to see what he would do.

He said, "I am going to show them my rag friend again." As he rode up to one of their tents, three white men came out to him, then they took him to a large tent. Quite a number of white men came out to him. I saw him take out the paper he called his rag friend and give it to one of the men who stood looking at it, then he looked up and came toward him and held out his hand to my grandfather, and then the rest of the white men did the same all round. Then the little children and the women did the same, and I saw the little ones running to their tents and back again with something in their hands, and they were giving it to each man.

The next morning I could not eat, and said to my mother, "Let us go back to father. Let us not go with grandpa, for he is bad."

My poor mother said, "We can't go alone; we would all be killed if we go, for we have no rag friend as father has. And dear, you must be good, and grandpa will love you just as well as ever.

You must do what he tells you to do."

Oh, how badly I did feel! I held my two hands over my face and was crying as if my heart would break.

"My dear, don't cry. Here comes grandpa."

I heard him say, "Well, well, is my sweetheart never going to stop crying? Come, dear, I have something for my baby. Come and see what it is."

So I went to him with my head down, not because I was afraid he would whip me, no no, for Indians do not whip their children. Oh, how happy I was when he told me he would give me something very beautiful. It was a little cup, and it made me very glad indeed, and he told me it was to drink water out of, not to wear.

He said, "I am going to tell you what I did with a beautiful gift I received from my white brothers. It was of the same kind, only it was flat and round, and it was as bright as your cup is now."

He said to his wife, "Give me my bright hat," and she did so. "You see, I used to wear it on my head, because my white brother did not tell me what it was for." Then he began to laugh, and he laughed so long! Then he stopped and said, "It was not to wear, but to eat out of, and I have made myself a fool by wearing it as a hat. Oh, how my brothers did laugh at me because I wore it at our first fight with Mexicans in Mexico. Now, dearest children, I do not want you to think my brothers laughed at me to make fun of me; no no, it was because I wore the tin plate for a hat, that's all."

He also said they had much prettier things than this to eat out of. He went on and told us never to take anything belonging to them or lying outside of his white brothers' houses. "They hang their clothes out of doors after washing them, but they are not thrown away, and for fear some of you might think so and take them, I tell you about it. Therefore, never take anything unless they give it to you; then they will love you."

So I kept thinking over what he said to me about the good

white people and saying to myself, "I will make friends with them when we come into California."

When we came to Sacramento valley (it is a very beautiful valley), my grandfather said to his people that a great many of his white brothers were there, and he knew a great many of them, but we would not go there; we would go on to Stockton. There he had a very good brother who had a very big house made of red stone; it was so high that it would tire anyone to go up to some of the rooms. My uncle, my mother's brother, asked him how many rooms were up there.

My grandpa said, "We have to climb up three times to get to the top."

They all laughed, as much as to say my grandpa lied.

He said, "You will not laugh when I show you what wonderful things my white brothers can do. I will tell you something more wonderful than that. My brother has a big house that runs on the river, and it whistles and makes a beautiful noise, and it has a bell on it which makes a beautiful noise also."

My uncle asked again how big it was.

"Oh, you will see for yourself. We will get there tomorrow night. We will stop there ten days, and you can see for yourselves, and then you will know, my brothers, that what I have told you is true."

After traveling all day, we went into camp for the night. We had been there but a little while, and there came a great many men on horseback and camped near us. I ran to my mother and said I was sleepy and wanted to go to bed. I did so because I did not want to see them, and I knew grandpa would have them come to see us. I heard him say he was going to see them. I lay down quietly for a little while and then got up and looked round to see if my brother was going too. There was no one but my mother and little sister. They had all gone to see them.

"Lie down, dear," my mother said.

I did so, but I did not sleep for a long time, for I was thinking about the house that runs on the water. I wondered what it was like. I kept saying to myself, "Oh, I wish it was tomorrow now."

I heard mother say, "They are coming."

Pretty soon I heard grandpa say, "They are not my brothers."

Mother said, "Who are they?"

"They are what my brothers call Mexicans. They are the people we fought; if they knew who I was, they would kill me, but they shall not know. I am not going to show them my rag friend for fear my rag friend will tell of me."

Oh my! Oh my! That made me worse than ever. I cried so that one could have heard my poor heart beat. Oh, how I wished I was back with my father again! All the children were not afraid of the white people, only me.

My brothers would go everywhere with grandpa. I would not have been so afraid of them if I had not been told by my own father and grandmamma that the white people would kill little children and eat them.

Everything was all right, and the next day we went on our journey, and after a whole day's journey, we came within a mile of the town.

The sun was almost down when grandpa stopped and said, "Now, one and all, listen as you go on. You will hear the water-house bell ring." So we did, and pretty soon we heard the prettiest noise we had ever heard in all our lifetime.

It became dark before we got to the town, but we could see something like stars away ahead of us. Oh, how I wished I had stayed with my father in our own country.

I cried out, saying, "Oh, mother, I am so afraid. I cannot go to the white people. They are so much like the owls with their big white eyes. I cannot make friends with them." I kept crying until we came nearer the town and camped for the night.

My grandpa said to his men, "Unsaddle your horses while I go and see my friend." He came back in a few moments and said, "Turn your horses into the corral, and now we will go to bed without making any fire."

So we did, and I for one was glad. But although very tired, I could not sleep, for grandpa kept telling us that at daybreak we would hear the water-house's whistle. The next morning my mother waked me, and I got up and looked round me. I found no one but mother.

"Oh, where is sister, mother?"

"Oh, she has gone with the rest to see the water-house."

"Mother, did you hear it whistle?"

"Yes, we all heard it, and it made such a fearful noise! The one that whistled has gone on. But another came in just like it and made just such a noise. Your brother was here awhile ago. He said the water-house had many looking glasses all round it, and when it came in it was so tired, it breathed so hard, it made us almost deaf."

"Say, mother, let us go and see."

But mother said, "No, your brother said there were so many white people that one can hardly get along. We will wait until your grandpa comes, and hear what they all say. Ain't you hungry, my child?"

I said, "Yes."

"Your brother brought something that tastes like sugar."

It was cake, and I ate so much it made me sick. I was sick all day and night, and the next day I had the chills. Oh, I was very, very sick; my poor mother thought I would die.

I heard her say to grandpa one day, "The sugar-bread was poisoned which your white brother gave us to eat, and it has made my poor little girl so sick that I am afraid she will die." My poor mother and brothers and sisters were crying; mother had me in her arms.

My grandpa came and took me in his arms and said to me, "Open your eyes, dear, and see your grandpa!"

I did as he told me, because I had not forgotten what mother had said to me, to do whatever he told me to do and then he would love me. The reason I had not opened my eyes was because my head ached so badly that it hurt me, so I shut them again. My poor mother cried the more, and all our people gathered around us and began to cry.

My mother said to grandpa, "Can there be anything done for her?"

"Dear daughter," he said, "I am sorry you have such bad hearts against my white brothers. I have eaten some sugar-bread, and so have you, and all the rest of us, and we did not get sick. Dear daughter, you should have blessed the strange food before you gave it to your child to eat. Maybe this is why she is sick."

It is a law among us that all strange food is blessed before eaten, and also clothing of any kind that is given to us by anyone—Indians or white people—must be blessed before worn. So all my people came together and prayed over me, but it was all in vain. I do not know how long I was sick, but very long. I was indeed poisoned, not by the bread I had eaten, but by poison oak. My face swelled so that I could not see for a long time, but I could hear everything.

At last someone came that had a voice like an angel. I really thought it must be an angel, for I had been taught by my father that an angel comes to watch the sick one and take the soul to the Spirit Land. I kept thinking it must be so, and I learned words from the angel (as I thought it). I could not see, for my eyes were swollen shut.

These were the words: "Poor little girl, it is too bad!" It was said so often by the pretty sweet voice, I would say it over and over when I was suffering so badly and would cry out, "Poor little girl, it is too bad!"

At last I began to get well, and I could hear my grandpa say the same words.

Then I began to see a little, and the first thing I asked my mother was, "What was the angel saying to me?"

Oh, how frightened my poor mother was! She cried out, "Oh, father, come here! My little girl is talking to the angels. She is dying."

My sister and brothers ran to her crying, and for the first time since I was sick I cried out, "Oh, don't, don't cry! I am getting well, indeed I am. Stop crying and give me something to eat. I was only asking you what the angel meant by saying 'Poor little girl, it is too bad!'"

"Oh," said grandpa, "it is the good white woman; I mean, my white sister who comes here to see you. She has made you well. She put some medicine on your face and has made you see. Ain't you glad to see?"

I said, "Can I see her now? "

"Yes, she will come pretty soon. She comes every day to see you."

Then my mother came with something for me to eat, but I said, "Wait, grandpa, tell me more about the good woman."

He said, "My dear child, she is truly an angel, and she has come every day to see you. You will love her, I know."

"Dear grandpa, will she come pretty soon? I want to see her."

Grandpa said, "I will go and get her. You won't be afraid, will you?"

So my grandpa went. I tried my best to eat, but I could not, it was so hard.

My sister said, "They are coming."

I said, "Mother, fix my eyes so I can see the angel. Has it wings, mother?"

Mother said, "You will see for yourself."

Just then they came, and grandpa said, "Here she is."

The first thing she did she put her beautiful white hand on my forehead. I looked at her; she was indeed a beautiful angel. She said the same words as before. I asked my grandpa what she was saying. Then he told me what she meant by it. I began to get well very fast, and this sweet angel came every day and brought me something nice to eat; and oh, what pretty dresses she brought me. When she brought the dresses, she talked to my grandpa a long time, and she cried.

After she went away, he said to my mother, "The dresses which my white sister gave my child were her dead child's clothes, so they should be burned."

I began to cry because I did not want them burned.

He said to me, "Don't cry, my child; you will get nicer ones than these if you learn to love my white sister." Of course the clothes were burned.

After I got well, my grandpa took great delight in taking us all to see his white brothers and sisters. I knew what he meant when he said "my little girls;" I knew he meant me and sister, and he also would say "my little boys" when he was talking about my brothers. He would say, pointing to my brother, "my natchez [boy];" he always said this. So the white people called one of my brothers Natchez, and he has had that name to this day. So I came to love the white people.

WE LEFT Stockton and went on farther to a place called San Joaquin River. It took us only one day to go there. We only crossed that river at that time.

One of my grandpa's friends was named Scott, and the other Bonsal. After we got there, his friend killed beef for him and his people. We stayed there some time. Then grandpa told us that he had taken charge of Mr. Scott's cattle and horses, and he was going to take them all up to the mountains to take care of them for his brothers. He wanted my uncles and their families and my mother and her two sons and three daughters to stay where they were; that is, he told his dear daughter that he wanted her two sons to take care of a few horses and cows that would be left.

My mother began to cry and said, "Oh, father, don't leave us here! My children might get sick, and there would be no one to speak for us, or something else might happen."

He again said, "I don't think my brothers will do anything that is wrong to you and your children."

Then my mother asked my grandfather if he would take my sister with him. My poor mother felt that her daughter was unsafe, for she was young and very good-looking.

"I would like to take her along," he said, "but I want her to learn how to work and cook. Scott and Bonsal say they will take the very best care of you and the children. It is not as if I was going to leave you here really alone; your brothers will be with you."

So we stayed. Two men owned the ferry, and they had a great deal of money. So my brothers took care of their horses and cows all winter, and they paid them well for their work. But, oh, what trouble we had for a while! The men whom my grandpa called his brothers would come into our camp and ask my mother to give our sister to them. They would come in at night, and we would all scream and cry, but that would not stop them.

My sister, my mother, and my uncles all cried and said, "Oh, why did we come? Oh, we shall surely all be killed some night."

My uncles and brothers would not dare to say a word for fear they would be shot down. So we used to go away every night after dark and hide and come back to our camp every morning. One night we were getting ready to go, and there came five men. The fire was out; we could see two men come into the tent and shut off the postles outside. My uncles and my brothers made such a noise!

I don't know what happened; when I woke I asked my mother if they had killed my sister. She said, "We are all safe here. Don't cry."

"Where are we, mother?"

"We are in a boarding house."

"Are my uncles killed?"

"No, dear, they are all near here too."

I said, "Sister, where are you? I want to come to you."

She said, "Come on."

I laid down, but I could not sleep. I could hear my poor sister's heartbeat.

Early the next morning we got up and went downstairs, for it was upstairs where we slept. There were a great many in the room.

When we came down, my mother said, "We will go outside."

My sister said, "There is no outlet to the house. We can't get out."

Mother looked round and said, "No, we cannot get out."

I as usual began to cry. My poor sister! I ran to her, I saw tears in her eyes. I heard someone speak close to my mother. I looked round and saw Mr. Scott holding the door open.

Mother said, "Children, come."

He went out with us, and pointed to our camp, and shook his head, and motioned to mother to go into a little house where they were cooking. He took my hand in his and said the same words that I had learned: "Poor little girl." I could see by his looks that he pitied me, so I was not afraid of him.

We went in and sat down on the floor. Oh, what pretty things met my eyes. I was looking all round the room, and I saw beautiful white cups, and every beautiful thing on something high and long, and around it some things that were red.

I said to my sister, "Do you know what those are?" for she

had been to the house before with my brothers.

She said, "That high thing is what they use when eating, and the white cups are what they drink hot water from, and the red things you see is what they sit upon when they are eating."

There was one now near us, and I thought if I could sit upon it I should be so happy! I said to my mother, "Can I sit on that one?"

She said, "No, they would whip you."

I did not say any more but sat looking at the beautiful red chair. By and by the white woman went out, and I wished in my heart I could go and sit upon it while she was gone. Then she came in with her little child in her arms. As she came in she went right to the very chair I wanted to sit in so badly and set her child in it.

I looked up to my mother and said, "Will she get a whipping?"

"No, dear, it belongs to her father."

So I said no more. Pretty soon a man came in. She said something to him, and he went out, and in a little while they all came in and sat round that high thing, as I called it. That was the table. It was all very strange to me, and they were drinking the hot water as they ate. I thought it was indeed hot water. After they got through, they all went out again, but Mr. Scott stayed and talked to the woman and the man a long time. Then the woman fixed five places and the men went out and brought in my brothers and kept talking to them.

My brother said, "Come and sit here, and you, sister, sit there."

But as soon as I sat down in the beautiful chair, I began to look at the pretty picture on the back of the chair.

"Dear, sit nice and eat, or the white woman will whip you," my mother said.

I was quiet but did not eat much. I tasted the black hot water; I did not like it. It was coffee that we called hot water.

After we had done, brother said, "Mother, come outside; I want to talk to you." So we all went out.

Brother said, "Mother, Mr. Scott wants us all to stay here. He says you and sister are to wash dishes and learn all kinds of work. We are to stay here all the time and sleep upstairs, and the white woman is going to teach my sister how to sew. I think, dear mother, we had better stay, because grandpa said so, and our father Scott will take good care of us. He is going up into the mountains to see how grandpa is getting along, and he says he will take my uncles with him."

All the time brother was talking, my mother and sister were crying. I did not cry, for I wanted to stay so that I could sit in the beautiful red chairs.

Mother said, "Dear son, you know if we stay here, sister will be taken from us by the bad white man. I would rather see her die than see her heart full of fear every night."

"Yes, dear mother, we love our dear sister, and if you say so we will go to papa."

"Yes, dear son, let us go and tell him what his white brothers are doing to us."

"Then I will go and tell Mr. Scott we want to go to our papa." He was gone some time, and at last came back.

"Mother," he said, "we can't go; that is, brother and I must stay. But you and sister can go if you wish to."

"Oh no, my dear children, how can I go and leave you here? Oh, how can that bad man keep you from going? You are not his children. How dare he say you cannot go with your mother? He is not your father; he is nothing but a bad white man, and he dares to say you cannot go. Your own father did not say you should not come with me. Oh, had my dear husband said those words, I would not have been here today and see my dear children suffer from day to day. Oh, if your father only knew how his children were suffering, I know he would kill that white man who tried to take your sister. I cannot see for my life why my father calls them his white brothers. They are not people; they have no thought, no mind, no love. They are beasts, or they would know I, a lone woman, am here with them. They tried to take my girl from me and abuse her before my eyes and yours too, and oh, you must go too."

"Oh, mother, here he comes!"

My mother got up. She held out her two hands to him, and cried out, "Oh, good father, don't keep my children from me. If you have a heart in you, give them back to me. Let me take them to their good father where they can be cared for."

We all cried to see our poor mother pleading for us. Mother held on to him until he gave some signs of letting her sons go with her; then he nodded his head they might go. My poor mother's crying was turned into joy, and we were all glad. The wagon was got ready, we were to ride in it.

Oh, how I jumped about because I was going to ride in it! I ran up to sister and said, "Ain't you glad we are going to ride in that beautiful red house?" I called it house.

My sister said, "Not I, dear sister, for I hate everything that belongs to the white dogs. I would rather walk all the way. Oh, I hate them so badly!"

When everything was got ready, we got into the red house, as we called the wagon. I soon got tired of riding in the red house and went to sleep. Nothing happened during the day, and after a while mother told us not to say a word about why we left, for grandpa might get mad with us.

So we got to our people, and grandpa ran out to meet. us. We were all glad to see him. The white man stayed all night and went home the next day. After he left us, my grandpa called my brothers to him.

"Now, my dear little boys, I have something to tell you that will make you happy. Our good father (he did not say my white brother, but he said our good father) has left something with me to give you, and he also told me that he had given you some money for your work. He says you are all good boys, and he likes you very much; and he told me to give you three horses apiece, which makes six in all. And he wants you and your brother to go back and to go on with the same work, and he will pay you well for it. He is to come back in three days; then if you want to go with him, you can."

Brother said, "Will mother and sisters go too? "

"No, they will stay with me."

My brothers were so happy over their horses.

Now, my dear reader, there is no word so endearing as the word *father*, and that is why we call all good people father or mother, no matter who it is—negro, white man, or Indian—and the same with the women. Grandpa talked to my mother a long time, but I did not hear what he said to her as I went off to play with the other children. But the first thing I knew, the white man came and stayed four days. Then all the horses were got up, and he saw them all, and the cattle also. I could see my poor mother and sister crying now and then, but I did not know what for.

So one morning the man was going away, and I saw mother getting my brothers' horses ready too. I ran to my mother, and said, "Mother, what makes you cry so?"

Grandpa was talking to her. He said, "They will not be hurt; they will have quite a number of horses by the time we are ready to go back to our home again."

I knew then that my brothers were going back with this man. Oh, then I began to cry and said everything that was bad to them. I threw myself down upon the ground. "Oh, brothers, I will never see them anymore. They will kill them, I know. Oh, you naughty, naughty grandpa, you want my poor brothers to be killed by the bad men. You don't know what they do to us. Oh, mother, run, bring them back again!"

Oh, how we missed our brothers for a long time. We did not

see them for a long time, but the men came now and then. They never brought my brothers with them.

After they went away, grandpa would come in with his rag friend in hand and say to mother, "My friend here says my boys are all right, not sick."

My mother said, "Father, why can you not have them come and see us sometimes?"

"Dear daughter, we will get ready to go home. It is time now that the snow is off the mountains. In ten days more we will go, and we will get the children as we go by."

Oh, how happy everybody was! Everybody was singing here and there, getting beautiful dresses made, and before we started we had a thanksgiving dance.

The day we were to start, we partook of the first gathering of food for that summer. So that morning everybody prayed, and sang songs, and danced, and ate before starting. It was all so nice, and everybody was so happy because they were going to see their dear country and the dear ones at home.

Grandpa took all the horses belonging to the white men. After we got home, the horses were put into the corral for all night, and the two white men counted their horses the next morning. They gave my grandpa eight horses for his work, and two or three horses each to some of the people. To my two brothers they gave sixteen horses and some money.

After we all got our horses, grandpa said to his people, "Now, my children, you see that what I have told you about my white brothers is true. You see we have not worked very much, and they have given us all horses. Don't you see they are good people?"

All that time, neither my uncles nor my mother had told what the white men did while we were left all alone.

So the day was set for starting. It was to be in five days. We had been there three days when we saw the very men who were so bad to us. Yes, they were talking to grandpa.

Mother said to sister, "They are talking about us. You see they are looking this way."

Sister said, "Oh, mother, I hope grandpa will not do such a wicked thing as to give me to those bad men."

Oh, how my heart beat! I saw grandpa shake his head, and he looked mad with them. He came away and left them standing there. From that day my grandma took my sister under her care, and we got along nicely.

THEN WE started for our home, and after traveling some time, we arrived at the head of Carson River. There we met some of our people, and they told us some very bad news indeed, which made us all cry. They said almost all the tribe had died off, and if one of a family got sick, it was a sure thing that the whole family would die. He said the white men had poisoned the Humboldt River, and our people had drank the water and died off.

Grandpa said, "Is my son dead? "

"No, he has been in the mountains all the time, and all who have been there are all right." The men said a great many of our relations had died off.

We stayed there all night, and the next day our hair was all cut off. My sister and my mother had such beautiful hair!

So grandpa said to the man, "Go and tell our people we are coming. Send them to each other, and tell my son to come to meet us."

So we went on our journey, and after traveling three days more, we came to a place called Genoa, on the west side of Carson River, at the very place where I had first seen a white man. A sawmill and a gristmill were there, and five more houses. We camped in the very same place where we did before. We stayed there a long time waiting for my father to come to meet us.

At last my cousin rode into our camp one evening and said my father was coming with many of his people. We heard them as they came nearer and nearer; they were all crying, and then we cried too, and as they got off their horses they fell into each other's arms like so many little children and cried as if their hearts would break,. They told what they had suffered since we went away and how our people had died off. As soon as one would get sick, he would drink water and die right off. Every one of them was in mourning also, and they talked over the sad things which had happened to them during the time we were away. One and all said that the river must have been poisoned by the white people, because they had prayed, and our spirit-doctors had tried to cure the sick. They too died while they were trying to cure them.

After they had told grandpa all, he got angry and said, "My dear children, I am heartily sorry to hear your sad story, but I cannot and will not believe my white brothers would do such a thing. Oh, my dear children, do not think so badly of our white fathers, for if they had poisoned the river, why, my dear children, they too would have died when they drank of the water. It is this, my dear children, it must be some fearful disease or sickness unknown to us and therefore, my dear children, don't blame our brothers. The whole tribe have called me their father, and I have loved you all as my dear children, and those who have died are happy in the Spirit Land, though we mourn their loss here on earth. I know my grandchildren and daughters and brothers are in that happy bright Spirit Land, and I shall soon see them there. Some of you may live a long time yet, and don't let your hearts work against your white fathers; if you do, you will not get along. You see they are already here in our land; here they are all along the river, and we must let our brothers live with us. We cannot tell them to go away. I know your good hearts. I know you won't say kill them. Surely you all know that they are human. Their lives are just as dear to them as ours to us. It is a very sad thing indeed to have to lose so many of our dear ones, but maybe it was to be. We can do nothing but mourn for their loss."

He went on to say, "My dear children, you all know the tradition says: 'Weep not for your dead, but sing and be joyful, for the soul is happy in the Spirit Land.' But it is natural for man or woman to weep, because it relieves our hearts to weep together, and we all feel better afterward."

Everyone hung their heads while grandpa talked on. Now and then one could hear some of them cry out, just as the Methodists cry out at their meetings, and grandpa said a great many beautiful things to his people. He talked so long, I for one wished he would stop so I could go and throw myself into my father's arms and tell him what the white people were. At last he stopped, and we all ran to our father and threw our arms around his neck and cried for joy; and then mother came with little sister. Papa took her in his arms, and mother put her hand in his bosom, and we all wept together, because mother had lost two sisters, and their husbands, and all their children but one girl; and thus passed away the day. Grandpa had gone off during our meeting with father, and prayer was offered, and everyone washed their face, and was waiting for something else.

Pretty soon grandpa came and said, "This is my friend," holding up his paper in his hand. "Does it look as if it could talk and ask for anything? Yet it does. It can ask for something to eat for me and my people. Yet it is nothing but a rag. Oh, wonderful things my white brothers can do. I have taken it down to them, and it has asked for sacks of flour for us to eat. Come, we will go and get them." So the men went down and got the flour. Grandpa took his son down to see the white men, and by and by we saw them coming back. They had given my father a red blanket and a red shirt.

CHAPTER II

DOMESTIC AND SOCIAL MORALITIES

OUR CHILDREN are very carefully taught to be good. Their parents tell them stories, traditions of old times, even of the first mother of the human race, and love stories, stories of giants, and fables. And when they ask if these last stories are true, they answer, "Oh, it is only coyote," which means that they are make-believe stories. Coyote is the name of a mean, crafty little animal, half wolf, half dog, and he stands for everything low. It is the greatest term of reproach one Indian has for another. Indians do not swear; they have no words for swearing till they learn them of white men. The worst they call each is bad or coyote, but they are very sincere with one another, and if they think each other in the wrong they say so.

We are taught to love everybody. We don't need to be taught to love our fathers and mothers. We love them without being told to. Our tenth cousin is as near to us as our first cousin, and we don't marry into our relations. Our young women are not allowed to talk to any young man that is not their cousin, except at the festive dances, when both are dressed in their best clothes adorned with beads, feathers, or shells, and stand alternately in the ring and take hold of hands. These are very pleasant occasions to all the young people.

Many years ago, when my people were happier than they are now, they used to celebrate the Festival of Flowers in the spring. I have been to three of them only in the course of my life. Oh, with what eagerness we girls used to watch every spring for the time when we could meet with our hearts' delight the young men, whom in civilized life you call beaux. We would all go in company to see if the flowers we were named for were yet in bloom, for almost all the girls are named for flowers. We talked about them in our wigwams as if we were the flowers, saying, "Oh, I saw myself today in full bloom!" We would talk all the evening in this way in our families with such delight and such beautiful thoughts of the happy day when we should meet with those who admired us and would help us to sing our flower-songs, which we made up as we sang. But we were always sorry for those that were not named after some flower, because we knew they could not join in the flower-songs like ourselves, who were named for flowers of all kinds.

At last one evening came a beautiful voice which made every girl's heart throb with happiness. It was the chief, and everyone hushed to hear what he said today.

"My dear daughters, we are told that you have seen yourselves in the hills and in the valleys in full bloom. Five days from today, your festival day will come. I know every young man's heart stops beating while I am talking. I know how it was with me many years ago. I used to wish the Flower Festival would come every day. Dear young men and young women, you are saying, 'Why put it off five days?' But you all know that is our rule. It gives you time to think and to show your sweetheart your flower."

All the girls who have flower names dance along together, and those who have not go together also. Our fathers and mothers and grandfathers and grandmothers make a place for us where we can dance. Each one gathers the flower she is named for, and then all weave them into wreaths and crowns and scarves, and dress up in them.

Some girls are named for rocks and are called rock-girls. They find some pretty rocks which they carry, each one such a rock as she is named for, or whatever she is named for. If she cannot, she can take a branch of sagebrush, or a bunch of ryegrass, which have no flower.

They all go marching along, each girl in turn singing of herself, but she is not a girl anymore; she is a flower singing. She sings of herself, and her sweetheart dancing along by her side helps her sing the song she makes.

I will repeat what we say of ourselves. "I, Sarah Winnemucca, am a shellflower, such as I wear on my dress. My name is Thocmetony. I am so beautiful! Who will come and dance with me while I am so beautiful? Oh, come and be happy with me! I shall be beautiful while the earth lasts. Somebody will always admire me. Who will come and be happy with me in the Spirit Land? I shall be beautiful forever there. Yes, I shall be more beautiful than my shellflower, my Thocmetony! Then, come, oh come, and dance and be happy with me!" The young men sing with us as they dance beside us.

Our parents are waiting for us somewhere to welcome us home. And then we praise the sagebrush and the ryegrass that have no flower, and the pretty rocks that some are named for, and then we present our beautiful flowers to these companions who could carry none. And so all are happy, and that closes the beautiful day.

My people have been so unhappy for a long time they wish now to *disincrease* instead of multiply. The mothers are afraid to have more children for fear they shall have daughters, who are not safe even in their mother's presence.

The grandmothers have the special care of the daughters just before and after they come to womanhood. The girls are not allowed to get married until they have come to womanhood. That period is recognized as a very sacred thing and is the subject of a festival and has peculiar customs. The young woman is set apart under the care of two of her friends, somewhat older, and a little wigwam called a teepee, just big enough for the three, is made for them, to which they retire. She goes through certain labors which are thought to be strengthening, and these last twenty-five days. Every day, three times a day, she must gather and pile up as high as she can five stacks of wood. This makes fifteen stacks a day. At the end of every five days, the attendants take her to a river to bathe. She fasts from all flesh-meat during these twenty-five days and continues to do this for five days in every month all her life. At the end of the twenty-five days, she returns to the family lodge and gives all her clothing to her attendants in payment for their care. Sometimes the wardrobe is quite extensive.

It is thus publicly known that there is another marriageable woman, and any young man interested in her or wishing to form an alliance comes forward. But the courting is very different from the courting of the white people. He never speaks to her or visits the family but endeavors to attract her attention by showing his horsemanship, etc. As he knows that she sleeps next to her grandmother in the lodge, he enters in full dress after the family has retired for the night and seats himself at her feet. If she is not awake, her grandmother wakes her. He does not speak to either young woman or grandmother, but when the young woman wishes him to go away, she rises and goes and lies down by the side of her mother. He then leaves as silently as he came in. This goes on sometimes for a year or longer if the young woman has not made up her mind. She is never forced by her parents to marry against her wishes. When she knows her own mind, she makes a confidant of her grandmother, and then the young man is summoned by the father of the girl, who asks him in her presence if he really loves his daughter and reminds him, if he says he does, of all the duties of a husband. He then asks his daughter the same question and sets before her minutely all her duties. And these duties are not slight. She is to dress the game, prepare the food, clean the buck-skins, make his moccasins, dress his hair, bring all the wood—in short, do all the household work. She promises to "be himself," and she fulfills her promise. Then he is invited to a feast and all his relatives with him. But after the betrothal, a teepee is erected for the presents that pour in from both sides.

At the wedding feast, all the food is prepared in baskets. The young woman sits by the young man and hands him the basket of food prepared for him with her own hands. He does not take it with his right hand but seizes her wrist and takes it with the left hand. This constitutes the marriage ceremony, and the father pronounces them man and wife. They go to a wigwam of their own, where they live till the first child is born.

This event also is celebrated. Both father and mother fast from all flesh, and the father goes through the labor of piling the wood for twenty-five days and assumes all his wife's household work during that time. If he does not do his part in the care of the child, he is considered an outcast. Every five days his child's basket is changed for a new one, and the five are all carefully put away at the end of the days, the last one containing the navel-string, carefully wrapped up, and all are put up into a tree, and the child put into a new and ornamented basket. All this respect shown to the mother and child makes the parents feel their responsibility and makes the tie between parents and children very strong. The young mothers often get together and exchange their experiences about the attentions of their husbands and inquire of each other if the fathers did their duty to their children and were careful of their wives' health.

When they are married, they give away all the clothing they have ever worn and dress themselves anew. The poor people have the same ceremonies but do not make a feast of it, for want of means.

Our boys are introduced to manhood by their hunting of deer and mountain sheep. Before they are fifteen or sixteen, they hunt only small game, like rabbits, hares, fowls, etc. They never eat what they kill themselves but only what their father or elder brothers kill. When a boy becomes strong enough to use larger bows made of sinew and arrows that are ornamented with eagle feathers for the first time, he kills game that is large—a deer, or an antelope, or a mountain sheep. Then he brings home the hide, and his father cuts it into a long coil which is wound into a loop. The boy takes his quiver and throws it on his back as if he was going on a hunt, and takes his bow and arrows in his hand. Then his father throws the loop over him, and he jumps through it. This he does five times. Now for the first time he eats the flesh of the animal he has killed, and from that time he eats whatever he kills, but he has always been faithful to his parents' command not to eat what he has killed before. He can now do whatever he likes, for now he is a man and no longer considered a boy. If there is a war, he can go to it, but the Paiutes, and other tribes west of the Rocky Mountains, are not fond of going to war.

I never saw a war dance but once. It is always the whites that begin the wars for their own selfish purposes. The government does not take care to send the good men; there are a plenty who would take pains to see and understand the chiefs and learn their characters and their goodwill to the whites. But the whites have not waited to find out how good the Indians were and what ideas they had of God, just like those of Jesus, who called him Father, just as my people do, and told men to do to others as they would be done by, just as my people teach their children to do.

My people teach their children never to make fun of anyone, no matter how they look. If you see your brother or sister doing something wrong, look away or go away from them. If you make fun of bad persons, you make yourself beneath them. Be kind to all, both poor and rich, and feed all that come to your wigwam, and your name can be spoken of by everyone far and near. In this way you will make many friends for yourself. Be kind both to bad and good, for you don't know your own heart. This is the way my people teach their children. It was handed down from father to son for many generations. I never in my life saw our children rude as I have seen white children and grown people in the streets.

The chief's tent is the largest tent, and it is the council tent where everyone goes who wants advice. In the evenings the head men go there to discuss everything, for the chiefs do not rule like tyrants; they discuss everything with their people, as a father would in his family. Often they sit up all night. They discuss the doings of all if they need to be advised. If a boy is not doing well, they talk that over, and if the women are interested, they can share in the talks. If there is not room enough inside, they all go out of doors and make a great circle. The men are in the inner circle, for there would be too much smoke for the women inside. The men never talk without smoking first. The women sit behind them in another circle, and if the children wish to hear, they can be there too. The women know as much as the men do, and their advice is often asked. We have a republic as well as you. The council tent is our Congress, and anybody can speak who has anything to say, women and all. They are always interested in what their husbands are doing and thinking about.

And they take some part even in the wars. They are always near at hand when fighting is going on, ready to snatch their husbands up and carry them off if wounded or killed. One splendid woman that my brother Lee married after his first wife died went out into the battlefield after her uncle was killed and went into the front ranks and cheered the men on. Her uncle's horse was dressed in a splendid robe made of eagles' feathers, and she snatched it off and swung it in the face of the enemy, who always carry off everything they find, as much as to say, "You can't have that; I have it safe." She stayed and took her uncle's place, as brave as any of the men.

It means something when the women promise their fathers to make their husbands *themselves*. They faithfully keep with them in all the dangers they can share. They not only take care of their children together, but they do everything together, and when they grow blind, which I am sorry to say is very common for the smoke they live in destroys their eyes at last, they take sweet care of one another. Marriage is a sweet thing when people love each other. If women could go into your Congress, I think justice would soon be done to the Indians. I can't tell about all Indians, but I know my own people are kind to everybody that does not do them harm, but they will not be imposed upon, and when people are too bad, they rise up and resist them. This seems to me all right. It is different from being revengeful. There is nothing cruel about our people. They never scalped a human being.

The chiefs do not live in idleness. They work with their people, and they are always poor for the following reason. It is the custom with my people to be very hospitable. When people visit them in their tents, they always set before them the best food they have, and if there is not enough for themselves, they go without.

The chief's tent is the one always looked for when visitors come, and sometimes many come the same day. But they are all well received. I have often felt sorry for my brother, who is now the chief, when I saw him go without food for this reason. He would say, "We will wait and eat afterward what is left." Perhaps little would be left, and when the agents did not give supplies and rations, he would have to go hungry.

At the council, one is always appointed to repeat at the time everything that is said on both sides, so that there may be no misunderstanding, and one person at least is present from every lodge, and after it is over, he goes and repeats what is decided upon at the door of the lodge so all may be understood. For there is never any quarrelling in the tribe, only friendly counsels. The subchiefs are appointed by the great chief for special duties. There is no quarrelling about that, for neither subchief or great chief has any salary.

It is this which makes the tribe so united and attached to each other and makes it so dreadful to be parted. They would rather all die at once than be parted. They believe that in the Spirit Land those that die still watch over those that are living. When I was a child in California, I heard the Methodist minister say that everybody that did wrong was burned in hell forever. I was so frightened it made me very sick. He said the blessed ones in heaven looked down and saw their friends burning and could not help them. I wanted to be unborn and cried so that my mother and the others told me it was not so, that it was only here that people did wrong and were in the hell that it made, and that those that were in the Spirit Land saw us here and were sorry for us. But we should go to them when we died, where there was never any wrongdoing, and so no hell. That is our religion.

MY PEOPLE capture antelopes by charming them, but only some of the people are charmers. My father was one of them, and once I went with him on an antelope hunt.

The antelopes move in herds in the winter, and as late in the spring as April. At this time there was said to be a large herd in a certain place, and my father told all his people to come together in ten days to go with him in his hunt. He told them to bring their wives with them, but no small children. When they came at the end of ten days, he chose two men who he said were to be his messengers to the antelopes. They were to have two large torches made of sagebrush bark, and after he had found a place for his camp, he marked out a circle around which the wigwams were to be placed, putting his own in the middle of the western side and leaving an opening directly opposite in the middle of the eastern side, which was toward the antelopes.

The people who were with him in the camp then made another circle to the east of the one where their wigwams were and made six mounds of sagebrush and stones on the sides of it, with a space of a hundred yards or more from one mound to the next one but with no fence between the mounds. These mounds were made high so that they could be seen from far off.

The women and boys and old men who were in the camp and who were working on the mounds were told to be very careful not to drop anything and not to stumble over a sagebrush root, or a stone, or anything, and not to have any accident but to do everything perfectly and to keep thinking about the antelopes all the time, and not to let their thoughts go away to anything else. It took five days to charm the antelopes, and if anybody had an accident, he must tell of it.

Every morning early, when the bright morning star could be seen, the people sat around the opening to the circle with my father sitting in the middle of the opening. My father lighted his pipe and passed it to his right, and the pipe went round the circle five times. And at night they did the same thing.

After they had smoked the pipe, my father took a kind of drum, which is used in this charming, and made music with it. This is the only kind of musical instrument which my people have, and it is only used for this antelope-charming. It is made of a hide of some large animal, stuffed with grass so as to make it sound hollow, and then wound around tightly from one end to the other with a cord as large as my finger. One end of this instrument is large, and it tapers down to the other end, which is small, so that it makes a different sound on the different parts. My father took a stick and rubbed this stick from one end of the instrument to the other, making a penetrating, vibrating sound that could be heard afar off, and he sang, and all his people sang with him.

After that the two men who were messengers went out to see the antelopes. They carried their torches in their right hands, and one of them carded a pipe in his left hand. They started from my father's wigwam and went straight across the camp to the opening, then they crossed, and one went around the second circle to the right and the other went to the left till they met on the other side of the circle. Then they crossed again, and one went round the herd of antelopes one way and the other went round the other way, but they did not let the antelopes see them. When they met on the other side of the herd of antelopes, they stopped and smoked the pipe, and then they crossed, and each man came back on the track of the other to the camp and told my father what they saw and what the antelopes were doing.

This was done every day for five days, and after the first day, all the men and women and boys followed the messengers and went around the circle they were to enter. On the fifth day, the antelopes were charmed, and the whole herd followed the tracks of my people and entered the circle where the mounds were, coming in at the entrance, bowing and tossing their heads, and looking sleepy and under a powerful spell. They ran round and round inside the circle just as if there was a fence all around it and they could not get out, and they stayed there until my people had killed every one. But if anybody had dropped anything or had stumbled and had not told about it, then when the antelopes came to the place where he had done that, they threw off the spell and rushed wildly out of the circle at that place.

My brother can charm horses in the same way.

The Indian children amuse themselves a great deal by modelling in mud. They make herds of animals, which are modelled exceedingly well, and after setting them up, shoot at them with their little bows and arrows. They also string beads of different colors and show natural good taste.

CHAPTER III

WARS AND THEIR CAUSES

I WILL NOW stop writing about myself and family and tribe customs and tell about the wars and the causes of the wars. I will jump over about six years.

My sister and I were living at this time in Genoa with Major Ormsbey's family, who took us as playmates for their little girl. While with them we learned the English language very fast, for they were very kind to us. This was in the year 1858, I think; I am not sure. In that year our white brothers had their houses all along Carson River.

There were twenty-one houses there in our country. I know all the names of the people that lived in them. One man who was on the upper part of Carson River was Mr. Olds; the next man by the name of Palmer had a family. The third one, by the name of Job, also had a family. Another family was named Walters; another man, whose name was Dr. Daggett, had no family; nor had the next one, whose name was Van Sickle. The next one had more than one family; he had two wives, and his name was Thornton. The man who lived in the next house had still more wives. There

were two brothers; one had three wives, and the other five. Their
name was Reuse. The next man was named Nott, and had no
family. The next house had three brothers, named Sides, with no
families. The next was named Gilbert, and had no family. The
next was named Alridge, and had a family. Then came our friend,
Major Ormsbey. Next came Adams and brothers, who had no
wives. Then Jones and family; Miller and family; Brown, with
no family; Elsey, with no family; Mr. Ellis and family; Williams
brothers, no family; Mr. Cole and family; Mr. Black and family
at Humboldt Lake.

All these white people were loved by my people; we lived
there together and were as happy as could be. There was no stealing, and no one lost their cattle or horses; my people had not
learned to steal. We lived that way in peace for another year. Our
white brothers gave my people guns for their horses in the way of
trading, yet my people never said, "We want you to give us something for our land." Now, there were a great many of our white
brothers everywhere through our country and mines or farms
here and there. The Mormons came in a great many wagons and
settled down in Carson Valley, where now stands the great Carson
City, as it is called.

The following year, 1859, we were yet living with Major
Ormsbey, and mother and father were down at Pyramid Lake
with all our people, so sister and I were all alone there with our
dear good friend, Major Ormsbey.

LATE THAT fall there happened a very sad thing indeed. A white
man who was dearly beloved by my people started for California
to get provisions for the winter, as they all did every winter. Mr.
McMullen took a great deal of money to lay in large supplies, for
they had a store about thirty miles down Carson River. Two of

them, MacWilliams and McMullen, went off the same night and camped in the mountains. Someone came in the night and killed them both, and after they had shot them with guns or pistols, they placed arrows in the wounds to make it appear as if Indians had killed them. The next day news came in that Indians had killed John McMullen. They were asked how they knew that Indians had killed him, and they answered, "We know because it was done with arrows."

That same afternoon thirty men went to get the dead bodies of the two men. They brought them in, and the arrows too. Of course everybody said it was the Indians that killed them. My brother, Natchez, and our cousin, who was called Young Winnemucca, and one hundred others were sent for. In two days' time they came. My brother was then peace chief. Major Ormsbey asked if he knew what tribe of Indians those arrows belonged to. My cousin told his white brothers the arrows belonged to the Washoes.

So our good father Major Ormsbey said to my brother, "Will you help us to get the Washoe chief to come in and give up the men who killed the two white men?"

My brothers said they would help to find the men that killed poor John McMullen. So that evening my people had what they call a war dance, the first one I had ever seen. A great many white men and women came to see them. Lizzie Ormsbey kept saying, "Where is Natchez?" He was dressed up so we did not know him.

The white people stayed until it was all over, and when it was all over, the major called his men and said, "We will sing 'The Star Spangled Banner.'" It was not a bit like the way my grandfather used to sing it, and that was the first time I had heard it sung by the white people.

My cousin was the war chief. He sent five men to bring in the Washoe chief. The next morning they came in with about ten Washoes. As soon as they came in, the white men gathered round them. Major Ormsbey showed the arrows and asked them if they knew them.

The Washoe chief, who is called Jam, said, "You ask me if these are my people's arrows. I say yes."

Major Ormsbey said, "That is enough." He said to my brother Natchez, "Tell Captain Jam that his people have killed two men, and he must bring the men and all the money, and they shall not be hurt, and all will be right."

The Washoe chief said, "I know my people have not killed the men because none of my men have been away. We are all at Pine Nut Valley, and I do not know what to think of the sad thing that has happened."

"But here are your arrows, and you cannot say anything," said my cousin, the war chief. "We will give you ten days to bring the men who killed our two white brothers, and if you do not, we shall have to fight you, for they have been so kind to us all. Who could have the heart to kill them? Now go and bring in the men."

Poor, poor Washoes, they went away with very sad hearts. After they left, brother talked with all his men and asked them what they thought about it. They all said it was very strange indeed; time would tell whether they killed them or not.

Six days after, the Washoe chief came in with three prisoners. One of the prisoners had a wife, the other two had none, but their mothers came with them. The white men gathered round them and put handcuffs on them to lock them up in a small house for the night. Next morning all the white people came to see them. Some said, "Hang the red devils right off," and the white boys threw stones at them and used most shameful language to them. At about three o'clock in the afternoon came thirty-one white men, all with guns on their shoulders, and as they marched along, my brother and cousin ran to meet them.

One Washoe woman began to scream, "Oh, they have come

to kill them!" How they did cry! One could hear the poor things miles away. My brother went to them and told them not to cry. "Oh, dear chieftain, they did not kill the white men; indeed, they did not. They have not been away from our camp for over a month. None of our men were away, and our chief has given these three young men because they have no fathers."

One of the young girls said, "You who are the mighty chieftain, save my poor brother, for he is all mother and I have to hunt for us. Oh, believe us. He is as innocent as you are. Oh, tell your white brothers that what we tell you is true as the sun rises and sets."

And one woman ran to my cousin, the war chief, and threw herself down at his feet and cried out, "Oh, you are going to have my poor husband killed. We were married this winter, and I have been with him constantly since we were married. Oh, Good Spirit, come! Oh, come into the hearts of this people. Oh, whisper in their hearts that they may not kill my poor husband! Oh, good chief, talk for him. Our cruel chief has given my husband to you because he is afraid that all of us will be killed by you." She raised up her head and said to the Washoe chief, "You have given my innocent blood to save your people."

Then my brother said to the Washoes, "These white men have come to take the three Washoe men who killed John McMullen and MacWilliams to California to put them in jail."

Just then one of the women cried out, "Look there, they have taken them out. See, they are taking them away."

We were all looking after them, and before brother got near them, the three prisoners broke and ran. Of course they were shot. Two were wounded, and the third ran back with his hands up. But all of them died.

Oh, such a scene I never thought I should see! At daybreak all the Washoes ran to where they were killed. The wife of the young man threw herself down on his dead body. Such weeping was enough to make the very mountains weep to see them. They would take the dead bodies in their arms, and they were all bloody themselves.

I ran to Mrs. Ormsbey crying. I thought my poor heart would break. I said to her, "I believe those Washoe women. They say their men are all innocent. They say they were not away from their camp for a long time, and how could they have been the men that killed the white men?" I told her all I had heard the women say, and I said I believed them.

Mrs. Ormsbey said, "How came the Washoe arrows there? And the chief himself has brought them to us, and my husband knows what he is doing."

I ran back to see what they were going to do with the dead bodies, as I had heard my people say that the Washoes were like the Digger Indians, who burn their dead. When I got there, the Washoe chief was talking to my brother. I did not know what he said before I came, but I know from what I heard that he had been making confession.

He said, pointing down to the men that were innocently killed, "It is true what the women say; it is I who have killed them. Their blood is on my hands. I know their spirits will haunt me and give me bad luck while I live."

This was what the Washoe chief said to my brother. The one that was wounded also died, and the sister and the mother it was dreadful to see.

The mother cried out, "Oh, may the Good Spirit send the same curse upon you! You may all live to see the day when you will suffer at the hands of your white brothers, as you call them." She said to her girl, "My child, you have no brother now, no one to love you, no one to come with game and say, 'Here, sister, here is game for you.' You are left all alone. Oh, my sweet son, gone, gone!"

This was the first trouble the poor Washoes had with white people, and the only one they ever did have with them.

So the day passed away, and the two dead Washoes were taken away, and their bodies were burned. That is their custom. The other was taken to California. My poor little sister made herself sick she cried so much that day.

Two days afterward Major Ormsbey sent his men home; so he did my cousin, who is called Young Winnemucca, and brother stayed longer for us, because we had been with Major Ormsbey a long time, and we could talk very well.

My poor little sister was so very sick it was two weeks before we could go to our mother. When we got home it was winter. There was so much snow that we stayed in the mountains where now stands the great city called Virginia City. It was then our pine nut mountains. Sometime during the winter, the Washoe chief came and told us that the white men who killed McMullen and MacWilliams were caught.

My brother Natchez said, "Oh, have they been caught?"

"Yes, that is what Major Ormsbey said; so did all the others." The Washoe chief went on and said, "I have come to ask you to pay me for the loss of the two men. The white men have brought back the other men, and they say that they have hung two men."

My brother told the Washoe chief that his people had nothing to do with what the white people had done. "It is you who ought to pay the poor mother and sister and wife of your own tribe because you gave them up yourself; therefore, you must not blame us. We only did our duty, and we all know that the white men did nothing to us, and we did no more than what they would do for us."

Next day my brother went to see for himself. He gave the Washoe chief a horse to go with him, for the poor Washoes had never owned a horse in their lives. Ten men went with my brother.

CHAPTER IV

CAPTAIN TRUCKEE'S DEATH

MY GRANDFATHER was very sick at that time. My brother was away two days, and my grandfather was very low, so they had to send to him to come back. As soon as he came, word was sent everywhere that their mighty chief was dying. In two days' time, we could see the signal fires of death on every mountaintop.

My brother came back and told his people that it was true that their own white brothers had killed the men for their money. The way they were found out was this: They were playing cards for the money, and one of the men lost his. There were five of them. They were almost fighting about the money, and two men who were out hunting heard them and went near enough to hear all. One of the men went to town to bring someone to arrest them, and the other stayed to watch them.

The one that lost his money said, "If you won't give me back my money, I will tell of you. Are you going to give me back my money or not?"

They all swore at him and told him if he did not stop talking, they would shoot him. Then the sheriffs came and took them and all the money they had. Two of the men told how they got the Washoe arrows and placed them in the wounds as if the Indians had killed them.

This is what brother told his people; he said, "This is what our white brothers told me to say to you."

OUR PEOPLE gathered from far and near, for my poor, poor grandpa was going very fast. His beloved people were watching him. It was the most solemn thing that I ever saw, before or since. Now he sent for a dear beloved white brother of his named Snyder. My brother went for him.

When he came my poor, dear grandfather called him to his bedside and said to him, "I am now going to die. I have always loved you as if you were my dear son, and one thing I want you to do for me." He said to my father, "Raise me up; I want to see my children."

My father raised him up, and while he was looking around him, his eyes fell on me and my sisters. He just looked at us, and he said to the white man, "You see there are my two little girls and there is my big girl, and there are my two boys. They are my sons' children, and the two little girls I want you to take to California, to Mr. Bonsal and Mr. Scott. They will send them to school to the sisters at San Jose. Tell them this is my last request to them. I shall soon die. I shall never see them in person; they have promised to teach my two little girls when they become large enough." He looked up and said, "Will you promise to do this for me?" The white man took my grandfather's hand and promised to do as he asked. My grandfather then bade him good-bye and said, "I want to talk to my own people."

When he was gone, he looked at my father and told him what he must do, as he was to be head chief of the Paiute nation. He cautioned him to be a good father, as he had always been, and after talking awhile, he broke down. We all cried. He remained in that way all night and everyone watched him.

Next morning about ten o'clock, a great many of our people came. The doctor was called to lay hands on him and try to bring him to, but all efforts were in vain, so nothing could be done but watch him, which was done all day. Night came on, and still the watch was kept up. At midnight, which was told by the seven stars reaching the same place the sun reaches at midday, he turned and twisted without opening his eyes.

The doctor said, "He is dying. He will open his eyes in a minute."

Ten minutes passed when he opened his eyes in his usual bright and beautiful way, and his first words were, "Son, where are you? Come and raise me up. Let me sit up." My father raised him up. Then he called mother, saying, "Bring all the children."

Mother awoke my sister. I was not asleep, small as I was. I lay awake watching for fear he would die while I was asleep. We gathered around him. He looked around to see if there were any others but his family present. He saw the white man, the same one that had promised to take care of his little girls. He pointed to his feet when we gathered round him and motioned for him to cover them and he did so.

Then he said, "I've only a minute to spare. I'm so tired; I shall soon be happy. Now, son, I hope you will live to see as much as I have and to know as much as I do. And if you live as I have, you will someday come to me. Do your duty as I have done to your people and to your white brothers." He paused, closed his eyes, and stretched out.

My poor mother, thinking he was dead, threw herself upon his bosom but was aroused by the doctor's saying, "Hold on, the spirit has not left the body."

My mother rose up, and of course, all of us were crying, "Poor grandpa! Poor grandpa!"

Then he recovered himself again and, opening his eyes, said, "Don't throw away my white rag friend; place it on my breast when you bury me." He then looked at his wife as if he wanted to say something, but his voice failed.

Then the doctor said, "He has spoken his last words, he has given his last look, his spirit is gone. Watch his lips; he will speak as he enters the Spirit Land."

And so he did; at least, he seemed to. His lips moved as if he was whispering. We were then told by the doctor that he was in heaven, and we all knew he was. No one who knew him would doubt it.

But how can I describe the scene that followed? Some of you, dear reader, can imagine. Everyone threw themselves upon his body, and their cries could be heard for many a mile. I crept up to him. I could hardly believe he would never speak to me again. I knelt beside him, and took his dear old face in my hands, and looked at him quite a while. I could not speak. I felt the world growing cold; everything seemed dark. The great light had gone out. I had father, mother, brothers, and sisters; it seemed I would rather lose all of them than my poor grandpa. I was only a simple child, yet I knew what a great man he was. I mean great in principle. I knew how necessary it was for our good that he should live. I think if he had put out his hands and asked me to go with him, I would gladly have folded myself in his arms. And now, after long years of toil and trouble, I think if our Great Father had seen fit to call me with him, I could have died with a better opinion of the world.

In regard to the doctor's saying "He will speak as he enters the Spirit Land," I wish to say it is the belief of my people that the spirit speaks as it goes in. They say if a child has a mother or a father in the Spirit Land, he will cry as his soul enters.

Such a scene I never had seen before. Everybody would take his dead body in their arms and weep. Poor Papa kept his body two days. Now came the burial. Everything he had was put into the grave with him. His body was put into blankets when it was ready to be put into the grave, and after he was buried, six of his horses were killed. Now, my dear readers, I do not want you to think that we do this thing because we think the dead use what we put in or if we kill horses at any one's death that they will use them in the Spirit Land. No, no; but it is the last respect we pay our dead.

IN THE spring of 1860, my sister and I were taken to San Jose, California. Brother Natchez and five other men went with us. On our arrival we were placed in the sisters' school by Mr. Bonsal and Mr. Scott. We were only there a little while, say three weeks, when complaints were made to the sisters by wealthy parents about Indians being in school with their children. The sisters then wrote to our friends to come and take us away, and so they did—at least, Mr. Scott did. He kept us a week and sent word to brother Natchez to come for us, but no one could come, and he sent word for Mr. Scott to put us on the stage and send us back. We arrived at home all right.

Shortly after, the war of 1860 began in this way. Two little girls about twelve years old went out in the woods to dig roots and did not come back, and so their parents went in search of them. Not finding them, all my people who were there came to their help, and very thoroughly searched, and found trails which led up to the house of two traders named Williams on Carson River nearby the Indian camp. But these men said they had not seen the children and told my people to come into the house and search it; and this they did, as they thought, thoroughly.

After a few days, they sorrowfully gave up all search, and their relations had nearly given them up for dead when one morning an Indian rode up to the cabin of the Williamses. In those days the settlers did not hesitate to sell us guns and ammunition whenever we could buy, so these brothers proposed to buy the Indian's horse as soon as he rode up. They offered him a gun, five cans of powder, five boxes of caps, five bars of lead, and after some talk the trade was made. The men took the horse, put him in the stable and closed the door, then went into the house to give him the gun, etc. They gave him the gun, powder, and caps, but would not give him the lead, and because he would not take a part, he gave back what he had taken from them and went out to the barn to take his horse. Then they set their dog upon him. When bitten by the dog, he began halloing, and to his surprise he heard children's voices answer him, and he knew at once it was the lost children.

He made for his camp as fast as he could and told what had happened and what he had heard. Brother Natchez and others went straight to the cabin of the Williams brothers. The father demanded the children. They denied having them, and after talking quite a while, denied it again, when all at once the brother of the children knocked one of the Williamses down with his gun and raised his gun to strike the other. But before he could do so, one of the Williams brothers stooped down and raised a trap door on which he had been standing. This was a surprise to my people, who had never seen anything of the kind.

The father first peeped down but could see nothing; then he went down and found his children lying on a little bed with their mouths tied up with rags. He tore the rags away and brought them up. When my people saw their condition, they at once killed both brothers and set fire to the house.

Three days after, the news was spread as usual: "The blood-thirsty savages had murdered two innocent, hard-working, industrious, kind-hearted settlers." Word was sent to California for some army soldiers to demand the murderers of the Williamses. As no army soldiers were there just then, Major Ormsbey collected one hundred and sixty volunteers and came up, and without asking or listening to any explanation, demanded the men. But my people would not give them up. When the volunteers fired on my people, they flew to arms to defend the father and brother, as any human beings would do in such a case—and ought to do.

And so the war began. It lasted about three months, and after a few precious ones of my people and at least a hundred white men had been killed (amongst them our dear friend Major Ormsbey, who had been so hasty), a peace was made.

My brother had tried to save Major Ormsbey's life. He met him in the fight, and as he was ahead of the other Indians, Major Ormsbey threw down his arms and implored him not to kill him. There was not a moment to be lost.

My brother said, "Drop down as if dead when I shoot, and I will fire over you." But in the hurry and agitation, he still stood pleading and was killed by another man's shot.

Some other friends of my brother—Judge Broomfield and servant, and a Spaniard—lived in a small cabin about twelve miles off. They were not fighting against us, and my brother defended their lives and risked his own. He stood at their cabin door, and beat back the assailants with a club, and succeeded in driving them off. But my uncle and cousins were so angry with him for saving white men's lives that they whipped him with a horsewhip. We all knew my uncle loved us. He was always kind to us, but I never could love him again as I had done after he whipped my brother—my noble, patient brother, who bore his uncle no ill will but was satisfied that he had saved the lives of his friends.

Brave deeds don't always get rewarded in this world. There was another occasion when my brother saved the life of his friend,

Mr. Seth Cook of San Francisco, and of six others, but as I do not remember all the particulars, I will not attempt to relate it. Mr. Cook had often given my brother valuable assistance, and he is still living and can tell the story of his escape from death himself.

The regular troops at last reached the ground, and after fighting a little while, raised a flag of truce which was responded to by my brother. Peace was made and a treaty giving the Pyramid Lake Reservation to my people. I have no way of telling any of the particulars. The reservation was given to us in 1860, and we were to get large supplies as long as we were peaceful, but though there were thirteen agents there in the course of twenty-three years, I never knew of any issue after that first year.

AMONG THE traditions of our people is one of a small tribe of barbarians who used to live along the Humboldt River. It was many hundred years ago. They used to waylay my people and kill and eat them. They would dig large holes in our trails at night, and if any of our people traveled at night—which they did, for they were afraid of these barbarous people—they would oftentimes fall into these holes. That tribe would even eat their own dead—yes, they would even come and dig up our dead after they were buried, and would carry them off and eat them. Now and then they would come and make war on my people. They would fight, and as fast as they killed one another on either side, the women would carry off those who were killed. My people say they were very brave. When they were fighting, they would jump up in the air after the arrows that went over their heads and shoot the same arrows back again.

My people took some of them into their families, but they could not make them like themselves. So at last they made war on them. This war lasted a long time. Their number was about twenty-six hundred. The war lasted some three years. My people killed them in great numbers, and what few were left went into the thick bush. My people set the bush on fire. This was right above Humboldt Lake. Then they went to work and made tule or bulrush boats, and went into Humboldt Lake. They could not live there very long without fire. They were nearly starving. My people were watching them all round the lake and would kill them as fast as they would come on land.

At last one night they all landed on the east side of the lake and went into a cave near the mountains. It was a most horrible place, for my people watched at the mouth of the cave and would kill them as they came out to get water. My people would ask them if they would be like us and not eat people like coyotes or beasts. They talked the same language, but they would not give up. At last my people were tired, and they went to work and gathered wood and began to fill up the mouth of the cave. Then the poor fools began to pull the wood inside till the cave was full.

At last my people set it on fire. At the same time they cried out to them, "Will you give up and be like men and not eat people like beasts? Say quick; we will put out the fire." No answer came from them. My people said they thought the cave must be very deep or far into the mountain. They had never seen the cave nor known it was there until then. They called out to them as loud as they could, "Will you give up? Say so, or you will all die." But no answer came. Then they all left the place.

In ten days some went back to see if the fire had gone out. They went back to my third or fifth great-grandfather and told him they must all be dead, there was such a horrible smell. This tribe was called people-eaters, and after my people had killed them all, the people round us called us *Say-do-carah*. It means conqueror; it also means enemy.

I do not know how we came by the name of Paiutes. It is not an Indian word. I think it is misinterpreted. Sometimes we are called pine nut eaters, for we are the only tribe that lives in the country where pine nuts grow. My people say that the tribe we exterminated had reddish hair. I have some of their hair, which has been handed down from father to son. I have a dress which has been in our family a great many years trimmed with this reddish hair. I am going to wear it sometime when I lecture. It is called the mourning dress, and no one has such a dress but my family.

CHAPTER V

RESERVATION OF PYRAMID
AND MUDDY LAKES

T HE RESERVATION, given in 1860, was at first sixty miles long and fifteen wide. The line is where the railroad now crosses the river, and it takes in two beautiful lakes, one called Pyramid Lake, and the one on the eastern side, Muddy Lake. No white people lived there at the time it was given us. We Paiutes have always lived on the river, because out of those two lakes we caught beautiful mountain trout weighing from two to twenty-five pounds each, which would give us a good income if we had it all, as at first. Since the railroad ran through in 1867, the white people have taken all the best part of the reservation from us and one of the lakes also.

The first work that my people did on the reservation was to dig a ditch to put up a gristmill and sawmill. Commencing where the railroad now crosses at Wadsworth, they dug about a mile, but the sawmill and gristmill were never seen or heard of by my people, though the printed report in the United States statutes, which my husband found lately in the Boston Athenaeum, says twenty-five thousand dollars was appropriated to build them. Where did it go? The report says these mills were sold for the benefit of the Indians who were to be paid in lumber for houses, but no stick of lumber have they ever received. My people do not own any timber land now. The white people are using the ditch which my people made to irrigate their land. This is the way we are treated by our white brothers. Is it that the government is cheated by its own agents who make these reports?

In 1864–5 there was a governor by the name of Nye. There were no whites living on the reservation at that time, and there was not any agent as yet. My people were living there and fishing, as they had always done. Some white men came down from Virginia City to fish. My people went up to Carson City to tell Governor Nye that some white men were fishing on their reservation. He sent down some soldiers to drive them away. Mr. Nye is the only governor who ever helped my people, I mean that protected them when they called on him in this way.

IN 1865 we had another trouble with our white brothers. It was early in the spring, and we were then living at Dayton, Nevada, when a company of soldiers came through the place and stopped and spoke to some of my people, and said, "You have been stealing cattle from the white people at Harney Lake." They said also that they would kill everything that came in their way—men, women, and children. The captain's name was Wells. The place where they were going to is about three hundred miles away. The days after they left were very sad hours indeed.

Oh, dear readers, these soldiers had gone only sixty miles away to Muddy Lake, where my people were then living and fishing and doing nothing to anyone. The soldiers rode up to their encampment and fired into it, and killed almost all the people that were there. Oh, it is a fearful thing to tell, but it must be told. Yes, it must be told by me. It was all old men, women, and children that were killed for my father had all the young men with him at the sink of Carson on a hunting excursion, or they would have been killed too. After the soldiers had killed all but some little children and babies still tied up in their baskets, the soldiers took them also, and set the camp on fire, and threw them into the flames to see them burn alive. I had one baby brother killed there.

My sister jumped on father's best horse and ran away. As she ran, the soldiers ran after her, but thanks be to the Good Father in the Spirit Land, my dear sister got away. This almost killed my poor papa. Yet my people kept peaceful.

That same summer another of my men was killed on the reservation. His name was Truckee John. He was an uncle of mine and was killed by a man named Flamens, who claimed to have had a brother killed in the war of 1860, but of course that had nothing to do with my uncle. About two weeks after this, two white men were killed over at Walker Lake by some of my people, and of course soldiers were sent for from California, and a great many companies came. They went after my people all over Nevada.

Reports were made everywhere throughout the whole country by the white settlers that the red devils were killing their cattle, and by this lying of the white settlers the trail began which is marked by the blood of my people from hill to hill and from valley to valley. The soldiers followed after my people in this way for one year, and the Queen's River Paiutes were brought into Fort Churchill, Nevada, and in that campaign poor General McDermitt was killed. These reports were only made by those white settlers so that they could sell their grain, which they could not get rid of in any other way. The only way the cattlemen and farmers get to make money is to start an Indian war so that the troops may come and buy their beef, cattle, horses, and grain. The settlers get fat by it.

During this time my poor mother and sister died, and we were left all alone with only father. The two Indians were taken who had killed the two white men over at Walker Lake. It was said they killed those two white men because the soldiers had killed their fathers at Muddy Lake, but they had no right to say so. They had no proof.

I WILL tell you the doings of the agents in that agency. The first six who came I did not know. In 1866, after my poor mother and sister Mary died, I came down from Virginia City to live with my brother Natchez while there were some white men living on the agency. They had a great many cattle on the reservation at the time. My people did not know how to work as yet. The agent was living there and had a store of dry goods which he sold to my people. I stayed with my brother all winter and got along very poorly for we had nothing to eat half of the time. Sometimes we would go to the agent's house, and he would get my sister-in-law to wash some clothes, and then he would give us some flour to take home.

In the month of May, the agent sold an Indian man some powder. He crossed the river, when he was met by one of the agent's men, who shot him dead on the spot because he had the powder.

My brother and I did not know what to do. All our people were wild with excitement. Brother and I thought he did wrong to sell the powder to one of our men knowing it was against the law. Our people said they would go and kill him.

Brother said to me, "What shall we do?"

I said, "We will go and tell them all to go away this very night."

So we put saddles on our horses, and away we went to tell the agent what our people had said. The river was very high; when crossing it my horse fell down in the river, and I got very wet. Brother jumped off his horse and helped me on again.

We went up to the house, and I said to him, "Mr. Newgent, go away, quick! My people are coming here to kill all of you and tell all who are on the river to go too, for they will surely come and kill them all."

He said, "I am not afraid of them; they will be glad to stop before they do anything. We have a good many guns." He called to his men, saying, "Get your guns ready; we will show the damned red devils how to fight."

Brother said again to him, "We would like to have you go; please do not get us into any more trouble."

He told my brother and me to go away. We did so. As soon as we got to our home, my brother got all his people together and told them to get ten young men and go and watch the crossing of the river, and if any one tried to cross, to catch him. "If there is more than one, kill them if you can; by so doing we will save ourselves, for you know if we allowed our people to kill the white men, we should all be killed here. It is better that we should kill some of our own men than to be all killed here."

About midnight my brother called his people together again. They all came running. Brother said to them, "I had a dream, and it is true that our people who were coming to kill the agent and his men are not going to kill them, but they are going to the Deep Wells, and the deed is already done." The place he spoke of is about thirty miles from the place where we were then, near Virginia City, Nevada. He said, "I see only one dead; one is not dead, but he will die. I see a great many horses taken by them. It is only a dream, but nevertheless, it is true. Get your horses; we will go after them. We must do it or we will all be in trouble."

So brother took thirty of his men to go and head them off if they could. After he went away, I heard one of the men say, "I wonder if what our chief said is true!" Just then someone was seen coming. He gave an alarm of danger at hand. Everyone jumped to their guns. I jumped on a horse, barebacked, to go and meet him, and my men did likewise.

When we met him, my first word was, "What is it?"

He said, "We shall all die this very day."

"Why?" said I.

"Oh, somebody has killed a white man and another is almost dead."

"Where are they?" said I.

"At the Deep Wells."

One of the men said, "Did you see them?"

He said, "Yes, and that is not all; our agent has gone to get soldiers to come and kill us all."

I said, "Where did you see him?"

"Halfway to the soldiers."

Just then we heard another alarm. We all turned our heads toward the noise. We saw another of our men coming as if he was running for his dear life. We all ran to meet him.

He too said, "We shall all be killed." He told the same thing about one dead man and one almost dead. So we returned to the camp again.

The subchief sent out spies to watch and come in to tell us in time to meet our enemies. In this way passed the day. Newgent, our agent, had left his house at daybreak to go to the fort to see some of the officers there. He rode up to the house, got off his horse, and went in to tell them about the trouble he had on the agency. A fearful thing met his eyes. One man was really dead and the other almost dead. He asked what was the matter. The man answered, "Three Indians came here last night and shot us, and they thought they had killed both of us. They have taken all our things away, and they swore at us in good English language that the agent had their brother killed." Poor man, he did not know that he was talking to the very devil that had made all the trouble.

Very late that evening, two of our men came as before. They brought me a letter; these were the words:

Miss Sarah Winnemucca,

Your agent tells us very bad things about your people's killing two of our men. I want you and your brother Natchez to meet me at your place tonight. I want to talk to you and your brother.
    Signed,
    Captain Jerome,
    Company M, 8th Cavalry

It took me some time to read it, as I was very poor indeed at reading writing; and I assure you, my dear readers, I am not much better now. After reading it four or more times, I knew what it said. I did not know what to do, as brother had not returned. I had no ink to write with. My people all gathered round me waiting for me to tell them something. I did not say anything. They could not wait any longer. They asked me what the paper said.

I said, "The soldiers are coming; the officer wants me and my brother to see them at our place." At that time, brother and I had a place on the reservation.

They said, "Oh, it is too bad that he went off this morning; you and he might be the means of saving us. Can you speak to them on paper?"

I said, "I have nothing to write with. I have no ink. I have no pen."

They said, "Oh, take a stick, take anything. Until you talk on that paper, we will not believe you can talk on paper."

I said, "Make me a stick with a sharp point, and bring me some fish's blood." They did as I told them, and then I wrote, saying,

HON. SIR,

My brother is not here. I am looking for him every minute. We will go as soon as he comes in. If he comes tonight, we will come sometime during the night.
    Yours,
    S. W.

I sent the same man back with the letter. He had not been gone long when my brother came in with his men. Everybody ran to him and told him his dream had come true. Some of the men who were with brother said, "We knew it was true before we got here. We saw the horses' tracks, so it is nothing strange to us." Then I told him that the agent had a company of soldiers waiting for him and me at our place. Brother asked when Newgent went for them.

"Early in the morning," I guessed, "and your dream, dear brother, was true. Mr. Coffman and his man are killed."

"Oh, sister, do not fool with your brother."

I said, "Indeed, indeed, it is so."

Everybody cried out, "It is every word of it true."

"Get us fresh horses," said he, "and we will go and see them. Wife, get me something to eat before I go. I want twenty men to go with me and my sister. Dear sister, did you send them word that we would come as soon as I came home?"

"Yes, brother."

We were soon on the road to see the soldiers. We went like the wind, never stopping until we got there. The officer met us. I told him everything from the first beginning of the trouble. I told him that the agent sold some powder to an Indian and that his own men had killed the Indian. I told him how brother and I went to him and asked him and his men to go away, as we had heard that our people were going to kill him. I told him that he talked bad to brother and me because we went to tell him of it. I told this to the officer right before the agent. The agent did not have anything to say, and then the officer asked my brother what he knew about it and if he had seen anything during that day.

He asked, "How many head of horses do you think they have?"

"I don't know—a good many."

"Well, how many do you think?"

"Maybe sixty or more."

I think the officer did not speak to the agent while we were there. We did not stay long, because I was afraid of the soldiers, although the officer asked us to stop all night.

I said, "Brother, we will go back."

The officer said, "We will come down tomorrow and have another talk with your sister." So off we went.

Many of our people did not sleep that night. Brother called all his people together at one place. He told them the soldiers were their friends and not to be afraid of them, because if they had come to fight with them, they would have brought more with them. He told our people there were only a few. So we watched for their coming the next morning.

At last they came and camped alongside of brother's camp. The first thing he did was to tell us not to be afraid. If we wanted protection, the officer would send for his company to come down from Carochel. We said our people were very much afraid of the soldiers. He asked us what we had to eat. We told him we had nothing just then, but we hoped the fish would soon run up the river so that we might catch some. He saw that we had nothing at all. He said he would go up to the fort and tell the commanding officer about us. So he took two men with him and left the rest with us.

Two days afterward a soldier came in and told brother that

the captain had three wagons of provisions for him and his people. Oh, how glad we were, for we were very poorly off for want of something to eat. That was the first provision I had ever seen issued to my people!

The agent came to the officer and said, "If you want to issue beef to the Indians, I have some cattle I can sell you." The officer told him "to be off."

Five days after, five soldiers came down from the fort with a letter for the captain. After he read the letter, he called brother and me to him and said, "I have got a letter from the commanding officer at the fort asking me if your father is here with you."

Brother told him he had not been with us for a long time. I was crying, and I told him father had not been in since the soldiers killed my little brother. I told him that he sent word to us some six months ago that he had gone to live in the mountains and to die there. I was crying all the while I was talking to him. My people were frightened; they did not know what I was saying. Our men gathered all round us. They asked brother what was the matter. He told them what the officer said to me.

"Sarah, don't cry. You and your brother shall go with me, and we will get your father here. If he will come in, he will be cared for by the officers of the army. The commanding officer says you are to go with me to Camp McDermitt, and you can get your father and all your people to come into the army post, where you can be fed. Now, if you will go, we will start by the first of July."

Brother asked me what I thought about it. "Dear brother," I said, "I will do whatever you say. If you say so, we will go and get our father if we can. We can try it."

Brother told all to his people. Some said, "Maybe they will kill him. You and your sister know what liars the white people are, and if you go and get him and he is killed by the soldiers, his blood will be on you."

Brother said, "I believe what the officers say, and if father comes in, they will take good care of us."

They said, "Well, it is your father, and you two know best what to do. If anything happens to him, you will have no one to blame but yourselves."

Brother said, "What has my father done to the white people that they should harm him? Because white people are bad, that is no reason why the soldiers should be bad too." (Brother and my people always say "the white people," just as if the soldiers were not white too.) So we told the captain that we would go with him.

NOW, DEAR readers, this is the way all the Indian agents get rich. The first thing they do is to start a store; the next thing is to take in cattlemen, and cattlemen pay the agent one dollar a head. In this way they get rich very soon so that they can have their gold-headed canes with their names engraved on them. The one I am now speaking of is only a subagent. He told me the head agent was living in Carson City, and he paid him fifteen hundred dollars a year for the use of the reservation. Yet he has fine horses and cattle and sheep, and is very rich. The subagent was a minister; his name was Balcom. He did not stay very long, because a man named Batemann hired some Indians to go and scare him away from the reservation that he might take his place. The leader of these Indians was named Dave. He was interpreter at the Pyramid Lake Reservation. So Batemann got the minister away, and then he got rich in the same way.

While Batemann was agent, I was asked to act as interpreter to the Shoshones by a man called Colonel Dodge, agent for the Shoshone Indians. He was going to issue clothing to them at a place called Battle Mountain. My brother Natchez went all about to summon the people there. I told Colonel Dodge all about our agent at Pyramid Lake Reservation. He said he would go to see him, which he did.

It took three days for the people to come up. Oh, such an issue! It was enough to make a doll laugh. A family numbering eight persons got two blankets, three shirts, no dress goods. Some got a fishhook and line; some got one and a half yards of flannel, blue and red; the largest issue was to families that camped together, numbering twenty-three persons: four blankets, three pieces of red flannel and some of blue, three shirts, three hooks and lines, two kettles. It was the saddest affair I ever saw. There were readymade clothes of all kinds, hats, shoes, and shawls, and farming utensils of all kinds. Bales upon bales of clothing were sent away to Salt Lake City.

After the issue, the things were all to be put into one place. Holy songs were offered up to the Great Spirit Father. The things were blessed before they were to be worn, and all the young men put the blankets round them and danced. In the morning some of the men went round with only one leg dressed in flannel, which made all the white people laugh.

At this issue our agent, Mr. Batemann, gave the Shoshones one ton of flour before this new agent, which made me very angry, and I talked to him before Colonel Dodge.

I said, "You come up here to show off before this man. Go and bring some flour to my people on Humboldt River, who are starving, the people over whom you are agent. For shame that you who talk three times a day to the Great Father in Spirit Land should act so to my people." This man called himself a Christian too.

Then came another agent by the name of Spencer. He was a better one than we had ever had. He issued some blankets to some old men and women and blind people, and gave brother some pieces of land to work upon. He then gave my people wagons, about ten altogether, and he had his daughter brought as a teacher at the rate of fifty dollars a month.

But he soon died, and then came our present agent. He was not married at the time, but he very soon learned that there was money to be made, so he went back and got married. Of course he put his wife in as teacher. Mr. MacMasters, for that is his name, has his own method of making my people divide the produce. If they raise five sacks of grain, they give one sack for the Big Father in Washington; if they have only three sacks, they still have to send one. Every fourth load of hay goes to the Big Father at Washington, yet he does not give my people the seed.

The head farmer, who is called Mushrush, never shows my people how to work. This is why they said, "Why does the Big Father want us to pay him when he does not give us the seed? We have to pay for the seed ourselves." Both the agent and farmer told my people they would have to pay it or the Big Father would take away their wagons. So my people talked it over and said, "We will pay it."

Later they got up a paper which the agent and the farmer wanted my people to sign. The subchief would not put his hand to the pen. He said to the agent, "I have been working for so many years, and I have never received anything as yet. You say it is supplies you are sending me and my people; but I am sick and tired of lies, and I won't sign any paper."

Of course our agent, Mr. MacMasters, told him to leave the reservation. His wagon was taken from him. At this my people sent me down to San Francisco to tell the commanding officer. I did so. I gave General McDowell a full account of the doings, and he reported him to the authorities.

The following spring my poor brother Natchez went to the agent and asked him to help him to a plough and to give him a set of harness. He told my brother to go away. "You and your sister," he said, "talk about me all the time. I don't want you and your sister here."

At this my poor brother got angry and said to him, "This is my reservation, not yours. I am going to stay here just as long as I like. My poor father and I never got so much as an old rag from any agent that ever came here."

At this our minister got angry and telegraphed to the soldiers to come and take brother and carry him to the Acotrass Islands [Alcatraz]. He wrote a letter saying all my people wanted him to send my brother away where they could never see him any more. After he had written it, he called up all the head men of our people and told them he had written to their father in Washington for good clothing for them and wished them to sign the paper. Of course, they did not know any better; they put their names to the paper and signed their chief away! So the soldiers came and took brother to San Francisco. Brother was only there a little while when two white men whose lives he had saved went and took him out and sent him home, and wrote to our minister agent. Of course I knew not what was in the letter.

Dear reader, I must tell a little more about my poor people and what we suffer at the hands of our white brothers. Since the war of 1860, there have been one hundred and three of my people murdered, and our reservations taken from us; and yet we, who are called blood-seeking savages, are keeping our promises to the government. Oh, my dear good Christian people, how long are you going to stand by and see us suffer at your hands?

OH, DEAR friends, you are wrong when you say it will take two or three generations to civilize my people. No! I say it will not take that long if you will only take interest in teaching us; and, on the other hand, we shall never be civilized in the way you wish us to be if you keep on sending us such agents as have been sent to us year after year, who do nothing but fill their pockets and the pockets of their wives and sisters, who are always put in as teachers and paid from fifty to sixty dollars per month, and yet they do not teach. The farmer is generally his cousin, his pay is nine hundred dollars a year, and his brother is a clerk. I do not know his name. The blacksmith and carpenter have from five hundred to eleven hundred dollars per year. I got this from their own statements.

I saw a discharged agent while I was on my way here who told me all the agents had to pay so much to the Secretary of the Interior, who had to make up what he paid to the agents. This I know to be a true confession, or the Secretary of the Interior and all the government officers would see into the doings of these Christian agents. Year after year they have been told of their wrongdoings by different tribes of Indians. Yet it goes on, just the same as if they did not know it.

When I went to Carson City in 1870 to see about my people's affairs, I was sent by the officials from one to another. At last we went to San Francisco to see General Schofield, and he sent me back to see Senator Jones. So brother and I went to where he was living in Gold Hill. I told him how my people were treated by the agents. He said, "I will see to it." He then put into my hands twenty dollars, which I took gratefully, for we were always poor, and brother and I went away. I have never seen or heard from him since.

I CAN give you one example to show how easily the Indians are influenced by those they respect and believe in. In 1868 many of my people were at Camp C. F. Smith taking care of themselves, but under many difficulties and very destitute. There was no game in that region of any kind, except now and then a hare. They had no land to cultivate but were living upon anything they could do or gather.

Some citizens wrote to Colonel McElroy, who was at that time commanding officer at Camp McDermitt, that the Indians were starving, and they were afraid there might be some outbreak or depredations, and they asked him to have them taken to his post. I was interpreter at Camp McDermitt at that time. Five hundred of my people, men, women and children, were already there. There were four hundred at Camp C. F. Smith. Colonel McElroy asked me how many companies of soldiers it would take to escort them. I told him none, that he and I could escort them, or my brother Lee and I. He could not believe me at first, but I told him I knew my people, and he and I, with one servant, went for them.

I went into council with my people. My brother Lee, who was there, and I sat up all night talking with them and telling them what we wished them to do. We Indians never try to rule our people without explaining everything to them. When they understand and consent, we have no more trouble.

Some of the interpreters are very ignorant and don't understand English enough to know all that is said. This often makes trouble. Then I am sorry to say these Indian interpreters, who are often half-breeds, easily get corrupted and can be hired by the agents to do or say anything. I know this for some of them are my relatives. My people are very reasonable and want to understand everything and be sure that there is fair play.

For one thing, they said they had so many children they would find it hard to carry them sixty-five miles. Did I think Colonel McElroy would let them have some wagons? I said I would ask him. He said yes, and he furnished fifteen wagons, which transported the women and children comfortably in two days, and the men had their horses. The recruits who were watching the buildings at

Camp C. F. Smith (for there was not a large force there) furnished
rations for the two days, and Colonel McElroy was to replenish
them from Camp McDermitt.

There were now nine hundred in all at Camp McDermitt.
Every head of a family was furnished with a good tent of the requi-
site size for his family, such tents as are used by the soldiers, and
every morning at five o'clock, rations for the day were issued. A
pound and a half of meat was given to every grown person, and
good bread—for they actually baked good bread for them—and
once a month coffee, rice, sugar, salt, pepper, and beans were
issued. Each woman came to me every day with her basket and
her number on a tag fastened to a leather thong tied round her
neck and told the size of her family and took what she needed
from me; and everything was recorded, for that is the way things
are done in soldiers' camps. Everyone had enough.

My father was with us at that time. He told my people in
council one day that he thought it was an imposition to be living
entirely on the soldier-fathers when we could do something to
support ourselves. He wanted them to go on hunting excursions
in the summer and bring in dried venison, rabbits, and what other
game they could find, and the women to go out and gather grass
seed and dig roots and do what they could toward the supplies
of the next winter.

I told Colonel McElroy what my father had said to his people,
and he told them to go to the sutler's store and get what ammunition they wanted and bring him the record of it, and he would
see that it was paid for. My father knew that the army gave this
support for the Indians as prisoners out of its own supplies. My
people had enough, I said; they had more than enough, and by
being prudent about their rations, they could save and sell enough
to get calicoes and other necessary things for the women and
children, for these things are not found in army supplies. It is

this generosity and this kind care and order and discipline that make me like the care of the army for my people.

Colonel McElroy belonged to Company M, Eighth Cavalry. He had my people in charge three years and was then ordered to New Mexico, but before he could go, he died in San Francisco. He was the first officer I ever worked for as interpreter.

Can you wonder, dear readers, that I like to have my people taken care of by the army? It is said that I am working in the interest of the army and as if they wanted all this care. It is not so, but they know more about the Indians than any citizens do and are always friendly. Nobody really knows Indians who cheat them and treat them badly. They may be very peace-loving people, but that would make saints sin. They are the most sociable people in the world in their own camps, but they are shut up to white people because they are so often wronged by them.

I remained at Camp McDermitt after Colonel McElroy's death. They thought it best to buy a large herd of cattle for beef for the soldiers and my people, and for a time they hired some of the Indians for herdsmen, but this proved too expensive, and they were discharged from that service, which was given to some soldiers.

One night the whole herd was stolen and driven off. The greatest search was made for them, but all in vain. It seemed as if they had vanished. But at last, the commanding officer thought the Indians, who knew how to track a trail, would do better at such business than white men, who do not know how to find a trail of anything. My brother Lee was staying with me then, and he and five other men undertook to find the cattle.

They were gone five days, and at the end of the time came back and said they were found. They had traced them to a deep canyon, and they were driven by one single man. One man had stolen and driven away all those cattle. My people had come back to get soldiers to go with them to capture him. So he was arrested and brought back to the post with all the cattle. It was truly comical to think of it. I was very glad my people were successful, for it would surely have been believed that some Indians, if not mine, had driven those cattle off.

THE LAST time sister and I were on a visit to our people at our old home, just before I was married, we stopped with a white lady named Nichols at Wadsworth, Nevada, on Pyramid Lake Reservation, the head farmer named Mushrush, and the subagent at Walker River Reservation in Nevada.

Someone tried to break through our bedroom door, and my sister cried out to them, saying, "Get away from that door or I will shoot!" At my sister's words they went away.

The name of the subagent is Louis Veviers, who has been with my people about eight years. All my people call him dog, because there is nothing too bad for him to say to them.

After I was married, I went to let my people see my husband. While we were there, we stayed with my brother Tom. On New Year's evening we heard a great noise coming toward the house. They were trying to make a noise like my people who had just lost a son and were crying. They were mocking them as they came on. There were four men—the doctor, the carpenter, the blacksmith, and one of their friends. My brother's wife gave them some pine nuts.

By and by one of them gave my husband a bottle of firewater and asked him to pass it round. My husband replied, "Pass it round yourselves."

They said, "Give some to your brother-in-law."

My husband said, "Give it to him yourself." This is the kind of people, dear reader, that the government sends to teach us at Pyramid Lake Reservation.

My people wanted to cut the hay, but they were not allowed to sell it until within five years. My cousin, Captain Bill, and his brother had borrowed some seed by promising to divide the wheat after harvest, which they did, and then the farmer, who never showed them how to sow their grain, came to Bill, and said, "You must pay me for the use of the government land."

"What for?" said Bill.

"Well, that's what the Big Father in Washington says."

Then Bill said, "Take it all."

After Mr. Mushrush took his unjust share, my poor cousin had only three sacks left for himself.

Our present agent made my people give every third sack of grain and the same of everything else. Every third load of hay is given. My people asked why, as he had not given them seed for planting, nor did the farmer help them. They did not see why they should pay so much, but the agent told them that was the order from Washington. They refused to pay it. The agent told them they must pay it or he would take their wagons away. They went home to talk it over that night.

However, Jim, the subchief, told his people that the white men had been stealing from them for a long time, "and now I am going to steal from them this very night. I am going to have my family hide away half of my grain. I have sixty sacks of wheat and twenty-six of potatoes. As for the hay cart, I don't care. What do you think of me for talking so to you? I see I can't keep up with the white people. They think it right to steal all they can while they are with us. And I am going to do another thing: I am going to quit signing any paper, for I don't know what I have been signing all these twenty-two years."

My cousin Captain Bill and his brother said, "We will keep all our grain, and if he wants the wagon, he can take it."

Then all the rest of the men said, "We will do the same as

our chief, and what is left he can have."

Some of them said, "We have only a little, and what shall we do?"

The next morning they went to the agent's house to see if he had changed his mind, but he told them that was the law.

Bill told him that he might go and get his wagon. "I bought my seed and paid my own money for it, and you did not help me."

The agent replied, "If you won't do what the government orders, you must leave the reservation."

Jim, the subchief, said, "You may take all I have, leave my people theirs, and I will go away into the mountains, and there I will live and die."

But the agent would not hear to it, and they all had to pay their share.

My brother Tom said, "If we don't pay it, we shall have to leave the reservation."

The agent thought it necessary to make a show of some kind, and this is the way he did it. There are unprincipled men in all tribes, as I suppose there are among all people, and the agent found one for his work. He is known as Captain Dave. His Indian name is Numana.

The plan made and carried out was this: Captain Dave was furnished with money and appointed captain of police, a useless office, for Indians could not arrest either an Indian or a white man. They really were nothing but private servants to the agent. But this was promised to Captain Dave, provided he and six others would go to San Francisco and do what the agent wanted them to do.

They were furnished with a drawing of a bridge that had been built and told to go to the newspaper offices in San Francisco and say beautiful things of the agent and his men. Every reasonable person will see by reading this paper, which was published in a newspaper, that the most intelligent Indian could not have given such a description of a bridge without he bad been furnished with a memorandum of it.

CAPTAIN DAVE AND THE RESERVATION

Numana, better known as Captain Dave, one of the leading men of the Piute nation, called on us yesterday, and showed us several papers, among which was a letter of recommendation from Governor Kinkead, and an appointment from the Indian Commissioner as captain of the Indian police at Pyramid Reservation. Dave is a very intelligent Indian, and gave us the following facts connected with the Piutes and their doings: He and his body-guard of six Piutes have just returned from a trip to San Francisco, where they spent the holidays pleasantly. He had in his possession a very good cut of the bridge at the reservation and its dimensions, which are, length one hundred and sixty-five feet, width twenty feet, height fifteen feet above low-water mark. A flume crossing the river on the bridge which carries the water from their irrigating ditch on the east side of the river to the other measures as follows: length twelve hundred feet, width six feet, height above ground on trestle eight to fifteen feet. He showed us by a rough sketch the course of the river at the reservation, the position of the dam, and the route of the ditch, which is not finished as yet. The dam is so constructed as to allow a channel (whereby the fish can run up) about ten feet wide and three or four feet deep. From the head of the ditch to the bridge is about one and a quarter miles, from the bridge to the Reservation House, about two miles. The ditch, when completed, will measure four miles and will irrigate a large area of land. The Indians are not working now, but are devoting their time to fishing. Agent McMasters is well-liked by the Indians, and he has a system of dealing with them which they fully understand and appreciate. Mrs. McMasters has charge of the school, and teaches some thirty Indian children, many of them being apt scholars, and all seeming to like to attend school.

Mr. Mushrush, the farmer, is giving perfect satisfaction, showing the Indians how to work, and doesn't simply order, but takes a hand himself, which Dave says pleases them.

They intend to farm on a larger scale next year than at any time before. Mr. McMasters' method in dividing the produce is stated by Captain Dave to be in this way. The Indian raises five sacks of grain, he retains four, and gives the government one. If he has four loads of hay he gives one of them to the government. This is given by the Indians to help feed the government stock, which is kept at work hauling stone, lumber, wood, etc., etc. Dave is very desirous of having the Piutes in all parts of Nevada notified to come to the reservation, and help build it up. He claims that in one year's time they will have room and work for them, and they can come there and build a home. He is also very anxious that the whiskey traffic among them be stopped, and to that end asks that the officers in e very town will see that a drunken Indian be punished as severely as possibly. This, he claims, is a terrible curse among them, and is gaining ground.

No newspaper in San Francisco would publish this statement,

and they were obliged to have it done in Reno, Nevada, in a paper the civilized world knows nothing of.

I will only speak now of the character of Captain Dave. I said Mr. Batemann hired an Indian to frighten Mr. Balcom away. That Indian was this very Captain Dave. I have known him many years, and have always been ashamed of him as a Paiute. Twenty years ago I knew him to blow a young girl's brains out because she refused to marry him, and his behavior ever since has been in keeping with that. It is no secret among my people that he exposes his wife to bad white men for money. He is not a "leading man." No man can be a leading man among Indians, unless he is honorable and brave. Dave is neither. On the contrary, he has no character whatever and could always be hired to do a wicked thing. He is my own cousin.

Mr. Mushrush, the farmer spoken of in the printed article, does all his farming in the bar room at Wadsworth. We have a store at this agency kept by Mr. Eugene Griswold. He is the man who always gets the beef contracts. It may be in another man's name sometimes, but it is all the same.

It has always been a mystery to me what this beef contract is for. If they mean it for a license to sell beef, why don't they say so? I defy them to find a man, woman, or child outside their ring who has ever received a pound of meat of any kind from them. I have a brother who lives on the agency, and he has never got an ounce of meat that he has not paid for. The contractors—Griswold, McMasters, etc.—really keep a butcher's shop but call it a beef contract. Those that have money can come up and buy. Those that have none stand back and cry, often with hunger.

All this refers to the Pyramid Lake Agency. The contractors call it the "Nevada Agency."

BROTHER AND I started for Camp McDermitt, Nevada, at the time set, along with company M, First Cavalry. It took us twenty-eight days to reach Camp McDermitt. Nothing happened during our journey. We reached the camp late in the evening. Brother and I did not see anybody until the next day.

After we had something to eat in the morning, the commanding officer, Major Seward, sent for us to come to his office. We did so. He was a very nice man.

He said to brother, "Are you tired?"

Brother said, "Not much. I guess my sister is."

He said to me, "You find it pretty hard traveling, don't you."

I answered, "It is pretty hard, it is so very warm."

He said to my brother Natchez, "Do you think you can find your father, or don't you think you can get him and his people to come to this place? I would like to have him come, so he can be taken care of. He is too old to be out in this bad country. If General Crook should find him and his people, he might make him some trouble. The white settlers are talking very badly through the whole country, and they have sent for General Crook to come and kill all the Indians that are not on some reservation. I am afraid to have your father out there. Natchez, if you can bring him in, I will feed him and his people, and will give them clothes such as the soldiers wear. I will be his friend and fight for him if he and his people are good."

I said, "Colonel, my good papa has never done anything unkind to the white people yet, and the soldiers came to Muddy Lake and killed a great many of our people there without our doing any bad thing to them. They killed my little brother. This is what drove my poor papa away; we have not seen him for two years."

Brother then said, "Yes, Colonel, it is too bad the way the white people say all the time that Indians are bad, and that they have bad hearts, and that their hearts are very black. Colonel, if you will give me your heart and hand, I will go and try to get my father to come to you."

"Yes, Natchez, I will do everything I have told you. I will send one company of cavalry with you. Your sister can stay here and talk for those that are already here. She shall be my interpreter, and I will pay her sixty-five dollars per month, and I will pay you five dollars a day while you are away."

Brother said, "Colonel, I don't want to have any soldiers go with me. I will go all alone, because my people will think I have brought soldiers to fight them. For fear they will think so, I will go alone. I will find my father sooner by going alone, for I will make the son's signal fire as I go along, and my father will know it is I who is coming to see him (the signal fires are like so many telegraphs of many kinds and orders), and he will come to meet me. And Colonel, you will take good care of my sister. See that no soldiers talk to her, and Colonel, I want you to give me a paper to tell the white people I meet who I am so they will not kill me. You know, Colonel, the white men like to kill us Indians."

The colonel said, "All right, Natchez, I will give you a paper."

So the talk ended. My brother was to go in the morning.

The colonel said, "We will go now and see the prisoners. I have twenty-five Queen's River Paiutes here already." As we walked along he said, "They are very good Indians. They are always ready to do whatever I tell them to do that is in the line of work. You will see that I have given them such clothes as I give my soldiers, but the women and children I can't do much for, because the government does not give me anything for them. But we will see what can be done for them after your father comes in, and when your sister gets rested, she may be able to do something for them."

We got to the camp at last. They all ran out of their tents to see us. The men ran to brother, saying, "My brother, oh, my brother!" They threw their arms round him, calling him many endearing words. Then they would throw their robes down on the ground for him to sit upon. They had not said a word to me until my brother told them I was his sister. Then they held out their hands to me, saying, "Our sister, we are glad to see you too. Oh, how kind of you to come and see us so far away." Then the women came to me crying, and said the same, "Our sister, we are glad to see you. Oh, how kind of you to come and see us so far away." It is the way we savages do when we meet each other; we cry with joy and gladness. We told the officer to go, we would come back soon. We would be ready at seven o'clock. Our people said many beautiful things about their black-clothes fathers. They should have said blue-clothes. They said, "We are getting plenty to eat, and we men get nice clothes to wear, and we do very little work for the clothes. All the work we do is only child's play. We would do more if they would only ask us to. We are as happy as we can be."

Brother said, "I am so glad, my people, to hear you say so, because I was going to leave my poor sister here all alone with the soldiers. I was afraid they might abuse her."

Then some of the women said to me, "Oh, dear, you can stay with us. We will make you a nice place."

I said, "Oh, brother, why can't I stay here with our own people? I will be so happy here with the girls."

"Oh, yes! Stay here with us, we will have such a good time."

Brother told them he was going to see his father and try to get him to come and live there with them.

They all said, "How nice that will be!"

Some of the old men said, "Oh, if he could only forget the wrong that the white men did to him. But of course he cannot forget it. Oh, it is hard how the white people are treating us. We cannot help it, we have to stand it like a little mouse under a cat's paws. They like to see us suffer, and they laugh at us when we weep, but our soldier-fathers are good; we will go with you to get your father. We can tell him how kind the soldiers are to us."

While the talk was going on, a soldier came and said that the commanding officer wanted us. Brother told the commanding officer he wanted five men to go with him in the morning.

I was afraid. I said to brother, "Can't I stay here while you go and see what he wants with us?"

He went up. It was lunchtime. After lunch brother told the commanding officer that he had heard something good about him and his men.

He answered, "I am glad of it."

Brother told him he would take five men with him to speak for him. "I think I shall have no trouble," he said, "in getting my father to come."

The officer said, "All right, Natchez; you want six horses then."

So next morning very early they started out and left me alone. I felt so badly, and I cried so much that my eyes were all swelled up. I could not eat anything.

After my brother had gone, I went to the commanding officer and said, "Colonel, I am here all alone with so many men. I am afraid. I want your protection. I want you to protect me against your soldiers, and I want you to protect my people also; that is, I want you to give your orders to your soldiers not to go to my people's camp at any time, and also issue the same order to the citizens." Accordingly the order was issued, and posted here and there, and the result was that we lived in peace.

Soon after this my brother found and persuaded my father and four hundred and ninety of my people to come into Camp McDermitt. On their arrival they were kindly received by the commanding officer. Clothing such as the soldiers wear was given to them, and rations were also issued—good bread, coffee, sugar, salt, pepper, pork, beef, and beans. So we lived quietly for two years.

ONE NIGHT a man named Joe Lindsey crawled into our camp. It was reported by one of my men to the commanding officer, who had him arrested and confined that night. The next day he was released with the understanding that he would leave the reservation. Nothing of importance occurred for three weeks when a soldier who had been fishing, and having drunk more than was good for him, staggered through our camp. Although he troubled no one, he was corrected and tied up by the thumbs all day and then placed in the guardhouse all night. I tell this to show what is done to any one who violates the orders given by officers of the army.

The following winter the man Lindsey came back with the express purpose of killing the Indian who reported him. He met him in the post traders' store. There were several white men in the store at the time. The Indian could not understand English, so did not know that they were planning to kill him.

After some talk, Lindsey said, "I'll bet the whiskey for the crowd that I can shoot his eye out."

Someone took the bet, and without any more delay, he turned round and shot him just below the eye. He then coolly pulled out his knife and scalped him and put the scalp in his pocket, got on the stage, and went to Winnemucca, eighty-five miles. Then he went from saloon to saloon calling for drinks and offering to pay for them with a scalp of a good Indian—a dead one.

His partner put the body of the unfortunate Indian in the trader's buggy and tried to hide it, but the beautiful white snow was too pure to hide the cowardly deed. His blood could be seen for miles and miles, and so we tracked them and brought the body back, and such a time as I had to keep my people quiet!

Early the next morning, the warriors assembled, determined

to begin a war to the death. I talked and reasoned for hours and at last persuaded them to go to their camps. Every effort was made by the commanding officer, Major Seward, to bring those "hard-working, honest, and kind-hearted settlers" to trial, but in vain. All that could be done was done. Their den was broken up, and shortly after this very gang had the audacity to put in a bill of damages against the government because the commanding officer had their cabin torn down and moved away.

CHAPTER VI

THE MALHEUR AGENCY

IN 1875 I was in Camp Harney, Oregon, to see my father. It was in May. I had not been there but a little while when my brother Lee came from the Malheur Agency, bringing me a letter from the agent, Mr. Parrish, inviting me to come to Malheur Agency and act as his interpreter to my people. After I read the letter, I told my father I should not like to go there, but my brother Lee would not hear to my refusing. Then I asked my father if he would go with me. He said, "Yes, dear child, I will go with you."

So we got ready very early one morning, for we wished to make it in one day. It was fifty miles east of Camp Harney. We traveled all day and got to the Malheur Agency late. Mr. Parrish was very glad to see us. He gave me a very nice little room to live in and said he would pay me forty dollars per month to talk for him. I took that offer, for I had no other way of making a living for myself. The army had no more prisoners, and therefore they could not give me a place to interpret for them, so I went to work. My people, who had been under the other agent's care, did not know how to work.

This reservation in Oregon was set apart for my people in 1867. I am quite sure there had been one agent before Mr. Parrish and that he went to stealing too badly. His interpreter, my cousin, whose name is Jarry, reported his doings to the officers at Fort Harney in Oregon. So Colonel Otis sent some of his soldiers under a lieutenant with directions to go there and stay and watch him.

They had not been there but a month or two when the lieutenant went to the agent and said, "I want to buy some clothes for my men." So the agent sold him and his men some flannel shirts at the rate of three dollars apiece! This was reported to the Commissioner of Indian Affairs. So you see the soldiers are our friends at all times. After the agent was discharged, Mr. Parrish came to take care of my people, and then my poor cousin Jarry was taken sick with sore eyes, and my brother Natchez sent him to San Francisco to be under a doctor's care. So Mr. Sam Parrish had no interpreter at the time he sent for me. Then he and I called my people to his office, and he began to talk to them about work.

First he said, "Now you are my children. I have come here to do you good. I have not come here to do nothing; I have no time to throw away. I have come to show you how to work, and work we must. I am not like the man who has just left you. I can't kneel down and pray for sugar and flour and potatoes to rain down, as he did. I am a bad man; but I will try and do my duty and teach you all how to work so you can do for yourselves by and by. We must work while the government is helping us and learn to help ourselves. The first thing I want you to do is to make a dam and then dig a ditch. That is to irrigate the land. Some of you can dig the ditch, some can build the dam, some can go to the woods and cut rails to build fences.

"I want you all to work while the government is helping us, for the government is not always going to help us. Do all you can until you get helped, and all you raise is your own to do with as you like. The reservation is all yours. The government has given it all to you and your children.

"I will do more. I will build a schoolhouse, and my brother's wife will teach your children how to read like the white children. I want three young men to learn to be blacksmiths, and three to learn to be carpenters. I want to teach you all to do like white people. You see, the poor white man has no one to help him. He gets some land, and he works it as best he can. Now you see the government is good to you. It gives you land for nothing and will give you more—that is, it will give you clothes, and a store, and I want you, chiefs of the Paiutes, to ask all your people to come here to make homes for themselves. Send out your men everywhere and have them come to this place. This is the best place for you all, and as soon as we get started, I will write to your father in Washington to send us a mill to grind our grain. We will raise a little something this summer. We can plant some potatoes and turnips and watermelons. We will not plant wheat, because we have no mill, but we can raise barley and oats."

My father said to his people, "What do you all think of what this man, our new father, says?"

The subchief, Egan, said, "For my part I think it is very good if he will only carry it out. There has been so much said that has never been fulfilled by our other agent. But we have no other way only to do what we are told to do. Oytes, you have your men."

"I have my men, and our father Winnemucca has his," said Oytes. "I am not going to work. I and my men have our own work to do—that is, to hunt for our children. You all know we don't get enough to eat."

Of course I told Mr. Parrish everything each of the subchiefs said, and so did my father.

Mr. Parrish said, "All right, Oytes, you can do just as you like."

My father got up and said, "My son Natchez says if we do not do as we are told by the white people, we will not get along at all. My children are talking for you all, and they tell us just what our white fathers say. We will all work at whatever our white father says we must work at."

Egan said, "Yes, we will work. I and my men will go into the timber and cut rails."

My father said, "I will take the rest of the men to go to work upon the ditch."

One of the men belonging to Oytes said, "We will work; let this man go." He meant Oytes, who was always getting us into trouble.

So my people went to work with good heart, both old men and young women and children. We were as happy as could be. They worked five days when Mr. Parrish told me to go and call them in. I did as he told me, and they all came in. He told me to tell them how glad he was to see them so willing to do as he had told them.

He said, "I don't like to see the old men and the women work, and they must not do it. The men are too old, and the women must not work in the field like the men. They can work in another way. They can cook for their husbands and have their meals ready at noon and at supper and early in the morning." But the old men would not mind; they worked on with the rest of the men.

My people got flour, and beef, and sometimes beans. As for myself, I had to pay for my board, as I was making a great deal of money; that is, I was making forty dollars a month. At that time I only paid fifteen dollars a month.

The ditch was getting finished. It was two and a half miles long and ten feet wide, and they were getting it through nicely. They were only six weeks at it. This is quite a contrast to our Pyramid Lake Reservation. They only got three miles of ditch on that reservation, which is twenty-three years old. They have been building a dam and a ditch all this time. There have been twelve different agents there during that time who taught them nothing. When my people had finished the work Mr. Parrish gave them to do at the Malheur, he sent for Egan to come in with his men. They came two days after.

The next day Mr. Parrish sent for all the rest to come. They did so, and after they had sat down and smoked, he said to me, "Sarah, you may tell your people that I am glad to see them so willing to work; your other agent told me that you would not work, that you were lazy."

My father broke out laughing; they all laughed and said, "What can they expect from women who have never been taught to work?"

Our father, Parrish, went on talking, and said, "All my people say that you won't work, but I will show them that you can work as well as anybody, and if you go on as we have started, maybe the Big Father at Washington will now give us a mill to grind our corn. Do all you can, and I know government will help you. I will do all I can while I am with you. I am going to have a schoolhouse put up right away so that your children can go to school. After you have cut your hay, you can go out hunting a little while and get some buckskins; I know you would like that."

My father said to his people, "Now, don't you think this is the best father we ever had in all our lives?"

One and all of them said, "Yes, and we are all ready to do what he wants us to."

So they all went to him and shook his hands, and his brother's hands too, Charley Parrish, and he has a lovely wife. Mrs. Parrish is dearly beloved by my people and myself. She is a beautiful lady as well as a good one. Oh, if they had stayed with us for five or six years, my poor people would not have suffered so much, and those who have been frozen to death would be living today.

Now we wanted a road because our flour must be hauled here for the winter. My people went to work with good heart; in this way we lived for five months. We were happy and contented.

In the month of September, we had some visitors. They were Columbia River Indians, and they came to trade with my people every summer. They said, "We come to trade with you for your furs and your buckskins. We will give you horses for them."

My people said they would ask their father before they would trade with them. The Columbia River Indians were angry at this and went off. These Indians knew the value of the furs. They did not want our white father to know about their trading with us. The Indian who said he would not work (Oytes) went off with them, and they stopped about thirty miles away. Then the Columbia River Indians gave Oytes three horses, telling him to come back and get some of his men to come and trade with them; they would wait there for them.

So Oytes came back and told our people to go with him to the Columbia River Indians and trade. He said, "Take everything; your furs, and blankets, and buckskins too."

My father and Subchief Egan came to me and said, "We have come to tell our father, Parrish, what Oytes is doing. He wants us to go to those bad Indians and trade with them."

Egan said, "Yes, they are our enemies, and we must not have them coming here, for they will bring us trouble. We are afraid of Oytes; he is a very bad man."

I told Mr. Parrish everything that father and Egan had said about Oytes. Our good white father said the same thing as my father did. He said the Columbia River Indians were always making trouble and it was best that they should never come to the reservation at all.

Father and Egan said, "Our good father, we are afraid of

Oytes because he says he can make us all die here. Last winter we had some kind of sickness, and a great many of our children died. He said it was he who was making us sick, and he told us to pay him or else we would all die. Every one of us paid him, but a great many died anyhow."

"Well, I will talk to Oytes; you must not be afraid of him. I will see to him," Mr. Parrish said.

He told Egan to tell Oytes to come over, but while my father and Egan were talking with our agent, Oytes took thirty men off with him to the Columbia River Indians.

Everything went along very nicely, and Oytes came back with his men about twenty-one days afterward. Our agent sent for them all to come to him.

After my people gathered together, he got up and said, "Now, my children, I am glad that you have been so obedient. You have all done well but one, and I am sorry for him, but I think he will be good also. I know he will be ashamed of himself by and by.

"I want the men who cut the hay to come and stand on one side." They did so, six in number. "Now those that cut grain." There were ten of them. "Now there are two stacks of hay. How many stacked the small stack?"

"Two."

"And the big stack?"

"Four."

"All right. The small stack will be mine. I have two horses, and I will pay you for that stack. The big one is yours. There are six horses and two mules that work for you, and if it is a hard winter, you can feed your ponies too. And I will also pay for part of the grain. I want you all to understand me. The two horses are mine, and the six horses and two mules are yours. The government has given them to you. That is why I will pay you for what you cut, and the money I give for the grain I will give to your two chiefs;

that is, to your father Winnemucca and to Egan." He stopped and asked, "Is that all right?"

My people, one and all, said, "Yes, all right."

He then asked the two men how many days they took to cut and stack the hay. The men said eight days. "Very well, I will pay you one dollar a day. Now I want to tell you something more. If you work for me or any of my men, we are to pay you for it. If you cut or pile wood, we will pay you for it. If I send you to Canyon City for myself or my men, you shall be paid for it."

He asked them if they liked his law. They all got up and said, "Truckee, Truckee." That means very well, very well. Then he paid eight dollars apiece to the two men for the hay and gave my father twenty dollars and the same to Egan.

He then said, "How many of you want to go out hunting?"

They said, "We would all like to go."

"Well, you can go, and don't stay too long, because your potatoes will be ready to be dug." So he gave each man a can of powder and some lead and caps, and also to each one a sack of flour.

Oh, how happy my people were! That night we all got together and had a dance. We were not so happy before for a long time. All the young people went on the hunt, and the old stayed and drew their rations right along. The carpenter went on with the schoolhouse till he had to stop on account of having no lumber to go on with. At last my people came in with their ponies laden with dried venison. My father did not come in. He sent word by Egan to me that he would go to Pyramid Lake Reservation to see the rest of our people there. So I was left all alone. I felt very badly because he went away. I was afraid of Oytes, I don't know why; Oytes did not get any powder to go hunting with. Some of his men gave him some after they all got in.

Mr. Parrish told me to tell all my people to come next day to get their rations. While I was there talking to Egan, Oytes came and said, "I want you to talk to your father, as you call him. Tell him I and my men are going to live with our brothers; that is, the Columbia River Indians. I cannot call that white man my father. My father was black, like myself, and you are all white but me; therefore, tell him I quit my country."

I said to Egan, "I will go."

Egan said, "I will go with you."

When we had got over the river, we looked back and saw Oytes coming. I said to Egan, "I am so afraid of that man."

"Oh," he said, "he is nobody. Don't you mind him. If he can make you afraid of him, that is all he wants, but if you are not afraid of him, he will be one of the best men you ever saw. We will tell our agent what he said to us."

Oytes came riding fast and overtook us. "You are our good teacher; don't you think our agent has treated me badly, and do you blame me for wanting to go away?"

I said, "Oytes, I have lived a long time with the white people, and I know what they do. They are people who are very kind to anyone who is ready to do whatever they wish. You see the agent is kind to all but you. Why, can you tell me?" I said to him.

He said, "I don't know."

"You want me to tell you?"

He would not say, and I would not tell him until he said he knew why.

We got off our horses and went in to talk with our agent. I told him everything that Oytes had said.

Our good white father said to Oytes, "I am heartily sorry that you have such a bad heart. Let me tell you, Oytes, if you want to get your young men into trouble, you can. I have not come here to make you do what you don't want to do. I came to tell you all that government is willing to do for you, and if you will not do it, I cannot help you. I have men here to teach you all how to work, and now you want to take your men away with those bad Columbia River Indians. They are just like you. They don't want to work like other people. Now the sooner you go, the better. I don't want to say anything more to you. Get out."

After he was gone, Mr. Parrish said to Egan, "You will all get your rations, and day after tomorrow is Sunday. On Monday I want you all to come here. We will dig our potatoes, and some of you must make a place to put them in."

On Monday came men, women, and children, and they went to work to dig potatoes, and everything was put away for winter. They were told to come and get their potatoes whenever they wanted to, and soon my people were called again. This time women and children were to come too. What a beautiful time we had all day long issuing clothing to all, ten yards of calico to every woman, ten yards of flannel for underwear, and unbleached muslin also to every woman. Pantaloon goods were given to the boys, handkerchiefs, shoes, stockings, shawls, and blankets. Men got shirts, pants, hats, looking glasses, and shoes; some red shirts, some got red blankets, some white. They got whatever color they liked. It was the prettiest issue I had ever seen in my life or have seen since. Everybody got something but two, one man and one woman. He would look at me and smile, but he did not say anything till it was all over. Mr. Parrish did not say anything to him.

Everybody was gone but Oytes and myself. He came to me and said, "You and I are two black ones. We have not white fathers' lips."

I said, "No, we are two bad ones. Bad ones don't need any pity from any one."

He laughed and went away.

That same night my cousin came over and said, "Oytes is coming over to kill our agent. We have said everything to him; we have given him our blankets, but that won't do. What will we do?"

I said, "We will tell Mr. Parrish." So I ran and told him, and he told his brother and all his men, six altogether, and three women—the doctor's wife, C. W. Parrish's wife, and her servant girl—and three children. Twelve white persons, among seven hundred Indians to come.

Our good agent sent for Oytes to come over the next morning. Egan brought him, and Mr. Parrish said to him, "Oytes, I have three hundred dollars. If you will let me shoot at you, if my bolt won't go through your body, the money is yours. You say bolts cannot kill you."

Our agent shook him, and Oytes cried out, "Oh, my good father, don't kill me. Oh, I am so bad. Oh, I will do everything you say. I never will say no to anything you will say. I will do just as my men are doing. I will not go away if you will forgive me."

Our agent said, "All right, Oytes. Don't let me hear any more of your talk, do you hear? You shall not fool with me, and don't say any more to your own people."

"No, good father, I will not say anything more."

So they shook hands and were good friends afterward. Our good agent gave him a red blanket, and red shirts and hat, and pants and shoes. He gave him everything he could think of and told him to give back all the things belonging to his people. So we got along happily afterward, and Oytes was the first one to be ready with his men when our agent wanted work done.

WE WERE all good friends, and our agent liked my people, and my people loved him. All his men were good men.

My people did some work during the winter. There were three miles of a ditch to make, and they all worked on it. There was only half a mile to be finished when a very long letter came one day, and Mr. Parrish called all the men to come in the evening. He told us that we had two hundred and ninety-two enemies in Canyon City. He said the name of the captain of these men was Judge Curry. This man wanted the west end of our reservation, and our Big Father in Washington wanted to know what we thought about it.

"These white men," he said, "have talked to your Father in Washington, saying that you are lazy and will not work."

Leggins and Egan said, "Our father, you are here to talk for us. Tell our Big Father hat we don't want to give up any of our reservation. We want it all. The Pyramid Lake Reservation is too small for us all, and the white people have already taken all the best part of it. We cannot all live there, and in case they take it all, we can have this to live on. There are a great many of our people, and we do not want to give up any of our land. Another thing, we do not want to have white people near us. We do not want to go where they are, and we don't want them to come near us. We know what they are, and what they would do to our women and our daughters."

Our white father told us he would write and tell all we said to our Big Father in Washington, so we lived along happy all winter.

AT LAST our schoolhouse was done, and my people were told that it was ready, and for the little children to come to school. It was the first day of May, 1876. Mrs. Parrish was to be teacher, and I was to help her and get the same pay for teaching the children English. I had given up my position as interpreter to my cousin Jarry, because he was almost blind. I asked Mr. Parrish to give it to him because he had a wife and daughter and no way of making a living for them. So Mr. Parrish sent for him to come and take my place.

On the first of May, Mrs. Parrish and I opened the school. She had her organ at the schoolhouse and played and sang songs, which my people liked very much. The schoolhouse was full, and the windows were thrown open so that the women could hear too. All the white people were there to sing for them. I was told to tell the children to sing. All of them started to sing as well as they could. Oh, how happy we were! We had three hundred and five boys, twenty-three young men, sixty-nine girls, and nineteen young women. They learned very fast, and were glad to come to school. Oh, I cannot tell or express how happy we were! Mrs. Parrish, the dear, lovely lady, was very kind to the children. We all called her our white lily mother.

We had not been teaching but about three weeks when very bad news came. Our white father, Parrish, told me to tell all the people to come to the schoolhouse. They all came with sad faces, because I had already told them that our white father was going away to leave us. Then he told us that he had received a letter from our Big Father in Washington saying another man was to come in his place, a better man than he.

"I am sorry to leave you," he said, "because I know I can make a good home for you. The man who is coming here to take care of you all is a good man. He can teach you better things than I, and maybe he will do more than I can. You must do just as he want you to do. Go right along just as you have done while I was with you. You all know who he is. He used to live in Canyon City and have a store there."

My people began to say to one another, "We know him then."

The mail carrier said, "I know him, for I know he had a store there."

Egan, the subchief, said, "Our father says he is going away. Now I have been thinking that some of you may have said something against our father. You might have done it without thinking that something would come of it. You all know that white men make a mountain of little things, and some of them may have heard something and told it on him."

They all said, "We have had nothing to say against our father. Why should we do so when he has been so good to us?"

Oytes got up and said, "We will not let our father go; we will fight for him. Why should we let him go? We have not sent for another father to come here. He has been doing everything for us, and we have made no complaints against him. We will all stand by him. He has taught us how to work, and that's what we want, and the white lily is teaching our children how to talk with the paper, which I like very much. I want some of the young men to go and tell our father Winnemucca to come here as soon as he can. I know he will think as I do. I say once more, we will not let him go."

I told our agent everything that was said by my people. Then he told me to say to them that it was not because he had done anything that was not right that he must go away. It was because they said he was not a Christian, and all the reservations were to be under the Christian men's care.

"Before I go," he said, "I am going to plant for you and help you all I can. I will give Egan and Oytes land for peas—Oytes, just on the other side of the river for him and his men, and Egan at the Warm Spring, which is just half a mile away on the east—and to Jarry Lang, and Sarah Winnemucca, and others, on this side of the river. Come right along, just as before, and we will plant whatever you want for the winter. Your new father will not be here until the first of July."

He asked each one of us what we wanted planted.

Egan said, "I want potatoes and a little wheat." Oytes said the same.

My cousins asked me what I wanted. I said, "We have horses enough to need oats and barley."

Mr. Parrish said, "Just as you like."

I said, "I will have wheat, and you oats, and we will have all kinds of vegetables."

Then our white father said to Egan, "There are eight ploughs. Some of your men can help to plough, and we will get everything in." He also told Egan that he could not keep Jarry any longer as interpreter. My cousin was married to Egan's niece, and Mr. Parrish gave me back my place as interpreter. All my people went to work just as before. In a very short time, everything was put in.

During that time, General O. O. Howard and his daughter and Captain Sleighton came to visit us. We were all very glad to see him. He came to see if my people would allow him to build a military post at a place called Otis Valley, ten miles from the agency. He wanted to move Camp Harney to that place.

The subchief, Egan, said to him, "I like all the soldiers very much. We must see first what our brother Winnemucca says. We have sent for him, and we look for him every day. When he comes he can tell you whether you can build there or not."

General Howard said, "All right, you can tell Mr. Parrish, and he will write to me. I am very glad you are getting along so nicely here. I like to see all the Indians get along in this way. Go on just as you are doing; you will soon be like the white people."

Egan got up and said to him, "You are our big soldier-father. We would like to have you come and see us, and see that no bad men come and take away our land. You will tell your soldiers to keep them off the reservation."

He promised he would see to it, and he stayed all night.

The school stopped at this time. Our names were put each on our grain field or garden.

My father came and told him all, and we went to see the agent. My father took his hands in his, and said, "My good father, you shall not leave me and my people. Say you will not go."

He answered, "It is not for me to say. I would like to stay, but your Big Father in Washington says that I must go, and that a better man is coming here. You will like him, I know."

Father said, "I do not want anyone but you. I am going to see the soldier-father tomorrow. I know they will keep you here for me, or I think they can if they wish to."

Mr. Parrish said, "They can do nothing against the government."

My father sat a long time without saying a word.

At last Mr. Parrish said, "Come with me, Winnemucca, I want to give you some things. Come with me."

So we went to our storehouse. After we got there, father stood in one corner of the room like one that was lost.

Mr. Parrish said, "What kind of clothes do you want?"

Father said, "I don't want anything if you are not going to stay with me. I don't want anything from you because it will make me feel so badly after you are gone."

It is the way we Indians do. We never keep anything belonging to our dearest friends because it makes us feel so badly, and when any of our family die, everything belonging to them is buried and their horses are killed. When my poor mother was yet living, every time we went near the place where my poor grandfather was buried, she would weep. I told father the way white people did if they were to part for a long time was to give each other something to remember each other by, and they would also keep another's picture if he was dead.

"Father," I said, "you had better take what he gives you, for he will feel badly if you don't."

So father took everything he gave him, and the next morning, father, Egan, Oytes, and myself started for Camp Harney to see the officer there. We arrived at Camp Harney, distant fifty miles, at about five o'clock.

We rode up to the commanding officer's quarters, and I said, "Major Green, my father has come to see you and to have a talk with you."

"Well, Sarah, tell your father to come at ten o'clock tomorrow.

Have you a place to stop at while you are here?"

I said, "Yes, I have a lady friend here. Father and I can stop with her."

"And where will those two men stop?"

I said, "I don't know."

"But let me see," he said. "They can stop with my men. I will give them a note to the sergeant."

I then told Egan and Oytes to go to the place, and father and I went to Mrs. Kennedy, and she and her husband were very glad to see us. I told her all about our trouble at the Malheur Agency.

In the morning, at the appointed time, we went to the office. There were all the officers in waiting for us to hear what father had to say. They thought we had come to tell something against our agent, for they were the same officers that had the other agent sent away.

They were all astonished when my father said to Major Green, "My great soldier-father, I am in great trouble and want you to help me. You can if you will. I come to you in my trouble knowing that you are our best friends when I and my people are good. Your soldiers have always stood by us. You took us as your prisoners. You know how the white people are always saying Indians are bad and steal cattle. They tell you these things so you can kill us all off. Now they want my reservation. They are sending away my agent. My men and I have not sent for another agent. We all like our good agent Parrish. We don't want him to leave us. He gives us everything we want. He and his men are all friendly. They are teaching us how to work, and our children are learning how to read, just like your children. What more do we want? There can be no better man than he, and why send him away? Oh, my good soldier-father, talk on paper to our Big Father in Washington and tell him not to take him away. I tell you I never saw white men like them in all my life. I have a reservation at my birthplace called

Pyramid Lake. For so many years, not one of the agents ever gave me or my people an old rag. I am just from there. My people have nothing to live on there but what little fish they catch, and the best land is taken from them. I saw a great many of my people. They say they will come here to make homes for themselves." He stopped and then said, "Will you help me, Major Green?"

"I will send all you have said to your Father in Washington. I am sorry Mr. Parrish is to leave."

He then asked me all about it. I told him everything I knew and our new agent's name. Mr. Parrish called him Major Reinhard. Major Green told father he would do all he could for him and his people.

The next morning we went back. I told Mr. Parrish what my father said to the officer, and he laughed.

ON THE twenty-eighth of June, 1876, our new agent, Major Reinhard, arrived. My people were all very sad indeed. Our dear mother, as we called Mrs. Parrish, and all the rest were gone except Mr. Sam Parrish, our agent. He was with us yet with one man, the head farmer, Dayman by name. Our agent took Major Reinhard all over the place, showed him how he had got us fixed, showed him where the field of each one was. Our agent had had our names written on boards to show who the fields belonged to. After he had shown him all our gardens, he took him to our storehouse, told him all the goods were to be issued right away.

He said, "I was going to issue now because I have not done it this spring. Some of the goods for this year's issue have not come yet. I have sent for coats and pants and hats so the men need not wear blankets while they are working." He said to Major Reinhard, "These Indians are very good to work. They are always ready to do whatever I tell them to do. They are honest and will do what they can." He also told him how often he issued rations.

After he had turned everything over to the new agent, he was going to leave. At the dinner Mr. Parrish said to the new agent, "Sarah has nice fields of wheat, and the next field to hers is Jarry Lang's; his field has oats." Mr. Reinhard did not say anything.

After dinner, Mr. Parrish, who is dearly loved by my people, went away. That was the last my people saw of him.

Two days afterward, that is the thirtieth of June, Major Reinhard's men came, two men called Johnson, brothers. L. Johnson had a family. One came as schoolteacher, and the one with a family was blacksmith. They were the poorest-looking white people I ever saw. The two men did not have decent pants, but the next day I saw them with new ones such as Mr. Parrish gave to my people, and a woman came to me and asked me if I had any dress goods. I asked her what kind of dress goods she wanted. She said calico, and I sold her ten yards to make her a dress. Then came the farmer; his family name was Howell; then the clerk, our agent's nephew, and then the agent's family. In a few days they were all well clothed—men, women, and children.

I was now all alone, as my father left the next day after Mr. Parrish went away.

One day Egan and Oytes came to me and said, "We know this man who is going to be our father. He is a bad man. He used to be over at Canyon City. He has sold me many bottles of firewater."

"Yes," said Oytes, "we know him well."

Just then he came along toward us. He held out his hand to the two subchiefs and said, "How do you do?" He said to me, "Sarah, tell them I want them to come to me tomorrow. I want to have a talk with them. Tell them to tell old Winnemucca to come too."

I said, "My father is gone."

"Where is he gone?"

"To Pyramid Lake Reservation."

"Will he be back soon?"

"I don't know, sir."

Next morning Egan and Oytes came with their men.

"Now, Sarah," he said, "tell your people that the Big Father in Washington has sent me here. He told me how I must make you all good people. This land which you are living on is government land. If you do well and are willing to work for government, government will give you work. Yes, government will do more than that. It will pay you one dollar per day; both men and women will get the same. Boys who can do a day's work will get the same. This is what the Big Father in Washington told me to tell you."

All the time he was talking, my people hung their heads. Not one looked at him while he talked. He stopped talking. My people passed some jokes and laughed at him because he was trembling as if he was afraid.

Egan said to Oytes, "You had better talk to your father. I don't want to talk to such a man."

Oytes said, "I am not a boy, I am a man. I am afraid he will die if I talk to him."

I said, "Say something to him."

Then Egan got up and said, "Our father, we cannot read; we don't understand anything; we don't want the Big Father in Washington to fool with us. He sends one man to say one thing and another to say something else. The man who just left us told us the land was ours and what we do on it was ours, and you come and say it is government land and not ours. You may be all right. We love money as well as you. It is a great deal of money to pay; there are a great many of us, and when we work, we all work."

Our Christian agent got mad and said, "Egan, I don't care whether any of you stay or not. You can all go away if you do not like the way I do."

"Our good father does not understand me. I did not say I would not work."

Oytes said, "Don't say any more; we will all go to work, and then see how much he will pay us."

Then the agent said, "When I tell you to do anything, I don't want any of you to dictate to me but to go and do it."

When I told them what he said, they all jumped up and went away.

The next morning men, women, and boys went to work. Some went into the fields to cut the grain, some to mow hay, and some to cut rails for fences. Some went to cut wood and some to haul it in. Everybody was busy all the week. Saturday, at half past six o'clock, my people came right from their work to get their pay, men, women, and boys; thirty-eight women, forty-three boys, and nineteen hundred and nine men.

We all went to the agent's office. I went in first and said, "All my people have come to get their pay."

"Well, tell them to come in."

Then he began to write: blankets, six dollars; coats, six dollars; pants, five dollars; shoes, three dollars; socks, fifty cents; woolen shirts, three dollars; handkerchiefs, fifty cents; looking glasses, fifty cents; sugar, three pounds for one dollar; tea, one dollar per pound; coffee, two and a half pounds for one dollar; shawls, six dollars; calico, ten yards for one dollar; unbleached muslin, four yards. "The rations they have had are worth about four dollars a week, and then they have two dollars left to get anything they want out of the storehouse."

Some of my men said, "Let us go; why do we fool with such a man?"

A good many got up and left. Egan, the subchief, got up and said, "Why do you want to play with us? We are men, not children. We want our father to deal with us like men and tell us just what he wants us to do, but don't say you are going to pay us money and then not do it. If you had told us you wanted us to work for nothing, we would have done it just as well if you had said, I will pay you. We did not ask you to pay us. It is yourself that said you would see that government paid us, and we would like to have you pay us as you said. You did not say anything about the clothing nor about what we ate while we were working. I don't care for myself, but my men want their pay, and they will go on with their work just the same. Pay them in money, and then they can go and buy whatever they like, because our Big Father's goods are too dear. We can go to our soldier-fathers and get better blankets for three dollars than yours."

He said, "Well, I will give you an order on a store in Canyon City which belongs to your Big Father in Washington where you can get nice things."

Egan got up again and said, "Our good father Sam Parrish sent for those things which are in the store for us, and you want us to pay you for them. You are all wearing the clothes that we fools thought belonged to us, and we don't want you to pay anything." He turned round to his men and said, "Go home."

Then our Christian father again forgot himself and said, "If you don't like the way I do, you can all leave here. I am not going to be fooled with by you. I never allow a white man to talk to me like that."

My people all went away to their camps. They sent for me during the night. I went to see what they wanted with me. The head men were all together. Then Egan asked me what I thought about our new father.

I said, "I don't know. What do you think about him? Do you think what he tells us is true? Are we to lose our home? It looks that way, don't it?" I said, "I have nothing to say. I am only here to talk for you all. What do you think we had better do? Where shall we go? He tells us all to go away. We have no way of getting our living. If he would only give us what we have raised, we could live on that this winter."

Some of the women said, "Oh, our children will surely die of hunger."

I said, "We will wait and see what he will do."

Oytes said, "Let us go and tell our soldier-fathers about him!"

I said, "No, we must wait."

The next day was Sunday, and there was nothing to do. Some of my people came to make a home with us who were never on the reservation before. I went to them, and they said, "We have come to make a home with you. We heard that your white father was so good to all, so we thought we would come here."

I said, "Our good father has gone away, and there is another one here, and I don't know what he is going to do for us."

They said, "We have nothing to eat."

I said, "Today is the day when people don't work. It is called Sunday. It is the day when the white people talk with the Spirit Father, and the agent told me to tell my people never to come for anything on Sunday. Tomorrow is ration day. I will go and see him anyhow."

I went to him and said, "Mr. Reinhard, some of my people have come here to make a home with us. They were never here before. They say they have nothing to eat. This is why I came to speak to you. Excuse me for coming on Sunday to tell of my people's wants."

He told me to say to them that he was not going to issue any more rations to them.

I said, "Very well, I will tell them."

I went and got my horse and told one of my cousins to saddle it while I went to tell Jarry, my cousin, my father's sister's son. Our agent and he were talking about me. I heard him say, "I shall have her go away, and if you want to be my friend, I will give you a good living if you will do as I want you to."

I heard my cousin say, "I will do whatever you say."

I did not go in but went back and got upon my horse and went to the Oytes camp, and told them what the agent told me to say to them. We all went then to the subchief's camp and told them. I said, "You can talk it over amongst yourselves and think what it is best to do."

Egan told some of the young men to go with me and tell Jarry to come. Jarry was his son-in-law.

After I got home, as I was sitting in the doorway, I heard such a scream! I looked round, and to my horror saw our agent throw a little boy down on the ground by his ear and kick him. I did not go to the rescue of the little boy but sat still. At last the boy broke from him and ran, and the agent ran after him round the house. But the little boy outran him. The agent looked over at me and saw me looking at him. He then came toward me. I hung my head and did not look up.

He said, "Sarah, that little devil laughed at me because I asked him to go and tell Jarry that I wanted him to come to my house. I will beat the very life out of him. I won't have any of the Indians laughing at me. I want you to tell them that they must jump at my first word to go. I don't want them to ask why or what for. Now, do you understand what I am saying?"

I said, "Yes, sir, I will tell them." I said, "Mr. Reinhard, that little boy never meant to laugh at you. He thought you were saying something nice to him, and another thing, he cannot understand the English language. I am your interpreter. Whatever you say to me, I am always ready to do my duty as far as it goes."

After he went away, my cousin Jarry came to me and said, "Sister, I don't think it right that you should always tell everything to our people."

I said, "Dear brother, I have not told anything but what I was told to tell them."

We Indians always call our cousins brother and sister, just as if they were our own fathers' sons and daughters. Although we are savages, we love one another as well as the fairest of the land.

My cousin said, "My father-in-law and all the men are coming to talk to the agent, and don't you say a word."

I said, "Very well."

"They are going to ask him for the grain, but don't tell anybody about Reinhard's doings. What do we care whether he gives our people anything or not, so long as he gives us something to live on? What do you think our people care for us? Let them go wherever they like."

I said, "Dear brother, I am ashamed of you. You talk so heartlessly. I am going to see my people dealt rightly by and to stand by them, and I am going to talk for them just as long as I live. If you want to see your people starve, that is your own business. I am going to see that they get their wheat, and I am going to get mine too; that is, if he will give it to us. I am here to work for my people, and I am going to my work."

Just then the mother of the little boy came crying as if her heart would break. "Oh, my poor child," she was saying, "he will die, the only child I have left out of four."

I said nothing. I was feeling badly for the little boy, and his mother too. Jarry asked her what was the matter. She told him all and said the little boy's ear was swelling badly, and it was black and the boy would not speak. "Oh, I am so afraid he is going to die. I have come to see if the white doctor will come and do something for him."

I said, "Come with me," and went for the doctor. There were a great many there to see the boy. Two subchiefs were there, and Oytes was laying hands on him as we got there.

I said, "Here is the white doctor; maybe he can do something for him."

Egan said, "No, the white people hate us; he might poison him." His whole head and face and neck were swollen.

I said, "They don't want you to do anything for him."

The doctor asked me what was the matter with him. I did not say anything, for he knew well enough what it was. He asked again.

I said, "You know; why do you ask? You saw your Christian and your praying man take him by his ear and throw him to the ground."

He said, "Is that the boy?"

This doctor's name is Shoemaker. He lived fat while he was there. He had all the firewater he wanted to drink, which was sent there under the pretense that it was sent there for the benefit of my sick people. This doctor was there when our agent Parrish was still with us. I had a room next to the doctor's office and could hear everything that was said in there.

One morning, just before Mr. Parrish knew he was going away, he came into the office and I heard him say, "Doctor, how much wine and liquor have you on hand?"

The doctor said, "I have but a very little brandy left, and I have not any wine."

"Why, doctor, what has become of it all? I had so much of it for my sick Indians; it was here for that purpose, and I know my men don't drink; if I knew they did I would not have them stay here."

The doctor said, "I used the wine for my table, and since the wine ran out, we had to use the other."

"What are you going to do if an inspecting officer comes here?"

"Oh, well, I will make some more. I have alcohol, and I know how to make all kinds of liquor." I heard all this.

THE NEXT day was ration day. Many of my people came to get their rations. I saw our agent Reinhard and Jarry going here and there, and talking together. I went to see the farmer's wife, who is a dear, good, Christian lady. She and her husband and son often said to me, "Our hearts ache for your people." She said she should not stay there. I told her everything. That afternoon there came some more of my people; among them was my brother, Lee Winnemucca. They had come from Pyramid Lake Reservation. It was a long way and they were hungry, but I could do nothing for them. I had to buy everything I ate, and I told them our agent had stopped issuing rations to all.

Brother said, "Is there anything we can buy?"

I said, "Yes, I will go and see him."

I went to see him and said to Mr. Reinhard, "My brother Lee is here with ten men, and they have nothing to eat. Will you sell some flour and other things to them?"

He said, "Where is Johnny?" That was an Indian boy who could talk a little English.

I said, "I will go for him." So I ran and soon found him, and we went to see what the agent wanted.

He came to meet us and said, "Johnny, go and get some beef; here is the key."

Johnny started off; he got only a little way when the agent called him back, but Johnny kept on. He called him again and again, and at last was so angry, he ran after him.

But the boy would not stop. He looked back and saw him coming. He turned round and said these words: "What in hell do you want?"

He ran up to him and took him by his hair, but the boy was too quick for him and got away, the agent after him saying, "Stop, or I will shoot you." But Johnny ran all the faster and got away from him.

I went back to where brother Lee and the rest were standing. They all laughed and made all kinds of fun of the agent.

He came to me and said, "Sarah, I am going to shoot him. He shan't live to see another day."

"Mr. Reinhard," I said, "why do you ask me? Why tell me what you are going to do?"

He walked off at that. The rest of the white people were looking on. He went to the house, got his pistol, and came back and said, "Sarah, shall I shoot him? I never had anyone talk to me in that way. If a white man talked to me like that, I would kill him right off."

I said, "You know best what to do."

My brother then spoke and said, "We have come a long way to hear good things from the Good Spirit man. Why talk of killing? Is that the kind of good man Mr. Parrish told us of? Of course, that is the kind of men that are called good, men who talk to the Spirit Father three times a day but who will kill us off as they would kill wild beasts."

Brother stopped at that, and I said, "Brother wants to buy some things out of your store."

He took us there to get the things. As I walked along with him, he said, "Sarah, I will give the things to your brother, and you take the money, for they might think hard of me for it. It is not my fault, but the Big Father in Washington tells me to sell everything to your people."

After we went in, I told them what he wanted me to do. They all laughed, and I told them when they got all the things to go right to him and pay him. Brother bought one dollar's worth of sugar, same of coffee, one sack of flour at two dollars. After they got all they wanted, Lee went to pay him. He took out his money and counted it out to him. When he handed it to him, he pointed to me. Brother offered me the money.

I said, "I am not the Big Father in Washington. I don't own anything in the store, and why should I take the money?" At this I went out.

I heard him say to brother, "Lee, you take the things; it's all right."

The same night he took Johnny and put handcuffs on him, saying, "I will send you to Camp Harney and have the soldiers hang you, for you are a very bad boy." The boy did not cry or say anything, but his mother ran in crying and threw her arms round him.

She cried so hard I said, "Mr. Reinhard, I don't know what you are thinking of by the way you are acting. I think you had better let him go."

Then he took me out and told me that he would put him in the storehouse and keep him there all night, and let him out in the morning. He then took him and locked him up. I told his mother what he had said.

The next morning all Egan's and Oytes' men came to have a talk with him. Egan said, "My children are dying with hunger. I want what I and my people have worked for; that is, we want the wheat. We ask for nothing else, but our agent Parrish told us that would be ours."

The agent said, "Nothing here is yours. It is all the government's. If Parrish told you so, he told you lies."

I spoke up and said, "Mr. Reinhard, why did not you tell me right before him when he was telling you about my wheat? If you had then said it did not belong to us, I would not have told my people about it. I told them, for they asked me if Mr. Parrish said anything about our grain."

"Why, if you take the government wheat, you rob the government," he said.

I said, "I don't want to rob anybody."

Jarry, my cousin, was against us and said we ought to be ashamed to talk about anything that did not belong to us.

Then Egan got up and said to me, "I want you to tell everything I say to this man."

I did as he said.

"Did the government tell you to come here and drive us off this reservation? Did the Big Father say, go and kill us all off so you can have our land? Did he tell you to pull our children's ears off, and put handcuffs on them, and carry a pistol to shoot us with? We want to know how the government came by this land. Is the government mightier than our Spirit Father, or is he our Spirit Father? Oh, what have we done that he is to take all from us that he has given us? His white children have come and have taken all our mountains, and all our valleys, and all our rivers; and now, because he has given us this little place without our asking him for it, he sends you here to tell us to go away. Do you see that high mountain away off there? There is nothing but rocks there. Is that where the Big Father wants me to go? If you scattered your seed and it should fall there, it will not grow, for it is all rocks there. Oh, what am I saying? I know you will come and say, Here, Indians, go away; I want these rocks to make me a beautiful home with! Another thing—you know we cannot buy. Government gave. We have no way to get money. I have had only two dollars, which I gave you for a pair of pants, and my son-in-law gave you the same for his. That is all the money the government is going to get out of me, and tomorrow I am going to tell the soldiers what you are doing and see if it is all right." He sat down.

Then our agent said, "You had better all go and live with the soldiers. What I have told you is true, and if you don't like what the government wants you to do, well and good. If I had it my way, I could help you, but I cannot. I have to do government's will."

We started for Camp Harney the next morning and arrived

there before evening. The distance is twenty miles. We told the commanding officer everything about our *Christian* agent's doings, and he told me to write to Washington, and he would do the same. I did as I was told; and when I had written it all, the head men of my people signed it, and then our Christian agent discharged me from my office of interpreter for reporting to the army officers, for which I don't blame him. After he discharged me, I stayed there three weeks.

While I was still there, he had another trouble with one of my people. He beat an Indian man almost to death for no cause whatever. He asked him to help him carry a sick woman. The Indian was a little too long getting on his moccasins. The agent knocked him down with a great stick and beat him so shamefully I ran to him and caught hold of him, saying, "Do not beat him so." The man rose up, and as he did so, the agent raised the stick again to him. At this the Indian took hold of it; then the agent took out a pistol to shoot him; but white men came to him and said, "Do not shoot Jim."

AFTER THIS, my good friend Mrs. Howell went away. My cousin, Jarry, had not spoken to me all that time, and I too went away and had to leave my stove, for which I had given fifty dollars. Mr. Reinhard used it all the time, for which I tried to get paid; but I had to lose it, because he was a *Christian* man.

His men—Frank Johnson the schoolteacher, and his brother the blacksmith—were the two greatest gamblers that ever lived. They played with my people and won a great many of their ponies, and they kept the interpreter Jarry losing all the time. They carried cards wherever they went.

When I was going away, Mr. Reinhard said to me, "Sarah, I want you to give this letter to Mr. Maulrick, and he will give

Captain Scott whatever he wants out of the store. Captain Scott will go with you."

I said, "All right," and went away; and oh, what a wicked thing I did! I read the letter. It said, "Dear friend, as I have promised you, I will send you all the Indians. You know you are to pay them not in money but in clothes. I have given the bearer of this a thirty-dollar check. Write and tell me what kind of clothing you give so that I can report that it has been issued to him."

I kept the letter, and when we got there, I gave the money check to him, and he asked me if I wanted anything in his store. I said, "I will see afterward." So he gave me the money for the check, and I gave it to Captain Scott. He was so glad to get the money he went back without buying anything. I have often laughed over this. I kept the letter a long time, but I have lost it or I should put it here just as it was.

I went back six months afterward to see my cousin, but the agent sent word to me by his interpreter that he did not want me on the reservation. I said to the interpreter, who was my cousin, "I am only an Indian woman. Why does not he come himself and tell me to go away, and not tell you?"

There are only two agents who have been kind to me: Captain Smith, agent at Warm Spring Reservation, and agent Parrish. It was because they did not steal. Captain Smith is the only agent who can truly say, "I have civilized my Indians." They are a self-supporting tribe and very rich. When he first took them, they were the poorest kind of Indians. We Paiutes call them snakeheaded Indians, for their heads are so flat that when they are turned sideways they look just like snakes' heads. Every year this agent gave from five to ten wagons, and the same number of farming implements, till every one of the Indians had farms. Dear reader, if our agent had done his duty like that one, there would be peace everywhere, on every agency; but almost all the agents look out for their own pockets. Every agent that we Paiutes have had always rented the reservation out to cattlemen and got one dollar a head for the cattle, and if my people asked whose the cattle were, he would say they belong to the Big Father at Washington, and then my people would say no more.

CHAPTER VII

THE BANNOCK WAR

IN THE winter of 1878, I was living at the head of the John Day River with a lady by the name of Courly. On the 21st of April, I had some visitors from the Malheur Agency. They were my own people. There were three of them, and they said they had come to see their sister. They had had a hard time to get over the mountains. There was a great deal of snow at one place on the summit.

"You see, dear sister," they said, "don't we look like men who have lived a long time without eating?"

"Yes," I said, "you look poorly indeed. You had better come in and have something to eat so that you can talk better."

The good lady got them something to eat. Bread and meat tasted very good indeed. It put one in mind of old times when meat and bread were plenty.

One of the men said, "We have come to see if you can help us in some way. We know that you are always ready to help your people. We will tell you so that you can judge for yourself. Our agent, Reinhard, has been very unkind to us since you left us. He has not given us anything to eat; he is not issuing rations to us as our father Parrish used to do, and our poor children are crying to us for food, and we are powerless to help our little ones. Some two months ago, the agent bought a good many beef cattle, but the cattle were only three days at the agent's when they ran away and cannot be found anywhere in the country. So we are really starving over there, and we don't know what to do. Nor do we get any clothing, as we used to do long ago. They are shooting our ponies down, too, when they break down the fences. The interpreter and the mail carrier go and get everything they want to eat. But poor we! You know, Sarah, there is nothing to be gathered this time of year, so we are at loss to know what will become of us. Oh, dear sister Sadie, go with us to Camp Harney and see the officers there; see if they can help us in some way, or go to Washington in our behalf."

After they had told me their story, I said to them that I was very sorry for them as I had nothing to do with. Then they asked me what I meant by saying that.

I said, "In the first place, I have no money to go to Washington, but I would be most happy to do all I could for you. In the second place, you all know how Agent Reinhard discharged me for reporting him to the officers at Camp Harney. I will do all I can, but that is very little."

So they went back to the Malheur Agency on the 23rd of April, and I stayed with Mrs. Courly all along. Then they came back again on the 29th of May, the same men and three others, making six in all. They were very glad to see me, for they said they were afraid I had gone away. They had come back to tell me again about Agent Reinhard's doings. He had driven them away from the agency, and their people were all down the river, about twenty-five miles away from it.

"They are there trying to catch salmon to live upon, as they had nothing else to eat, and we can catch enough for all that are there. There are with us about fifteen families of Bannocks at the fishery. They came from Fort Hall.

"It is Bannock Jack's band. They have brought us very sad news from there. They say that all their ponies have been taken from them, and all their guns, too, for something two of their men had done. They got drunk and went and shot two white men. One of the Indians had a sister out digging some roots, and these white men went to the women who were digging, caught this poor girl, and used her shamefully. The other women ran away and left this girl to the mercy of those white men, and it was on her account that her brother went and shot them. They are the cause of all our trouble and caused us all to lose our horses and everything we had, and we all left there thinking your good agent was with you yet. We have come to make us a home with you, but we see that your new agent is very bad indeed for not giving you anything to live on. He knows you have not got anything and can get nothing unless you steal it somehow."

This is what the Bannocks told my people, and they brought it to me in John Day valley and asked me to go with them. I told them I could not go just then, but I would go about the last of the month.

They said, "We ourselves have lost some of our horses, and we would like to have you write us a letter that we can show to some of the whites who live round here. Maybe they could tell us something about it. But we think the Columbia River Indians have stolen them, or the Umatilla Indians—we don't know which, for a party of both of them were at the agency."

Very late in the fall, my people came again while I was living with Mrs. Courly, and once more they asked me to talk for them. I then told them I would do what I could. "If it was in my power, I would be too happy to do so for you, but I am powerless, being a woman, and yet you come to me for help. You have your interpreter; why does not he talk for you? He is the man for you to go to."

Then they said to me, "Sarah, we know that Jarry is in with the agent, and it is no use for us to ask him or the mail carrier, who have everything they want and enough to eat, and Reinhard does not care whether we get anything or not. So we came to you, for you are the only one that is always ready to talk for us. We know our sister can write on paper to our Big Father in Washington if she will."

I told them I would come over as soon as I could get over the mountains with my wagon, as I had a nice little wagon of my own. Then they said good-bye and went away.

ON THE first of June, two gentlemen called on me from Canyon City. They said they had heard down there that I was going over to the agency soon. I told them it was true.

"We heard that you have a team of your own, and we have come to ask you if you would take us over with you. From there we can go over to Malheur City."

One of the men said, "I have a daughter, and there will be three of us who would like to go with you if you will take us. We will pay you well. How much will you charge us to go with you?"

I told them I did not know. I could not tell just then. I then asked the gentleman who said he had a daughter to bring her to see me, and I would then tell him. So on the same day, he and his little daughter called on me, and he introduced her as Rosey Morton. She was only twelve years old and very pretty. I then told him I would take them to Malheur City for twenty dollars. He said, "I will give it to you," and I told them to be ready on the morning of the fourth of June.

They came. We started that afternoon and went on to the summit that night; we started early again the next morning and got to the agency about six o'clock in the evening. I took my passengers to the agent's house and left them there, then went to where the interpreter lived. It was about two miles and a half further.

As soon as I got there my cousin, the interpreter, sent for Oytes and Egan, as they were down at the fishery. I heard Jarry say to the men he was sending, "Tell them that Sarah is here. If they can come tonight, well and good. If not, tell them to be sure to come tomorrow. Tell the Bannocks to come too."

The interpreter did not tell me many things. He only said, "A great many of the Bannocks are here with us now, and I don't know what they are going to do here. They will tell you all about themselves."

It was some time in the night when they came. I heard Jarry, the interpreter, say to Egan, "Did you bring any salmon or anything to eat? Sarah went to bed without anything to eat. We have not anything at all down here."

"We have not caught any salmon for ten days," Egan said, "and therefore we had nothing to bring. What does that praying agent mean by not giving us our rations? What does he say about giving rations, anyhow? Or what does he say about giving us some of the wheat which we raised last year?"

"Well, Egan, he did not say anything when I told him what you and Oytes said about the wheat. I was there yesterday to see if I could buy some flour of him, but he won't sell me any. He told me to tell you and Oytes that he has written to Washington about the wheat, and just as soon as the order comes, he would send to your people."

"Well, what has Washington to do with the wheat, I'd like to know?"

"Well, Egan, that is what he told me to tell you and Oytes."

Then I heard Egan say, "Is Sarah asleep? We had better talk to her now for fear Reinhard will find out she is here and send her away, as he did before."

So my cousin came and told me that the chiefs Egan and Oytes wanted to have a talk with me. I did not dare to say no, so I got up and went to the council tent. As I went in, Chief Egan introduced me to the Bannocks. He told them I was their former interpreter at the agency and that I was their teacher also.

"She has done everything in her power for us," he said, "and our praying agent discharged her for no other cause than that Oytes and I took her to Camp Harney to report him. Therefore you need not be afraid to talk to her. She is our friend. Tell her all your troubles. I know she will help you."

Egan stopped talking, and then Bannock Jack went on and said, "You say our great chieftain's daughter is good, and you say she can talk on paper too, and therefore I will ask her if she heard what the papers are saying about our troubles at Fort Hall?"

When this question was put to me, I told them I had been living quite a way from Canyon City and had not seen the papers, and could not tell them anything about it.

"Well," said Bannock Jack, "you can talk on paper."

I said "Yes, I could."

Then he said, "Will you be so kind as to write down all I will tell you?"

Then I sent for some paper and a pencil to write it down as he asked me to. He went on and told me the very same thing that my people had already told me when they came to see me at John Day valley, except this: Bannock Jack said the white people had told their chiefs to go and get the two men who had killed the two white men. They said they must get two Indian men within ten days. If they did not, they would all suffer for it.

When this was told us, our chiefs sent our men to find them, and it took some little time to do so, and when they did find them, they were bringing them in. One more day would have brought them to Fort Hall. But some of the friends of the two men came and met them and said that all of their people were in prison. "Oh, everything was taken from them, their guns and their ponies, and they were guarded by a great many soldiers, and it is said they are all going to be killed."

"And what is the use," they said, "for us to go with these men? We had better keep away from them." Well, it was these men's friends who went on the warpath, and this was the beginning of the Bannock War.

Then Bannock Jack asked me if I had it all written down. I said, "Yes."

Then he said, "Will you be so kind as to send it to Washington and ask our Big Father in Washington to help us get back our guns and our ponies? They were not given us by our Big Father in Washington. If they had been, we would not say a word. They were bought by our own hard work. We think it very hard for a whole tribe to lose everything and to be all killed besides, and for what they did not give us time to do, and as if we had refused to get the men."

The second chief, Egan, got up again to talk. He began by saying, "My dear mother," for this is the way our people address any one who is their superior. If a woman, it is their mother; if a man, it is their father. So Egan began in this way. When he got up to talk to me, he said, "When our good father, Sam Parrish, was here, oh, then we were happy. Our children were not crying for anything to eat and causing our hearts to ache for them. We all had everything we wanted. We had plenty of clothes and were all doing well. And you, our dear mother, told us the truth. You told us that Sam was going away and that there was a Christian agent to be sent here in his place; but you said you new he would not do for us like our father Parrish. Oh, it was too true! Here we are all starving under this Christian man. He has not made any issues of clothing since he came here. After he discharged you and you were gone, he called for a council, and all went to hear what he had to say. He told us that if we did not like the way he did, all we had to do was to leave the place, that he did not care. He also said, 'If my interpreter does not do as I want him to, he can go too. The government is not going to fool with you. Now if you want to work, the government will pay you one dollar a day.'

"I, chief of the Snake River Paiutes, stopped the agent by saying, 'I want to talk a little.' I commenced by saying, 'You are a good man. You talk with our Great Father up in the Spirit Land. You look up to the sky and make us think you are a good Christian, and we want you to tell us the truth, not lies. We know nothing. We don't read, and therefore we don't know what to think. You, who are greater than anybody, say that this is government land, not land for us; you say we must work for government, and government will pay us one dollar a day for our work. Yes, we will work for the government for money, for we love money just as well as you do, you good Christian men who have come here. We were told by our good agent, Sam Parrish, that this land was ours for all to work upon and make us homes here. He also told us the government had set it apart for us Indians, and government would help us all if we would help ourselves, and that we must always be ready to go to work at whatever work he put us to, and that everything we raised on the place was ours, and the annuities that were sent here were given to us by our good father Parrish. He gave us everything our hearts could wish for. He also told me to tell all my people who had no homes to come here and go to work like white men. The white folk have to work very hard, and we must do the same. Our good agent never had any trouble with us because we would do everything we could to please him, and he did the same by us. He gave us our annuities without saying

'You must do this or that, or you leave here.' No, he treated us
as if were his children, and we returned his kindness by doing
everything he set us to do. He was with us two years, and we were
all happy. He did not shoot our ponies because the ponies broke
the fences, but he would say, 'Your horses have broken into your
grain; look out for them,' and then we would run and get them out
and mend the fences. He did not do like you, good Christian man,
by saying, 'Here, my men, go and shoot those Indians' horses!
They are in our grain.' Our father Parrish told us all to be good
and never take any stray horses that came on our agency, nor did
he want us to go and get stray horses. Have you done so? No. You
and your men have done everything that is bad. You have taken
up every horse that came along here, and you have them in your
stable, and you are working them.

"'And another thing—your men are doing what Parrish told
us not to do, that is, gambling. You and your men have brought
a book amongst us that has big chiefs' pictures and their wives'
pictures on the papers, and another picture which you call Jack,
and another something like it. And with these your men come
to our camps and gamble with your interpreter and your mail
carrier every time you pay them off. This is what your blacksmith
Johnson is doing, and your schoolteacher, Frank Johnson, instead
of teaching my people's children, does more gambling than teaching. What you pay to your interpreter and mail carrier, the two
Johnsons win back again with the book that you brought here.

"'So we are at a loss to know which of you are right: whether
Sam Parrish told us lies, or you, or our chieftain's daughter, Sarah
Winnemucca, about the land being ours. You who talk with our
Great Father in the Spirit Land three times a day have come here
and told us the land is not ours.'

"This is what I said to the agent after you left us, and now
you have come and found me almost starved.

"Now one and all of you, my men, give our mother what little money you have. Let her go and talk for us. Let her go right on to Washington and have a talk with our Big Father in Washington."

Then they all asked me if I would go if they would give me the money to go with. I told them I would only be too happy to do all I could in their behalf if they wanted me to. So they went to work and got together and everyone gave what they could, and all Egan got for me was twenty-nine dollars and twenty-five cents. This was got for me by Egan, the chief of the Snake River Paiutes. This was indeed very little to start with.

But as I had promised, I thought I would go to Elko, Nevada, with my horses and wagon and sell them there, and go to Washington and see what I could do for them. So our council ended on the 7th of June, 1878. And Mr. Morton asked me again if I would take him and his little daughter to Silver City, Idaho. I told him yes, if he would pay fifty dollars for the three of them, and pay one half of it down, which he did.

So we started on the morning of the 8th of June. We journeyed on for three days and heard nothing about an Indian war. But we saw houses standing all along the road without anybody living in them. We talked about it and did not know what it meant.

On the twelfth we met a man on the summit, just before getting to a place called Fort Lyon, who told us there was the greatest Indian war that ever was known. He said the Bannock Indians were just killing everything that came in their way, and he told us to hurry on to a place called Stone House. That was the first I heard that the Bannocks were on the warpath. So we hurried on to the place. We got to the stage road, and as we were going up the road, we met three men coming down. They told us that the stage driver had been killed. There had been no stage running for three days. He said there had been fighting going on at South Mountains, and a great many were killed, and some

Paiute Indians were killed too.

I said, "Are they on the warpath, too?"

They said, "No, they were with white men who went out to fight the Bannocks, and the Bannocks had whipped them. Everybody is at the storehouse with their families." He told me not to go any farther than there, for they would surely kill us if they came across us. "They want nothing better than to kill Chief Winnemucca's daughter."

So these men went on down the road, and we went on as fast as we could and drove up to the storehouse just at eleven o'clock. They ran out to my wagon. They all had their guns and one of the men asked me who I was and where I was going. I said I was Sarah Winnemucca, and I was going to Elko, Nevada.

As I told him who I was, he held out his hand and said, "I am Captain Hill, and I want you to stop here, for you are in great danger. Just drive in there."

I did so. I told Mr. Morton to take care of the team, and I took the little girl and went into the house. Then Captain Hill took me into the parlor and asked me if I knew anything about the outbreak of the Bannocks. I told him I did not know anything about it till yesterday, when a man met me at the summit beyond Camp Lyon, who told me. He then asked me if I knew Captain Bernard. I told him I did.

"He will be here tonight," he said, "or tomorrow sure, with his command." He asked me who the man was who was with me. I told him I did not know much about him, but he and his little daughter were going to Silver City. All this time I little thought of the talk that was going on about me until about twenty scouts arrived and with them a Paiute Indian. Then the captain of the scouts came to me and asked me to talk English with him, not Indian. So I asked him who he was.

He said, "Me name Paiute Joe."

"What is the matter?" said I.

"Me no see," he said, "here you all goin me hope no sauce."

I said, "Captain, what is the use of my talking to you? If you are afraid of me, there is a white woman who can talk my language well. You can call her, and she can tell you if I say anything wrong."

The captain said, "Where is she?"

"There she is."

So the lady's husband brought her forward. Then he said, "The Bannocks are all out fighting. They are killing everything and everybody, Indians and whites, and I and two more of my people went with these men out to South Mountain to fight them, and we came on to Buffalo Horn's camp and had a fight with them, and the scouts ran away and left him to the mercy of Bannocks. I saw that I could not get away when they were all mustered on me, so I jumped off my horse and placed my horse between me and them. I laid my gun over the saddle and fired at Buffalo Horn as he came galloping up ahead of his men. He fell from his horse, so his men turned and fled when they saw their chief fall to the ground, and I jumped on my horse again and came to Silver City as fast as I could. I tell you, my dear sister, my captain was surprised when he saw me coming, for he had left me to be killed by the Bannocks. The two other Indians were wounded, and I am wounded also."

Just then Captain Bernard came along on his way down to Sheep Ranch with his one company. All the soldiers looked at me as if I was some fearful beast when Captain Bernard came to talk to me after he had seen the two captains.

Captain Bernard said to me, "Sarah, these citizens say that you have a good deal of ammunition in your wagon."

Oh, can anyone imagine my feelings when he said this to me? My heart almost bounded into my mouth. I said, "Captain, they must know or they would not say so. Go and see for yourself, Captain, and if you find anything in my wagon besides a knife and fork and a pair of scissors, I will give you my head for your football. How can I be taking guns and ammunition to my people when I am going right away from them?"

I told Captain Bernard everything—why I was there and that I had started to go to Washington for my people, as they wanted me to do. I once more said to him, "Go to my wagon and see."

"No, Sarah, I believe what you tell me is true."

Then I told him what Paiute Joe had told me about his killing Buffalo Horn out at South Mountain. "Now, Captain, you do me a great favor by believing me. If I can be of any use to the army, I am at your service, and I will go with it till the war is over."

He said, "Well, Sarah, I will telegraph to General O. O. Howard. He is at Fort Boise, and I will see what he says about it. Do you know the country pretty well?"

I told him I did.

"Well, Sarah, I will send for you from the Sheep Ranch. You will come if I send, will you?"

I said, "I will come if the citizens don't kill me."

"Yes, Sarah, I would like to have you go as my guard, for I can get no Indian to go with me for love or money."

"Yes, Captain, I will go and do all I can for the government if General Howard wants me."

Then Captain Bernard said good-bye and went away with his company. I stayed at the place all night, and the citizens were mad because the captain did not search my wagon for the ammunition. They put a guard on my wagon that night. I cried and told them they ought to be ashamed of themselves. So passed the night quietly.

I got up in the morning, had my breakfast, and looked after my horses. I went to the captain and said, "Please come to my wagon with all of your men and women. I want to show you all how much ammunition I have in it."

Captain Hill asked me to forgive him for saying such a thing about me to the army officer. "I know your father is a friend to the whites. If I can do anything for you, I will be most happy to do it. If you want to go to the command, I will give you a horse any minute you want to go."

Just then there came four Indians and one white man. I ran to meet them. I knew them all. I asked where they came from.

They said, "We were sent by the commanding officer from Camp McDermitt with a dispatch to the chief of the soldiers."

"Which way did you come?"

"We came by Camp Three Forks of Owyhee River." They had to come that way because there was no traveling on the stage road since the driver was killed. The telegraph wire was cut, so there was no communication between Sheep Ranch and Camp McDermitt.

I then said to the captain, "I want to go with these men to the command."

"Yes, Sarah, I can let you have a horse and a saddle too."

Then I told my people I would go with them. Then George, one of the men, said, "Oh, Sarah, I am so glad you are going with us, for we are all afraid that the white people will kill us if we go alone, for just about here we met some men, and they would have killed us anyhow, only this white man saved us."

I ran to my wagon to get ready. I told Morton and his little girl that I was to leave them, and the little girl began to cry.

Her father talked to me and said, "Sarah, don't leave Rosey, for she has come to love you."

I told him I had to work for my people.

"Now, Sarah, as I have never talked to you before, will you be my wife? We will go to Silver City and get married right away."

I said to him, "You honor me too much by offering marriage to me, Mr. Morton. I thank you very much for your kind offer, but I cannot marry a man that I don't love. You and your daughter can go down tomorrow. I shall be at the Sheep Ranch, and there I will wait for you."

My horse was ready, and I bade him good-bye. This was on the 12th of June, 1878.

We rode full gallop most of the time. We had thirty miles to go to the command. Just as we got in sight of the camp at Sheep Ranch, we saw a man coming. He did not see us until he got pretty close to us. When he saw us, he stopped and looked at us. We were riding along slowly, and the white man that was with us was ahead of us, so that he could see there was a white man with us, but he turned round and ran as fast as he could. The white man who was with us called to him just as loud as he could. The other man ran on and turned to shoot. Our white man took off his hat to show him we were not his enemies, but he got worse.

Then I said, "Let us run after him, for he knows we are not Bannocks. Bannock women don't ride sideways, nor do they wear riding dresses."

So we put after him just as hard as we could, the white man and I riding side by side, halloing to him just as an Indian would do when he is after his enemy. I tell you we very soon made him stop his foolishness.

When Captain Bernard saw me coming with four Indians, he and other officers came to meet me. His first question was, "What is the matter with the Indians?" Without saying a word, I gave him the letter they had given me from Camp McDermitt, which explained all without my saying a word. Bernard told the men to take the Indians to their camp and give them something to eat, as it was eight o'clock, and he took me to his own tent. I was treated with most high respect by the captain and his officers. After supper he took me up to the hotel, and I stayed there all night.

The captain wanted me to help him get the Indians to go with a dispatch to Camp Harney or to the Malheur Agency and find out the whereabouts of the hostile Bannocks. He said if they would go, they would be well paid. I told them, word for word, what Captain Bernard had told me to say to them.

Then they said, "Sarah, we will do anything we can for the officers and you; we will go with dispatches anywhere but to the hostile Bannocks. We cannot go to them, for, Sarah, you don't know what a danger that is. Sarah, your brother Natchez was killed, or is dead, for the same morning on which we were to start, three white men said so. Natchez and they made their escape from the hostile Bannocks, and the Bannocks pursued them, and Natchez's horse gave out. And all your folks were crying the day we left Camp McDermitt. Dear sister, it is not safe to go to them. Of course we know only what the white men told us. Oh, we do hope it is not so. If Natchez is killed by the Bannocks, oh, it will be too bad indeed."

Oh, when they told me this sad news about my dear brother, my heart was dead within me. A thousand thoughts passed through my mind. I said to myself, "If my brother was killed by the Bannocks and we do go and be killed by them too!" Then I told Captain Bernard the Indian men would not go for love or money. I told the captain I would go if I had to go alone, and he would give me a good horse.

He said, "Sarah, you cannot go, can you?"

"Yes, I will go if there is a horse to carry me."

"Sarah, if you are in earnest, I will send a telegram to General Howard and see what he says about it."

On the morning of June 13, I got up very early and went down to the camp and had my breakfast. Then I called the Indians and asked George to accompany me to Malheur Agency or to the whereabouts of the hostile Bannocks.

"Are you playing with me, Sarah, or do you think I would let you go alone? No, no, I will go with you. John and I will go."

"Well, we will go as soon as the telegram comes from General

Howard. George, we will go, no matter what comes of it. There is nothing that will stop me."

Just as I got these words out of my mouth, Captain Bernard called me, and I went to him.

> *The saddest day hath gleams of light,*
> *The darkest wave hath bright foam 'neath it,*
> *And twinkle, o'er the cloudiest night*
> *Some solitary star to cheer It.*

"Now, Sarah," he said, "if you will go to your father, tell him and his people that they shall be taken care of and be fed. Get all the well-disposed of your people to come near the troops where they can be safe. Now, Sarah, if you can succeed, your reward shall be five hundred dollars. Don't forget to tell them that all who behave well shall be properly fed."

I said to the captain, "I came through the Malheur Agency on the 6th of the month and there is nothing for them to eat there."

He said, "Tell them all to come to the troops."

Then I asked him to write me a letter to take with me in case that my horses should give out and I should come to a ranch where I could get some horses. He wrote:

TO ALL GOOD CITIZENS IN THE COUNTRY:

Sarah Winnemucca, with two of her people, goes with a dispatch to her father. If her horses should give out, help her all you can and oblige.

CAPTAIN BERNARD

With this letter I started down the crossing of Owyhee River, about fifteen miles from the Sheep Ranch, at about a quarter of a mile from the place where the stage driver was killed. When we got there, the citizen-scouts were all asleep. If we had been hostile

Bannocks, we could have killed every one of them. Some of these scouts were getting from fifteen to twenty-five dollars a day, and this is the way the citizen-scouts earned their money during an Indian war. They go off a little way from the troops and lie down and come back and report that there are Indians within half a mile from the troops.

We went into the house and waked them up. I said to them, "Is this the way you all find the hostiles? We could have killed every one of you if we had been they. I want a fresh horse if you have one, as I don't think one of our horses will stand the trip, as we are going to the Malheur Agency or to the hostile Bannocks wherever they are. We are sent by General Howard, and here is a letter which Captain Bernard gave me."

One of them read it and said, "All right, Sarah, we will give you the best horse we have here."

Then they gave us our dinner, and we started on our work. We had not gone but about a mile beyond the crossing at Owyhee River when we struck the hostiles' trail. We followed it down the river as much as fifteen miles, and then we came to where they had camped, and where they had been weeping, and where they had cut their hair. So we knew that it was hereabout that Buffalo Horn had been killed, for they had been tearing up clothes, cutting off hair, and breaking up beads there. Here they left the river and struck off toward Barren Valley. They had to go up a hill, and here I found the poor stage driver's whip, which I took with me.

We rode very hard all day long—did not stop to rest all that day. The country was very rocky and no water. We had traveled about fifty miles that day. Now it was getting dark, but we rode on. It was very difficult for us to travel fast, for our horses almost fell over sometimes.

I said, "Boys, let us stop for the night, for our horses will surely fall over us and kill us, and then the hostile Bannocks will not have the pleasure of killing us."

Here my men laughed at me, so we stopped for the night and ate our hard bread without any water. Then I gave my orders by saying, "John, you stand guard, George and I will sleep a little, and then wake him and let him stand guard the rest of the night. We must start just as soon as we can see to travel."

So I lay down to have a little sleep using my saddle for a pillow. I did not sleep, as my horse kept pulling me, as I had tied him to my arm.

I heard John come and say to George, "It is daylight."

I jumped up and said, "We will go. I am almost dead for water."

We started on the full jump across Barren Valley toward Mr. G. B. Crawley's ranch. As we came nearer and nearer, I said, "I can't see the house."

So we rode on until I saw it was burnt down, and the men said, "Yes, and we see the smoke yet." Yes, it was still burning. We saw a fresh track here and there. I saw by the look of everything that it was set on fire the morning of the 13th of June.

George said to me, "Sarah, let us not stop here, for they must be close by."

I saw that they were afraid. I said to them, "It is of no use to be afraid; we have come to see them and see them we must. If they kill us, we have to die, and that is all about it. Now we must have something to eat. George, you go and look out while John and I make some coffee, and when it is ready, we will call you."

John said, "Sarah, let us kill some of the chickens."

I said, "No, John, we will not, for they do not belong to us."

So we made our coffee as quickly as we could. We made it in one of the tin cans that had been burnt, and we called George, who came down, and we all ate our breakfast as fast as we could.

I said to my boys, "What do you two think? Had we better

go to the Malheur Agency or follow up the trail, which looks as if all the Indians were going towards Stein's [Steens] Mountains. You are men, you can decide better than I can."

"Now, Sarah, you know this country better than we do, and you know what to do, and if we say go this way or that way, you would blame us if anything should happen. And another thing— we have come with you and are at your command. Whatever you say, we will follow you."

"Well, since you have left it all to me, we will follow up the fresh trail that goes toward Stein's Mountains. I think it is our people going to Camp McDermitt."

It was now about six o'clock in the morning of the 14th of June. So we started again and rode as fast as our horses could travel. We had about sixty miles to go to find some white people. We traveled on and found a clock on their trail at a place called Juniper Lake, and we all knew it was the hostile Bannocks we were following. The next thing we found was a fiddle, and I took it along with me.

About noon I saw something coming down the mountain. "Oh," said I, "oh, look there! What is it?"

"Oh, it is mountain sheep."

We galloped up toward them. They came close to us, and John shot and killed one. We took some of the meat. There I lost my fiddle, and it is there to this day, as I never went back to find it.

As we rode on, about five miles from Juniper Lake, we saw someone upon the mountains as if they were running, so we waved our handkerchiefs at them. There were two of them. As we came nearer to them, I said to George, "Call to them." He did so; I saw them rise to their feet.

I waved my handkerchief at them again, and one of them called out, "Who are you?"

I said, "Your sister, Sarah."

It was Lee Winnemucca, my brother, who had called out. So they jumped on their horses and came to us. The minute he rode up, he jumped from his horse and took me in his arms and said, "Oh, dear sister, you have come to save us, for we are all prisoners of the Bannocks. They have treated our father most shamefully. They have taken from us what few guns we had, and our blankets, and our horses. They have done this because they outnumber us, and we are all up in the mountains with them. Oh, sister, have you brought us some good news? Have you come for us? Oh, dear sister, here I am standing and talking to you, knowing the great danger you are in by coming here, and these men too. The Bannocks are out in the mountains looking out. Take off your hat and your dress, and unbraid your hair, and put this blanket round you so if they should come down they would not know who it is. Here is some paint. Paint your face quick. Here, men, hide your guns and take off your clothes and make yourselves look as well as you can."

All this was done as quickly as possible, and we were all dressed like the hostile Bannocks.

I asked, "Where is our father? "

"We are all up over that mountain. We are but six miles from here."

"I must go to him. I have a message for him and for all our people too."

"Oh, no, dear sister, you will be killed if you go there, for our brother Natchez has made his escape three days ago. They were going to kill him because he had saved the lives of three white men. Oh, dear sister, let me pray you not to go, for they will surely kill you, for they have said they will kill everyone that comes with messages from the white people, for Indians who come with messages are no friends of ours, they say every night."

"But, dear brother, they will not know me."

"Yes, Oytes will know you, for he is their chief now since Buffalo Horn is killed."

"Dear brother, I am sorry to tell you that I must go to my father, for I have come with a message from General Howard. I must save my father and his people if I lose my life in trying to do it, and my father's too. That is all right. I have come for you all. Now let us go."

The mountain we had to go over was very rocky and steep, almost perpendicular. Sometimes it was very hard for us to climb up on our hands and knees. But we got up at last and looked down into the hostile encampment.

Oh, such a sight my eyes met! It was a beautiful sight. About three hundred and twenty-seven lodges, and about four hundred and fifty warriors were down Little Valley catching horses, and some more were killing beef. The place looked as if it was all alive with hostile Bannocks. I began to feel a little afraid.

I looked down upon them, and I said, "Brother, is our father's lodge inside the line? We must leave our horses here and go on foot. I can run down the mountain very fast."

Brother said, "If you are discovered, how will you get out?"

"Oh, well, our horses are almost given out anyway; so, dear brother, we must trust to good luck, and it is not so very far. Let us go quick and be back, for I have no time to lose."

So we ran all the way down the mountain. Before I went into my father's lodge, I sent brother in to tell him I was coming. He did so, and I heard him whistle, and I then said to the men, "We will go in."

Oh, how glad my father was to see me! He took me in his arms and said, "Oh, my dear little girl, and what is it? Have you come to save me yet? My little child is in great danger. Oh, our Great Father in the Spirit Land, look down on us and save us!" This was repeated by everyone in the tent.

Everyone in the lodge whispered, "Oh, Sadie, you have come to save us!"

I said, "Yes, I have come to save you all if you will do as I wish you to and be quiet about it. Whisper it among yourselves. Get ready tonight, for there is no time to lose, for the soldiers are close by. I have come from them with this word: 'Leave the hostile Bannocks and come to the troops. You shall be properly fed by the troops.' Are you all here? I mean all the Malheur Reservation Indians."

"Yes, all are here, and Oytes is the chief of them."

"Father, you tell the women to make believe they are gathering wood for the night, and while they are doing that, they can get away."

And while I was yet talking, I saw the women go out, one by one, with ropes in their hands, until we were left alone; that is, I was left alone with eight men: my father, and my brother Lee, and my cousins George Winnemucca, Joe Winnemucca, and James Winnemucca, and the two men that were with me.

"Now, father, let us go, as it is getting dark."

Then father said, "Now, dear son, go and get as many horses as you can get, and drive them down as fast as you can. We shall wait for you at Juniper Lake."

My brother Lee jumped up, rope in hand, and went out of the tent. Then my father gave orders to his nephews, and we four started out, leaving father's lodge all lonely. It was like a dream. I could not get along at all. I almost fell down at every step, my father dragging me along. Oh, how my heart jumped when I heard a noise close by. It was a horse running toward us. We had to lie down close to the ground. It came close to us and stopped. Oh, how my heart beat! I thought whoever it was would hear my heart beat. It stood a little while, and someone whistled.

"Yes," the whistle said, "where is father?"

It was dear little Mattie, my sister-in-law. She had waited for her husband in the woods, and he came out. She went with him, and he sent her to me with a horse. Oh, how thankful I was to Mattie for the horse! So my father helped me on to the horse. We went on faster, and got to where we had left our horses, and found them all right.

"George," I said, "take off my saddle and put it on this horse, the horse my brother has sent me, and you take my horse. It is better than yours."

The men led the horses down the mountain while Mattie and I ran down hand in hand. We could run down the mountain faster than horses could. When we got down to the Juniper Lake, Lee was there all ready waiting for us, also the women. Lee also had had the women cook the mountain sheep meat we had left there for me, for I assure my readers that I did not know what hunger was all that time. I had forgotten all about eating.

I said, "Come, women, take some in your hands and get on your horses, and eat while you are traveling, for we have many miles before us tonight. Tie your children to your backs. If they should sleep so, they will not fall off, for we must travel all night."

Lee came up to me and said, "Sarah, I am going back to get Jarry Lang." That was our cousin, Agent Reinhard's interpreter. "He is a close prisoner. I will go and see if I can get him."

I said, "Lee, if you go, try and get all you can." I turned round and said, "Are you all ready?"

"Yes." My father gave the order by saying, "Ride two by two, keep close together. Men, march your children and your wives. Six men keep back, for fear we will be followed."

So father and Mattie and my two men and myself led at the head of my people. We marched for some six hours. Mattie and I saw a track, and father called out "Halt!" And the men came forward and lighted a light. It was a herd of cattle. We marched all night long. Just at daybreak, we got to a place called Summit Springs.

I said, "Father, we will stop here and wait for Lee as we promised we would." So we unsaddled our horses, and I lay down to have a little sleep, having had no sleep for two nights.

No sooner did I lie down and fall asleep than my father called me and said, "Eat something." They had cooked some of the sheep meat. "You cannot sleep until your brother comes."

I tell you I did eat, for indeed I was really starved. When I got through, I asked if the men were out watching. Just as father said "Yes" came a warning alarm. Everybody jumped for their horses. Mattie and I ran and got our horses, jumped on their bare backs, and went to meet the man who brought the warning.

I said, "What is the matter?"

"We are followed by the Bannocks." His horse was almost falling from under him.

I said, "Jump on behind me." He did so. We galloped up to the camp. "Oh, father, we are followed."

"Yes," said the man behind me, "we are followed. Egan and his whole band is overtaken and are taken back. I looked back and saw Lee running, and they firing at him. I think he is killed. Oytes is at the head of this. I heard him say to the Bannocks, 'Go quickly, bring Sarah's head and her father's too. I will show Sarah who I am. Away with you, men, and overtake them.'" This is the news that came to us the morning of the 15th of June.

My father said, "If my son is killed, I will go back to them and be killed too. If we are to be killed off for what the white people have done to them, of course we cannot help ourselves."

I said, "Father, it is no time to talk nonsense now. Be quick, let us go; for my part, my life is very dear to me, though I would lose it in trying to save yours, dear father."

My stepmother was crying; so was poor little Mattie, Lee's wife.

"Come, father, give me your orders, as I am going back to the troops. What shall I tell General Howard, as I am going to where he is this very day if the horse can carry me?"

"Tell him to send his soldiers to protect me and my people." With this message I left my father on the morning of the 15th of June.

Poor little Mattie cried out to me, "Oh, dear sister, let me go with you. If my poor husband is killed, why need I stay?"

I said, "Come on!"

Away we started over the hills and valleys. We had to go about seventy-five miles through the country. No water. We sang and prayed to our Great Father in the Spirit Land, as my people call God. About one o'clock we got to the crossing of a creek called Muddy Creek. We got off our horses and had a drink of water, and tied our horses till they got cooled off while we gathered some white currants to eat, for that is all we found. Now we watered our horses and found a narrow place to jump them across, and off again toward our soldiers as fast as our horses could carry us. We got to the crossing of Owyhee River at three o'clock and stopped twenty minutes to eat some hard bread and coffee while they saddled fresh horses for us. We jumped on our horses again, and I tell you we made our time count going fifteen miles to the Sheep Ranch. We whipped our horses every step of the way till we were met by the officers. Captain Bernard helped us off. I saw one of the officers look at his watch; it was just 5:30 p.m.

I told the general everything: how I got my people away, how we were discovered and followed by the Bannocks. Oytes, one of the Snake River Paiutes, a leading chief, had overtaken Egan, a subchief, and his band and driven them back. "Maybe my brother Lee was killed. My father is on his way here and wants you to send him some soldiers for protection."

When I said this, the officers looked at each other, and so

did the soldiers and also the volunteer scouts, just as much as to say, "You are lying to us."

I saw Lieutenant Pitcher wink at Lieutenant Wood. The general asked me how many Indians I thought there were in all. I told him that my brother Lee thought there were about seven hundred in all, men, women, and children. Then the general called the captain of volunteers, Mr. Robbins, and ordered him to take all his men and go and bring Chief Winnemucca to the troops. I called Paiute Joe, who had killed Buffalo Horn, and told him in a few words which way to go to meet my father.

This was the hardest work I ever did for the government in all my life, the whole round trip, from ten o'clock June 13 up to June 15, arriving back at 5:30 p.m., having been in the saddle night and day; distance, about two hundred and twenty-three miles. Yes, I went for the government when the officers could not get an Indian man or a white man to go for love or money. I, only an Indian woman, went and saved my father and his people.

> Let us then be up and doing,
> With a heart for any fate;
> Still achieving, still pursuing,
> Learn to labor and to wait.

The next morning was Sunday. The general called me, and said, "I want you to go with me as my interpreter and guide."

I said, "Can I go with Captain Bernard's company?"

He said, "Do so. I want you and Mattie with the headquarters."

I said, "Which is the headquarters?"

He said, "We will go to Camp Lyon. The headquarters will be habitually with the right column."

The general's staff in the field consisted of Major Edwin C. Mason, 21st Infantry, Acting Assistant Inspector General; Captain Lawrence S. Babbitt, Ordnance Department Engineer and Ordnance Officer; Assistant Surgeon General, Perkins A. Fitzgerald, Chief Medical Officer in the field; First Lieut. Ebenezer W. Stone, 21st Infantry, Chief Commissary of Subsistence in the field; First Lieut. Fred H. G. Ecstein, 21st Infantry, R.I.M., Chief Quartermaster in the field; First Lieut. Melville C. Wilkinson, 3d Infantry, Aide-de-Camp; Second Lieut. Charles E. S. Wood, 21st Infantry, Aide-de-Camp, Assistant Adjutant General in the field.

With these officers, Mattie and I started for Camp Lyon, and I was as mad as could be because I wanted to go right after the hostile Bannocks. Mattie and I had to ride in a wagon going to Camp Lyon. We met three or four companies of cavalry half-way. Some of the soldiers cried out, "Oh, I see they have Sarah Winnemucca a prisoner." Mattie and I laughed at this.

We got to Camp Lyon about three o'clock. It was Sunday. Captain Lawrence S. Babbitt and Lieutenant C. Wilkinson came down from Silver City, Idaho. Later we had prayers and singing in the evening, as they were all Christians but Captain Babbitt and the soldiers by the name of Moffatt and Musenheimer and Goodwin, and Mattie, four. White men, educated, not Christians; men that are almost born with the Bible in hand. What! not Christians? Yes, that is just what I mean.

Poor General! He had some hard words with a citizen who owned a stage, because he wanted thirty-five dollars a day to take us to Reinhard's crossing of Malheur River.

I stood by them when they were talking, and I could hold in no longer. "That is the way with you citizens. You call on the soldiers for protection, and you all want to make thousands of dollars out of it. I know if my people had a herd of a thousand horses, they would let you have them all for nothing."

The general looked at me so funny and said, "Yes, Sarah, your people have good hearts, better ones than these white dogs have." The man would not give in, so they had to give him thirty-five dollars and pay all expenses besides.

So we left Camp Lyon. The second night we slept at Henderson's Ranch, near Keeney's ferry, where Lieutenant Ecstein, field quartermaster, joined us, and we went the next day to Reinhard's crossing, just in time to meet Stuart's column, which had already reached that point a few hours before us and had been kept under arms ready to move. The weather for the poor soldiers and for us had been hot and dry, and the roads very dusty. The country of our route was characterized by the usual alkali and sage brush, much of it bare and mountainous.

At the stone house at Reinhard's crossing were gathered a number of families from the country around. Here I met an enemy, whom I had met about eleven days before, to whom I had given something to eat when he was almost starved. Then he paid it back to me by telling General Howard that he saw me at the Malheur Agency and that I was the one that started my people on the warpath. General Howard brought him to me and told me what he had said about me. I told the general where I had met him. It was about forty miles this side of Malheur Agency. He and another man came to my camp almost starved, and I gave them their supper and breakfast.

"I know the other man will not say that of me," I said. I was crying when he was talking.

Then he came forward and said, "Oh, Sarah, I did not mean it. Forgive me, Sarah."

I said right out, "You brute."

He turned out afterward to be the best friend I had. We stayed there all night, the 18th of June. A citizen came in and reported Indians close by. The general asked me what I thought about it. I told him I did not think there were any Indians within ten hundred miles of us.

On the morning of the 19th, we marched up toward Malheur City about twenty-five miles and camped. General Howard asked me if I would be afraid to go with a dispatch to Camp Harney. Camp Harney had not been heard from for some time. A story having the appearance of truth was brought to us that Captain McGregor's company had had a disastrous engagement and had lost the most of their horses. The news also reached us that the hostiles had abandoned the Stein's Mountains and gone to Harney Valley, and it was probable that the left column of Captain Bernard's company had pushed after them.

Later in the evening, General Howard and Lieutenant Wilkinson came to us again and said, "Well, Sarah, what do you think about going?"

I said, "I am always ready to go anywhere you wish me to go."

"Do you think you would want an escort?"

I said, "No, Mattie and I will go alone, for no white man can keep up with us. We can go alone quicker than with soldiers."

But Lieutenant Wilkinson said he would go with us, for they could not let us go alone, as there were bad white men who might harm us, and he would take two soldiers besides. "Supposing we were to meet the hostiles and they were to kill me, what would you do?"

Poor Mattie was the first to speak. "Sister and I will throw ourselves on you, and they should kill us first, then you."

This made the officers laugh.

So on the 20th, Sister and I started for Camp Harney with Lieutenant Wilkinson, Aide-de-Camp, Corporal Moffatt, and Private Musenheimer. After we had traveled about twenty miles, Sister Mattie's horse gave out, and Lieutenant Wilkinson took a stage horse for her. At twelve o'clock we stopped for something to eat, for it was the last place we should see or where we should find anything until we got to Camp Harney, a hundred miles farther. Here I met another enemy of mine who was unlooked for. We three went in when dinner was ready, and the two soldiers had their lunch outside.

We sat down, and the woman came in with coffee. She looked at me and then said, "Well, I never thought I should feed you again. I hope they will not let you off this time." She then turned to Lieutenant Wilkinson and said, "Why do you take so much trouble in taking her to Camp Harney? Why don't you take her and tie one part of her to a horse and the other part of her to another horse and let them go? I would see the horses pull her to pieces with good grace."

All this time Lieutenant Wilkinson tried to stop her, saying, "You don't know what you are talking about. This is Sarah Winnemucca."

She replied, "I don't care. Rope is too good to hang her with."

Lieutenant Wilkinson said to me, "Never mind her. She is crazy."

But I could not eat anything. Dear reader, this is the kind of white women that are in the West. They are always ready to condemn me.

After dinner, Lieutenant Wilkinson brought me another horse.

"Now," I said, "it is about sixty miles to the agency." We went past there just a little after dark for fear some of the Bannocks were hiding there somewhere. We rode on as fast as we could, took a great many shortcuts which helped us along greatly, and stopped to rest for half an hour. We stood guard while Lieutenant Wilkinson slept a little while, called him up at the appointed time, and went on without stopping again. As we passed the agency, everything was dark and still, as if every living thing was dead, and there was no living thing left. This is the way it felt as we passed. We traveled on until our lieutenant gave out. He would get off his horse and walk awhile.

We traveled all night long and got to Camp Harney at ten o'clock on the following day. Oh, how tired I was! Mattie and

I went to bed without anything to eat. In the evening Major Downey's wife called on me to see if I wanted anything. She found me very poorly off for dress and went and got one of her own dresses, for which I was very thankful.

The next day was Sunday. Lieutenant Wilkinson was a minister. He was going to preach to the soldiers at ten o'clock, but a courier came riding very fast and reported Bernard's engagement. Bernard had attacked the hostiles that morning, Sunday at nine o'clock a.m., surprised and charged their camp, formed and recharged. The enemy rallied. Bernard asked for reinforcements and pressed every man with the utmost speed to his and the enemy's position on Silvery Creek, near Camp Curry, forty-five miles from Harney. Bernard reported only one soldier killed at the time the messenger left him. He had four companies of cavalry: his own, Whipple's, McGregor's, and Perry's under Bomus.

This is the report we brought to General O. O. Howard at eleven o'clock on Sunday night, distance about forty-five miles back on the way we had come Saturday night. I was asked to go back that same night, but I was so tired I could not. So Lieutenant Wilkinson was ordered back. Very early the next morning, Lieutenant Wilkinson and Lieutenant Wood, his Aide-de-Camp, left us with Major Mason and Major Babbitt to stop with the troops.

We traveled all day without stopping and got to where sister and I had hidden our rations when on our way to meet the troops. They were hard bread and canned baked beans. On the outside it said "Boston baked beans." It was about three o'clock in the afternoon, and all the officers were very hungry. We dined as well as we could. Each man gave one dollar. Just think of it. It only cost one dollar a plate for beans baked in Boston.

We got into Camp Harney very late that night. It took us three days to overtake the troops. The same night we got there, an

Indian woman was taken prisoner. They brought her to our tent. I asked her about everything. She did not want to tell me at first.

Sister Mattie said, "If you do not tell us, we will see why you had better tell us."

She was a Bannock woman. Then she was afraid and told us everything. She said her people were going right to Umatilla Reservation, and as the Umatilla Indians had told Oytes they would help them to fight the white people, this was why they were going there. She said Oytes had taken her nephew's place as chief over the Bannocks. She cried and said her nephew Buffalo Horn was killed at South Mountain. I told General Howard what she said. The next morning she was taken to Camp Harney, as she was blind, and the troops were ordered to go and have a fight with Bannocks about fifteen miles above us. The volunteer scouts kept coming to report. They said the Bannocks were waiting to fight there.

General Howard asked me what I thought about it. All I said was, "General, if you find any Indians within two hundred miles of here, you may say Sarah is telling lies."

"Then you think these scouts are not telling the truth, do you?"

"That is what I mean."

So we pushed on ahead of the troops for a while, and sister and I saw something on a high hill above us and ahead of us. It looked as if there were a great many there. We knew what it was, but we did not say anything for we wanted to see what they would do.

At last the bugle sounded. "Halt!" Sister said. "Now we will have some fun." We just laughed, for we knew what was coming.

The captain of the volunteer scouts rode up to General Howard and said, "General, don't you see them on that hill yonder?"

The general said, "I see something, but I don't see them moving."

"I do. They are there to fight us. They have a good place up there."

Then General Howard called me, and I went up to him. All the officers were there together. He said, "Sarah, what have you got to say now? The Indians seem to be there."

"I have the same thing to say as before. I see nothing but rocks put there to deceive you."

The officers took out their field glasses and looked up and said, "Sarah, it surely looks like people there."

I said, "Well, I can't say any more. Do as you think best." One of them gave me a field glass and told me to look. I said, "I will show you that there are no Indians there. I will go up there."

So I started to go when General Howard called me back and said, "I don't want you to get killed. I will send the troops up."

They found everything just as I had told them.

How they did laugh that evening when we camped for the night. It is a way by which we Indians do deceive the white people by piling rocks on each other and putting round ones on the top to make them look like men. In this way we get time to get away from our enemy.

In the morning we took up the trail in good earnest. At the dawn of the 28th, we were at the end of the wagon road in the direction where the Bannocks were moving. Yet rough and impassable as the way appeared, it was necessary, with the means of transportation then existing, to move the wagons across this mountain region. Just think—we were going to overtake them, with wagons and well-mounted on fresh horses every day, and we with our wagons only. We might as well say an Indian will overtake white men in building railroads.

On the morning of the 28th of June, we were riding on. At six a.m. a rough wagon trail was all the road. We arrived in camp at eight p.m. Bernard went some miles further. He sent back word of Indian pony tracks just ahead, and that they turned back suddenly. Sister and I again said, "Not so." We were again on the way.

The 29th of June was very cold, snowing all day. We went on ahead of the troops. At this place we came to a large camp. From fifteen hundred to two thousand Indians had been there, and there I found they had left a scalp behind them. It was the first scalp I had seen in my life, for my people never scalped anyone. The Bannocks had left it there. We waited there until the troops came up. I ran to the general and showed him what I had found. All the officers gathered round to look at it. They all said it was a real scalp.

Colonel Bernard said, "Sarah, you have done more than any of us. You have rescued your father and your people, captured the stage driver's whip, and now you have captured a scalp from the Bannocks."

General Howard said, "Yes, Sarah, you must keep them."

All this time Mattie was looking round. She called to me. I ran to her and left my scalp, and when I went back to get it someone had taken it, for which I was very glad. We camped here, and the cavalry went on ahead of us. General Howard ordered Colonel Bernard to go in hot pursuit of the Bannocks and overtake them if he could, but he only went a little way and camped. The cavalry pursued through the deep canyon of the south fork of the John Day River. Wagons crossed a mountain range gradually working to the highest ridge.

Oh, such a time as we did have! On July 1, great difficulty was encountered in getting the wagon train into the deep valley of the south fork, the hill being five miles in descent and so steep as to cause constant sliding of the wagons. It took from two o'clock p.m. until after ten o'clock at night to worry the train down this hill into the camp. The cavalry was four days ahead of us. On

July 2, we proceeded down the south fork about thirty miles to Stewart's Ranch on Murderer's Creek and saw evidences of a skirmish between volunteers and Indians. Here sister and I went on ahead and came to where the bodies of two men were buried by our advanced scouts. On the 3rd of July, the infantry went into camp in John Day valley, near the mouth of the south fork. The wagon train was replaced by pack mules that came to us from Canyon City. July 4, General Howard with his staff and sister and I pushed on to the advance and came up with the McGregors, and came on with them to Fox Valley.

While we were marching along in the hot sun, someone came running his horse toward us just as if he was running for his dear life. He said, "Oh, somebody shot at me. They are after me." General Howard asked him if they were Indians. He said, "I don't know, but I think they are white men."

"No wonder; you look just like an Indian, and they take you for such and shoot at you. Take your feathers off your horse."

This man would tie everything he could find belonging to Indians—feathers, beads, and red rags—on the mane and tail of his horse. He was no other than the man who talked so badly to me at the crossing of Malheur River, who I said was my best friend afterward. He was a newspaper reporter of the name of Parker from Walla Walla. It was he who sent word to the *Chronicle* that there were no Indians on the reservation after the Bannock War.

The next day we went on with McGregor's company and overtook Bernard and the remainder of the cavalry. On July 6, the cavalry reached Canvass Prairie in Oregon, passing through much timber. At this place a scout came and told us of another encounter of the volunteers with the Bannocks, and a rumor that the Umatillas had not joined the hostiles but fought them. Just then came up another party of scouts saying the Indians were coming right over the hill. All the cavalry drew up in line of battle.

Sister and I put whips to our horses and rode up the hill. Colonel Mason and Major Babbitt rode up also. We could not see anybody. About two miles off on a mountain, we saw some scouts going up with white linen coats. These are the reporters of the so-called noble citizens. Then Colonel Mason waved his hat to the troops to come on.

The evening of the seventh brought our advance to Pilot Rock, where a junction was formed with the troops sent thither by Colonel Wheaton. At this place I told General Howard we had passed the Bannocks. Maybe they would go back the same way they came or would go through the Blue Mountains. They know all the troops are on this side of the mountains.

Just then three volunteer scouts rode up and said the Indians were about fifteen miles from there. General Howard asked how many they thought they were. They said, "We think fifteen hundred, maybe more." General Howard asked me if I would go to them and see if they would surrender without fighting.

I said, "I will."

"I will see after supper," he said. All the officers had a talk over it. At supper he said, "Sarah, I will not send you. If you should get killed, your father will blame me. I will send some scouts to watch their camp during the night."

At the Battle of Birch Creek, General Howard formed a junction with his troops. Here they thought they would have an effective battle with the Bannocks and capture the fugitives. I did not think so because the Bannocks had the best of it. They had the timber on their side. I knew they would go into the timber and get away, and this I told the general, but he would not believe it. Seven companies of 1st cavalry and twenty of Robbins's scouts, with a Gatling gun, proceeded some three miles toward Battle Creek, when we met the two scouts who reported that the Indians were in position on a height about three miles from us. Bernard, taking the trail, moved quickly into position over the troublesome front hill, the east of which was fenced by a canyon and over a mile in the ascent. The cavalry sped from hill to hill till in the vicinity of the enemy, strongly posted on a rocky crest.

Oh, what a feeling I had just before the fight came on! Every drop of blood in my veins went out. I said to sister, "We will see a great many of our people killed today, and soldiers too."

Then the bugle sounded "Fire!" I heard the chiefs singing as they ran up and down the front line as if it was only a play, and on our side was nothing but the reports of the great guns. All my feeling was gone. I wanted to go to them. During the engagement the advance was made along several approaches in a handsome manner, not a man falling out of the ranks. The different sides of the hill were steeper than Missionary Ridge; still, the troops, though encountering a severe fire that emptied some saddles and killed many horses, did not waver but skirmished to the very top, the enemy abandoning his position and running to the next height in the rear, slightly higher and specially crowned with natural defenses of lava rock. In twenty minutes this height was charged from different sides and taken. Then the soldiers commenced a rapid pursuit of the flying Indians, who abandoned their spare horses that were in the field, perhaps two hundred. They were mostly jaded and worthless. They also left provisions and ammunition and camp material. The hostiles struck for the thick pines which crest the Blue Ridge and again made a stand, using the trees for defenses. Again the cavalry pressed them in the front and on the flanks, and in a few minutes dislodged them a third time and pushed them four or five miles further into the mountains. The rough country and the great exhaustion of horses and men caused a cessation of the pursuit for that day.

In this battle I did not see an Indian fall nor one killed, and there were five enlisted men wounded and probably twenty horses killed. The Indian women and their children and their best horses in droves were well out of the way before the battle began, and all the officers and scouts said they were making for Grande Ronde, but I for one said, "No, they will go back or through Blue Mountains and Malheur Agency, and back to their own country," but they all said the flight was in that direction. Captain Bernard was entitled to special credit for this engagement; yes indeed, for the entire campaign and his officers and men did as well as brave and true men can do. Dear reader, if you could only know the difficulties of this wilderness, you could then appreciate their loyal service.

The fight commenced at 8 a.m. under a hot sun and with no water. The whole of it was watched by the general commanding. The bullets were whistling all round us, and the general said to me and Mattie, "Get behind the rocks, Sarah. You will get hit." I did not feel any fear. I asked the general to let me go to the front line where the soldiers were fighting.

At last I heard Oytes say, "Come on, you white dogs. What are you waiting there for?"

I again asked the general if I might go to the front line to hear what Oytes was saying, and he said, "Go, Sarah." I put the whip to my horse and away I went to where the Gatling gun was placed. I jumped off my horse and stood alongside of it, but Oytes did not speak again. Then General Howard rode up and took his stand at the Gatling gun. This battle lasted from 8 a.m. to 12:30 p.m. Where do you think the citizen volunteer scouts were during the fight? The citizens, who are always for exterminating my people (with their mouths only), had all fallen to the rear, picking up horses and other things which were left on the battlefield, and after the battle was over they rode up to where we were and asked where were the Indians. General Howard said, "Go look for them."

Sometimes I laugh when I think of this battle. It was very exciting in one way, and the soldiers made a splendid chase and deserved credit for it; but where was the killing? I sometimes think it was more play than anything else. If a white settler showed himself, he was sure to get a hit from an Indian, but I don't believe they ever tried to hit a soldier. They liked them too well, and it certainly was remarkable that with all these splendid firearms, and the Gatling gun, and General Howard working at it, and the air full of bullets, and the ground strewn with cartridges, not an Indian fell that day.

One scout came running in to General Howard and said an Indian was lying in a stream at the bottom of a deep canyon tied to the tail of a horse and dead. General Howard always sent sister and me to look after the Indians when he heard any were killed, and he sent us down that steep canyon that day to see if we knew the dead Indian, but we found nothing though we went two miles along the stream. It was a false report, just such an one as citizen-scouts give. They take good care not to go too near Indians, and the officers know well enough what they are good for. If they wanted to find enemies, they would not send them to reconnoiter. They know very well that they would shirk any such duty.

Have not the Indians good reason to like soldiers? There were no Custers among the officers in Nevada. If the Indians were protected, as they call it, instead of the whites, there would be no Indian wars. Is there not good reason for wishing the army to have the care of the Indians instead of the Indian Commissioner and his men? The army has no temptation to make money out of them, and the Indians understand law and discipline as the army has them, but there is no law with agents. The few good ones cannot do good enough to make it worthwhile to keep up that system. A good agent is sure to lose his place very soon, there are so many bad ones longing for it.

We camped here for the night. Here the poor soldier who was wounded so badly was brought to us, and Mattie and I watched over him. I asked him if I could do anything for him, but he shook his head. Later in the evening, General Howard came with a book and read, and prayed with him. There was no one with him during the night. Sister and I went to see him once, but at four o'clock in the morning, he cried out for someone to come to him. We went to him, poor fellow, and I asked him again if I could say or do anything for him. He looked at me but could not speak, and died in a few minutes. He was buried at the same place under a beautiful pine tree. Late in the fall, he was taken up by the Odd Fellows and carried to Walla Walla, Washington Territory.

On the morning of the 20th of July, we struck the Indian rear guard in the canyon of the north fork of the John Day River. This canyon is about one thousand and two hundred feet deep; and as the walls are nearly perpendicular, our command actually slid down the trail that we were following into the stream, which rushed down the bed of the canyon. We had to climb up the opposite side leading our horses, the ascent being so steep that several of our pack animals fell over backward into the stream and were lost while trying to follow the puzzling zigzags of the trail.

The Indians that constituted their rear guard numbered about forty. They had fortified themselves near the brow of the hill on the trail, so as to command it for several hundred feet below their line of work. The scouts, numbering about eight, were a short distance ahead of us, who were in the advance guard. The Indians, who were in ambush, permitted them to get almost up to their line when the accidental discharge of a carbine in the advance guard caused them to believe that they were discovered, and they at once fired upon the scouts, killing H. H. Froman, a courier, who was with the advance, and severely wounding a scout, John Campbell. The advance guard was Company E, 1st Cavalry, under Captain W. H. Winters. At the sound of the firing, he deployed his company, dismounted, and took a strong position, which was re-enforced by sending forward Company H, under

Lieutenant Parnell, and Company L, under Lieutenant Shelton, and they extended the line to the right by pushing Company G, under Captain Bernard and Lieutenant Pitcher, up the side of the canyon to a projecting point which commanded and protected the trail and the bench of land upon which we had corralled our stock. As soon as this formation was completed, which occupied us about an hour and a half and was made under fire of the enemy, the line moved forward, and the crest of the precipitous hill—or more properly speaking, bluff—was reached. Not soon enough, however, to give us a chance at the foe, who had mounted and fled.

At this fight, a little girl baby was found by a sergeant, who picked it up. He said it was lying on its little face. He carried it to the officers, and Captain McGregor was the first who gave it something to eat. It was gingersnaps, sugar, and water. They also took two Indian women. One of them I knew. She had returned during the night looking for her lost children, and the other was a Bannock woman. I asked the woman I knew if she would be so kind as to look out and care for the baby for me. She said she would, and General Howard ordered some condensed milk for me so that the woman might feed it, and I told her how to fix it. General Howard also told me to take good care of its little shirt and all its beads, and if they should ever surrender, we could find its mother. We had the little baby three months.

Now we went on as quickly as possible to form a junction with all the troops at what is called Burnt River Meadows. There were only eight companies of soldiers. We went in hot pursuit of the Indians, crossed the Blue Mountains range by very steep and difficult trails, and descended through the Granite Creek Valley.

We camped here. All the troops were out of rations. We were waiting for the return of the commissary from Baker City when we met at Burnt River Meadows. Sanford divided his rations with all, after which the command took up the Indian trail and moved on rapidly on Wednesday and Thursday.

On Thursday morning we met with Mr. Parrish. We had stopped to rest the cattle at Little Creek. He came right up to me and held out both his hands, saying, "Oh, Sarah, little did I think when I left you all, it would come to this! Oh, it is too bad! I can't believe it!"

The tears were running down his cheeks, and Mattie and I could not stop our tears. This is the only time and the last that I have seen him since he left us. He rode with us awhile, but at last said good-bye to us and went back to Granite City. We went on and camped for the night. About four o'clock a citizen rode up. It was Reinhard's blacksmith, A. L. Johnson. He sold some horses here which once belonged to my people. They were bought by Mr. Parrish while he was with us. After he sold them he stayed with the troops a long time.

On Friday we went to the vicinity of Ironsides Mountain. Here we camped at the crossing of Canyon City and Malheur City wagon road. That night General Howard asked me if I would go to the agency to ascertain if some of the flying Indians had not put in an appearance there, about twenty miles down the canyon. So very early next morning, sister and I started with eight Indian scouts and Lieutenant Wilkinson. We got to the agency about eleven o'clock; not a sign of anybody had been there since June. We stayed there all night, and next morning we went back the other way, that is, on the east side of the mountain called Castle Rock, and back to our place of starting.

Oh, what a hard ride we had that day! To my sorrow we found the troops had left the same day. We had gone the day before and thought no one was left behind, and I said to Lieutenant Wilkinson, "I am so tired! Can Mattie and I stop a little and rest?"

"Oh, Sarah, I am afraid something might happen to you."

I said I did not think I could go any farther.

"Well, then, Sarah, I would not stay long, will you?"

We had not been there but a little while when three men rode up. One of them said, "Come, boys, here are the girls, and the lieutenant is not with them."

At this I said to sister, "Quick, get on your horse," and off we went without stopping.

They called out to each other, saying, "Catch them, boys, let us have a good time."

Over the rocks and down the hill we went without stopping and got to the agency at six o'clock. As soon as I rode up, the general knew something was the matter. I told him all, and the men were discharged right there and then.

This was the second visit of the troops to the Malheur Agency, July 27. We found still a little flour, and the gardens comparatively undisturbed. It was very hard to see the poor, weary, and hungry troops. The next day Captain Miller with his company of the 4th Artillery reached us by the shortest road from Bucher City with plenty of rations. At this time the general told me to send one of the women to her people and tell them to come in and be peaceful. If they would lay down their arms and be good, they could have their reservation back to live upon all their lives, and then they could be well fed by the government. This is what General Howard told me to say to the woman. I did as I was told, and I said more than he did. I said, "Tell them I, their mother, say come back to their homes again. I will stand by them and see that they are not sent away to the Indian Territory." With this word the woman went away.

Oh, I saw the most fearful thing during that summer's campaign. Poor Egan, who was not for war, was most shamefully murdered by the Umatilla Indians. He was cut in pieces by them, and his head taken to the officers, and Dr. Fitzgerald boiled it to get the skull to keep.

A man by the name of Rattlesnake Jack scalped an old Indian who was lost because he was almost blind, and his wife was blind too. He was leading his wife the best he could through the woods. At last they came to the road. They had gone but a little way when the man rode up to them, and the poor woman could only hear her husband's groans as the man was cutting him to pieces. At last his groans died away. She felt so thankful that she could not see! She said every minute she cried out to her Spirit Father that he might kill her right away and not let her person be outraged, for she would rather die a hundred deaths than be outraged by a white man. At last she heard his footsteps coming toward her, "and I knelt down," she said, "and held my head down for the blow, for my heart was already dead within me. Instead of giving me a blow on my head, he put his foot on the back of my neck and brought my head down to the ground. I felt him take hold of my hair and the top of my head and felt his knife cutting off my scalp. Then the blood ran down my hands and face, for I had my two hands over my face. He kicked at me and stamped my head to the ground, and then I heard him go away. Oh, if he had only killed me, but he left me to starve and to die a slow death. I was left in this way for a long time and lay just where I was left. It must have been some days, for my mouth and throat were dry, and I was dying. To my great joy I heard some noise I thought so but was not quite sure, but I heard it again more plainly. It sounded like a wagon coming. Yes, it was a wagon. Oh, I was so glad, it was the white people, and that they would kill me. 'Oh, come quick and kill me!' Then I heard them talking very softly. It was a white woman and her children. Oh, if she would be like the wife of our agent, Parrish's brother, who used to come and give me sugar and coffee because I was blind [that was our white lily]. I heard them come nearer and nearer until they drove up close to where I was lying. I tried to get up but could not. I tried to speak but I could not. I wanted to say, 'Kill me quick.' I heard the woman make a noise as if she was crying. Someone came and raised me up. Of course I did not know whether it was a woman or a man. They tried to make me stand up, but I could not. 'Oh, my Good Spirit Father, speak to their hearts that they may kill me. I want to go where my husband has gone. For many years he has taken care of me. I don't want to live.' This was my thought when someone came and put a cup to my lips. I quickly swallowed some, thinking it might be poison, but it was only water. The first swallow almost killed me. Then they gave me more, then a little while after more, then they took me up and put me in the wagon and took me away. It was a long time before they stopped, and then I was taken out of the wagon. Then food was given into my hands which I did not care to eat, but the good woman kept putting something into my mouth. Afterward she went away, and when she came again, I held out my hands to feel of her dress, and for the first time I cried out, saying, 'Oh, my sister, who are you? Sarah Winnemucca? Have you come to save my life? Oh, dear sister, I don't want to live—don't try to save me.' I said all these things thinking it was you. When she did not answer me, then I knew it was not you. Whoever that woman was she took good care of me for a long time. She would often wash my head, and when I got well again, I thought of my poor husband. Oh, I can hear him now!"

This is what the poor blind woman told me after the war was over, and she is still living at the Yakima Reservation where I saw her last. Her husband had always taken such beautiful care of her.

On the night that Egan was murdered, I saw it all in my sleep. I had a vision, and I was screaming in my sleep when Mattie waked me and asked what was the matter. I told her that Egan was murdered, and I saw it all—saw his head cut off and saw him cut in pieces. This is true. Many of my family have seen things in their dreams that were really happening.

ON THE 27th of July, Mattie and I left General O. O. Howard and went with General Forsythe. We left Malheur Agency, and we left my baby, as they called it, with the rest of the prisoners. General Forsythe and myself were ordered to go throughout the whole country and pick up small parties of hostiles. General Howard said all captives would be held as prisoners of war, subject to the orders of the department commander. So we marched from the Malheur Agency to Stein's Mountains. We marched along the north fork of Malheur, at noon crossed the big Malheur River, traveled along its banks about five miles, and camped. No sign of my people. We took up our march again the next day, went about thirty miles, and on the next day about forty miles, for there was no water any nearer. Some of the poor soldiers had to leave their horses, which gave out, and walked in the hot, burning sun. My heart used to ache for the poor soldiers. The next day we camped at the very place where my brother Lee had met me and threw a blanket over me to hide me from the Bannocks, at Juniper Lake, Stein's Mountains. On the fifth day we camped east of Stein's Mountains. A good many of the soldiers went on foot. After leaving this camp, we had to go across a desert of forty-five miles without water. I told General Forsythe how far we should have to go without water, but I said, "About six miles ahead of us is a man who has a farm that has a great many horses and cattle on it. If he is there, maybe you can buy some horses for your men, or maybe he will let you have a wagon."

The general gave orders to his men that they must change about with their horses.

I also told him, "If there is nobody living there, Mattie and I will go on ahead about twenty miles. There used to be a spring there, and if it is not dried up, maybe there would be enough for the men to drink, but not for the horses. We would put up a white flag at the spring and go on. It will be at the left. If the spring is dry, we will not put up any flag."

We got up to the man's place, and he was not at home, but thanks be to God, the good man when he came gave General Forsythe two wagons and barrels to take water in, so we were all right.

About two o'clock, my sister's horse gave out. It could not walk at all, so we took the saddle off and left him. Sister would have to walk, and then I would walk a while. In this way the march was kept up all day, till we camped at a place called Old Camp C. F. Smith. All that time there were no fresh signs of my people, and the citizens living along the road reported that no Indians had been seen by them for ten or twelve days. We had traveled from the Malheur Agency one hundred and forty-four miles. The first night we camped there, sister Mattie and I saw a signal fire of distress and loneliness, and for help also. All the officers came to me and asked me the meaning of it. I told them it was the signal fire of one Indian.

They asked me how I knew. I said, "I am an Indian woman and understand all kinds of signal fires."

"Well, what do you think? Shall all the companies go over there and send out scouting parties to find out the fact that the signal fires were built by only one Indian?"

I said, "Just as you think best."

They went off by themselves and had a long talk. By and by General Forsythe came to me and said, "Sarah, are you in earnest in telling me there is only one Indian there?"

I said, "General Forsythe, if what I have told you is not true, I have never told a truth in all my life. I want you to go over there and hunt the mountain over and over, and if you find more than one Indian there, you can say Sarah has deceived you."

He said, "Well, Sarah, I will send some citizen-scouts tomorrow."

The scouts were sent the next day, and they were gone two days, and came back and reported the signal fire made by one Indian on foot. They said they could not find him.

Some citizen who came said there were some of my people at his house, so the general sent me up there to get them to go after the one Indian. I got four of them to come and see the general. He told them to go and get the man; he would give them ten dollars each if they brought him. They were willing to go if he would give them horses. They went, and on the second day they brought him. I knew him. He was one of the best Indian men Mr. Parrish had to work for him.

Fresh horses were got here from citizens, and everybody was ready to go on. Later I said to Mattie, "I think I had better go and see father and my brothers at Camp McDermitt. You can stay with General Forsythe and come on with him tomorrow. If you say so, I will go tonight and get there some time during the night. Will you let me, Mattie?"

She said, "Why, dear sister, you can go, I am not afraid; and another thing, my brother will be here in a little while, and therefore I will not be alone." We had sent for her brother to come to us.

It was seventy miles to Camp McDermitt. I said to the general, "I want to go to Camp McDermitt to see my father and brothers, and Mattie will stay with you. I will meet you at Antelope Springs."

General Forsythe said, "Can Mattie talk English well enough to talk to me?"

I said, "Yes."

"Well, you will want someone to go with you to see that no harm comes to you."

I said, "No, General, I can go alone. It will be night."

"No, Sarah, I must send someone with you. I will send Lieutenant Pitcher and two soldiers."

I said, "Very well, but I had as soon go alone as not."

So everything was made ready for my going. About four o'clock, nine of my people came. Among them was Mattie's brother. We were both made happy by it. At six o'clock we were ready for our journey. I kissed my sister, and away I went. Oh, what riding we did, all night long. We did not stop to rest all night long, nor did the lieutenant stop our horses from trotting from the time we started. About four o'clock the next morning, he stopped and said to the men, "Fix my saddle."

I said, "Lieutenant, can I go on?"

He said, "Yes."

Oh, what a relief it was to gallop my horse! At last I stopped and looked back, but could not see them coming. I would not wait for them and got to Camp McDermitt just at daybreak. I saw a great many encampments there—yes, as many as six hundred camps. I rode up to one camp and said, "Here, you are sleeping too much; get up."

One of the women jumped up and said, "Who is it? What is it?"

"Where is my brother's camp? Where is Natchez?"

"Ah, here, next to us."

I rode up to the camp. "Halloo! Get up. The enemy is at hand!"

My brother jumped up and said, "Oh, my sister!" He helped me off my horse and said to his wife, "Jump up, wife, and make a fire, sister is so cold." I had nothing on but my dress. A blanket was put around me. Fire was soon made, and I sat down to warm myself.

Brother stood up and said, "My children, I hope none of you have forgotten your duty to your Spirit Father in your sleep.

I hope you have passed the beautiful night in peaceful sleep and are all ready to do his work during the day. I am sorry to say there is no report yet from the young men saying that we are all safe; no one to say there is no enemy here; none of them have come and said, 'I have done my duty.' I am afraid, my young men, you are not doing your duty; for I have here in my camp a warrior who has just arrived. Come, one and all, and see for yourselves."

My poor papa was the first one who came up. He ran up and took me in his arms and said, "Oh, my poor child! I thought I never would see you, for the papers said you were killed by the Bannocks. We have all mourned for you, my child. Oh, when I heard you, my darling, who saved my life for a little while longer, had gone first, I thought my heart would break!" I put my face down on his bosom. He said, "Look up, dear; let me see if it is really my child."

I looked up. The tears were running down his cheeks. I looked round, and I saw tears in everyone's eyes. I told them everything: who was killed, what their names were, and how many prisoners we had, about our baby, and the four women, and the poor blind woman who was scalped, and about poor Egan, who was cut to pieces. I told them about Oytes too, and they all said they hoped when the soldiers caught Oytes, they would hang him.

"If they don't, we shall kill him ourselves," they said, "for he is to blame for all."

It was Oytes who first carried some of my people over to the Bannocks.

I told them the soldiers did not kill Egan, but the Umatilla Indians, who made General O. O. Howard believe they were friendly to the whites, and at the same time they were helping the Bannocks, because they are more civilized and know the value of money. They would go out nights for them, and lay out plans for them, and made them believe they were their best friends, and

then U-ma-pine, who was acting as chief, and the Umatillas that
were with the Bannocks got word that the white people offered a
reward of one thousand dollars to any one who would bring Egan,
alive or dead. This is why U-ma-pine, the Umatilla Indian, killed
poor Egan, and I said, "He is with us."

"What, with you?"

"I mean with the troops, and there are three more besides him."

After I was through talking, Leggins, my cousin's husband,
got up and said, "My brothers, I think we ought to go and kill
him. We have never done them any harm and have always been
kind to them when they came on our reservation. We have given
them presents, yes, more than they ever gave us. Oh, my brother
Winnemucca, and you, my dear Natchez, you are great friends
to our soldier-fathers. You and your sister can demand of them
to give him up to us."

Here I jumped up and said, "I have not told you all. At the
time they took Egan, they also took a great many women prisoners,
and most of them are young girls."

I sat down. My brother Natchez got up and said, "My children, this is a very sad thing indeed, and if we should go and kill
this U-ma-pine, I am afraid we will never get back our women
and girls. I want you all to listen well to what I am going to say of
what I think it is best for us to do. We will go and have a talk with
them right before General Forsythe's whole command, and say to
them, 'Friends, we have come to talk to you. Now tell us what our
subchief Egan has done to you that you should kill him and have
him cooked in the way you did. Was he good to eat? Oh, my dear
friends, some of you will suffer the same as Egan did at your hands.
If we had made war with you and had taken prisoners in battle, we
would not say anything, but you helped the thing along, and for
four years you have come on the Malheur Reservation and told
Egan and Oytes to make war against the whites. You have called

them fools for staying on the reservation to starve. And another thing, you have helped the Bannocks to fight the soldiers. You are nothing but cowards; nothing but barking coyotes; you are neither persons nor men. We were never your enemies, for we have let you come to our country and always welcomed you. We have never been to your country. Now we cease to be friends, and after the soldiers quit fighting with the Bannocks and with Oytes' men, we will make war with you for the wrong you have done us if you do not return our women and girls whom you have taken as prisoners. As soon as the war with the Bannocks is over, we want you Umatillas to bring us our women and children. We will then show you what fighting is. My friends, it must be a beautiful sensation to cut a man or a woman to pieces and then skin their beads and fasten them on a pole and dance round them as if you were indeed very happy. Do you know there is not money enough in the world to make me go and fight a people who have not done me any harm? You have done this year after year against your own people. Are you never going to stop? You and the Snakeheaded Indians, who are called the Wascoe Indians, and the Columbia River Indians, and the Nez Perces are about alike: you are always ready to take up your arms against your own people. And what do you gain by it?

"'You neither get praised by the so-called government, nor do you get anything more than we do. No: you are as poor as we are, we who have never taken our own brother's scalp and fastened it on a pole and danced round it to show our white brothers how brave we are.

"'My friends, here I stand before you, an old man, the snow has fallen upon me and it has left its mark, and my hair is white. My hands are clean from the shameful work you have done to Egan.

"'Why, friends, our great soldier-fathers, General Howard and General McDowell, have asked me to furnish them twenty-five of my men as scouts for them. General Howard and General McDowell are my best soldier-fathers, yet they could not give me money enough to take up arms against any tribe of Indians.'

"Now, my dear children, I will go with my sister, and I will say all to the Umatillas that I have said to you, right before General Forsythe and all the officers. I think it is right and just, and I also think it is the only way we can get back our women and girls."

This is what my brother Natchez said to his men, and one and all of them said they were always ready to hear our chief and to do what he says.

Brother then said, "How many want to go with me?"

They answered, "We will all go."

Brother said, "I am afraid the soldiers will think we have come to fight them if they see so many of us coming; therefore, I think about thirty of us will be enough to go."

While the talk was going on, Lieutenant Pitcher came and said, "Sarah, we will be ready to go back this afternoon at one o'clock."

"All right, Lieutenant," I said. Then I said, "Lieutenant, this is my father Winnemucca, and this is my brother Natchez. Father and brother and thirty men are going with us to see the Umatillas who are with you."

The lieutenant said, "Very well, they can go with us."

I had had no sleep yet. In those days I never knew what it was to be tired or sleepy.

My father then got up and spoke, saying, "I am ashamed to have to speak to you, my children. I am ashamed for you, not for myself. Where is one among you who can get up and say, 'I have been in battle and have seen soldiers and my people fight and fall.' Oh! For shame! For shame to you, young men, who ought to have come with this news to me! I am much pained because my dear daughter has come with the fearful things which have happened in the war. Oh, yes! My child's name is so far beyond yours; none of you can ever come up to hers. Her name is everywhere, and everyone praises her. Oh I how thankful I feel that it is my own child who has saved so many lives, not only mine, but a great many, both whites and her own people. Now hereafter we will look on her as our chieftain, for none of us are worthy of being chief but her, and all I can say to you is to send her to the wars and you stay and do women's work and talk as women do.

"Now we will go and see the man-eaters. I have never shot anything in all my life but what is good to eat. In my way of thinking and in my father's way of thinking, no man ought to kill anything unless it is good to eat. We were obliged to fight our white brothers at one time. It was only five months after my poor father's death. If he had lived, it might not have happened. I have promised to be a friend to white people, and I have done just as I said, although they have killed my people here and there. I have not unburied my bow and arrows yet, and I hope, my children, that you will keep our promise to the end of the world, and then it will be well with us. Now we must get something to eat before we go. You have all heard what your chief has said. There is one among you who did not go out to help defend his people. He is tall and strong, but he is a coward. Put a woman's dress upon him and give him woman's work to do. Let him dig roots, and prepare food, and make moccasins, and all the rest of his life let him wear women's clothing and not go among the men."

My dear readers, such is the respect my people have for their chiefs that that man still wears a woman's dress and does women's work, and will continue to do so all his life. My people, and I think no Indian people, feel the same respect for a *made* chief. Sometimes chiefs are chosen by others and set over a tribe. There is no respect felt for such chiefs. That breaks up the family life that is the best thing for Indians. I do not like to think of my people separated from each other. Their love for their chief holds them together and helps them to do right. A tribe is a large family. If a chief appoints subchiefs to help him take care of his people; they are respected unless they do wrong. But as I said before, no man can be a leader among Indians who is not a good man. His band may break away from him at any time if he does not do as his great chief does.

My father went on to say, "Some of the young men can go now and get our horses, and then we will go to see the scouts."

We got ready and started to go to a place called Antelope Springs, where we met the troops. All the officers were glad to see my father and brothers and all my people. Rations were issued to them. I told General Forsythe what my people came for, and he was glad.

After they had had their supper, all the officers were called, and the Umatillas also. They all came but one, and that was U-ma-pine. General Forsythe asked them where U-ma-pine was. They said they did not know. "Well, we want him here," the general said, "go and get him. These chiefs want to talk to you all."

One of them went but soon came back and said he could not find him. He was afraid and stayed in the hills that night, and my brother had to talk to the others. I have already told you, my readers, what he meant to say to them. The officers all cheered my brother after the talk was over. They told him that U-ma-pine and his people would suffer yet for what they had done. "General Howard," they said, "is not going to let them off as easily as they think. We will see that they turn all the prisoners over to us after the Bannocks all surrender."

My people stayed all night with us. The next morning, very early, we were ready to go on. But Mr. U-ma-pine could not be found anywhere. My people went along with us some ten miles to get a sight of the brave man who killed Egan. At last they gave it up and said good-bye to me and went back to Camp McDermitt.

Here my brother Lee said, "Sister, can I go with you and my wife?"

I said, "You can if you wish to."

We traveled about forty miles that day on account of no water. A good many of the soldiers' horses gave out. We camped here at a place called The Three Forks of the Owyhee River. The canyon is very deep; on the right-hand side of the river are very high mountains.

My brother told me a very funny story about the soldiers' doings at this place. "A few years ago, we were on that hill yonder. The soldiers were on that steep mountainside. We then called out to them. They stopped, and they were so frightened that they shot at us across, and one and all of us called out to them again."

Here my brother laughed so that I thought he would never stop. At last he said, "Dear sister, they had a cannon on a mule, and they shot at us before they took it off the mule's back, and the poor mule fell down the steep mountain." Here we all laughed. Brother said, "Some of our people said if the soldiers were going to shoot mules at them, they had better go away, and they traveled all night without stopping. They only said that to make fun."

After traveling three days we got to Silver City. We went to Tinker's Mill, on Tinker's Creek, and camped for the night.

General Forsythe received instructions to divide his command, Sanford to accomplish what had been given the whole, and Bernard to deviate southward and gather up the Indians who might be lurking in the neighborhood of Duck Valley, South Mountain, and the region on to McDermitt. General Forsythe himself was to go at once to Boise City to take command of the troops to the south and east of Boise City. I was ordered to go with Captain Bernard and Captain Winter's company to Duck Valley to gather up my people, and brother Lee, with his wife, to go with some of our people who were there. They were told to go with them to Camp McDermitt, Nevada.

Two days after we left Silver City, we went to Duck Valley and found some of my people there. They were very glad to see me. I told them that the order was that all our people were to go to Camp McDermitt. The captain told me to tell them that they must go because the citizens might mistake them for Bannocks and would kill them. He told me to say that the citizens were very angry with the soldiers because they would not kill all the Indians they could find. "We don't want," he said, "to kill good Indians, but we want to be your friends, and we don't want to see the citizens kill you. That is why I want you to go where the soldiers can look out for you all."

Among these was the father of Paiute Joe, who killed Buffalo Horn at South Mountain. He said to me, "Tell our soldier-father that we want to go but are afraid to. If he will send some of the soldiers with us, we will only be too glad to go, or give us a paper and then the citizens won't kill us."

I told Captain Bernard what Paiute Joe's father had said, and he gave him a letter and said, "We will go tomorrow."

The next day we went back the same way we came and camped at a place called Trout Spring. The officers caught a great many trout that afternoon. We stayed all night at that place. That evening the captain said to me, "Sarah, would you like to take a letter to Silver City for me? The companies will not go that way. We will cut across the country from here if you will go. You can get upon the stage and go to Boise City and leave your horse there. You will get there before we shall."

I said "Yes, I will go." The distance was fifty miles, so I started at seven o'clock in the morning. I said to myself, "I will see how fast I can ride and at what time I will get there." I did not meet anyone on the way.

I rode into Silver City at two o'clock in the afternoon, and the next morning I was in the stage on my way to Boise City, Idaho, and went to see General Forsythe. He found me a place to stop at and sent me to see the prisoners at Fort Boise. I went, but they would not speak to me. They were Shoshones. I went in first to see the men. While I was talking with the men, one of the women came in and said in Shoshone, "Don't tell her anything. She will tell the soldiers what you say." One of the men said, "I wonder who she is."

"I will tell you who I am if you will ask me; if you will tell me why you are here, maybe I can help you." I waited to see if they would say anything. I again said, "Will you tell me where you were when the soldiers took you?" They would not speak yet. "Your soldier-father sent me here to ask you what you want to do." But they would not say anything to me.

I went and told General Forsythe that his prisoners would not speak to me. I stayed in Boise City ten days. I was then told to go with Captain McGregor and Sanford's command, two companies of cavalry, going the way of Baker City, and then to Camp Harney, Oregon, where I expected to see a great many of my people, and Bannocks too, for it was reported that the old woman whom I had sent away to my people to tell them to come back to the Malheur Agency was there. After traveling six days in that burning sun, we arrived at Canyon City and camped about three miles down the river.

I thought to myself, I will go and see Mrs. Parrish, for she was living at Canyon City. I saw all the officers going up, and I wished to go too and see my dearest friends. I rode into the city and saw a negress that I knew who used to cook for a woman by the name of Moore. She ran up to me and said, "Oh, Sarah, I am afraid someone will do you harm. There is a woman living here who swears that the first Indian she sees she will shoot, because she had her husband killed during the war."

Just then a man came up to me and gave me a letter. I did not stop to read it, but ran with it to the officers who were right across the street from where I was. I gave it to Captain McGregor. "Come," said he, "go to the camp as fast as your horse can carry you." We ran across to get our horses. I got upon mine and rode down to the camp as if I was riding for dear life. I did not know why Captain McGregor sent me for till he came down from the city. He then told me it was the sheriff who wanted to arrest me as a witness against Oytes.

I did not see my dear friend Mrs. Parrish (the white lily) that time. We went on to Camp Harney and got there two days afterward and found all the Bannocks and the Snake River Paiutes there. After we got rested, I sent for the baby that was found on the battlefield. I went to every camp with the child but could not find its mother. The next day I got its little yellow shirt and its beads, as General Howard had told me to keep them so the little one's mother might find her child by its clothes and beads. I did as I was told by him, and again Mattie and I went to find its mother. At last we came to a camp where there was a young woman. I saw at once they were in deep mourning, and I knew them too. I said, "John Westler, I have here a little girl baby that was found on the battlefield, and if I can I want to find her father and mother. It may be a Bannock child."

The father of the little child got up and looked at the baby. He cried out, "Oh my baby, my child, my lost little girl!" Its mother got up also and came. They wept with joy. They said everything that was beautiful to Mattie and me for saving their little child. They told me most fearful things that happened the same day that the child was lost. They said there was a little baby that was crushed against the trees as the soldiers fought them through the thick timber. They said they were running for their dear lives through the timber for miles and miles. The timber was very dense; so much so that it was impossible to travel with pack animals except by packing them on top and not on the side as my people usually pack them. In that timber these children were crushed, and this little one was thrown from its basket and left on the road in the hurry and confusion.

All my people and the officers called this little baby my baby, and they named it Sarah.

EVERYTHING WENT on aright until October, when an order came from Washington saying that all the Indians that belonged to the Malheur Agency should be gathered together at Camp Harney and be ready to go to the Malheur Reservation for the winter. So I was told to go to Camp McDermitt and bring all my people to Camp Harney. Company A was first to go with me. So everything was got ready, and we started for Camp McDermitt. It took six days. At last we arrived at the camp. I told my people what the Big Father in Washington said. Some of my people said, "We know there is something wrong. We don't like to go." But the officers told them there was nothing to fear. They would be sent to the Malheur Agency.

My people asked me over and over again. I told them I did not know any more than they did; therefore, I could not say. At last I said, "What need have you to be afraid? You have not done anything. All the officers know that you have acted for the whites. General Howard knows all about you. None of you have fought the whites. You have all done your duty to the whites during the campaign."

After talking with them so long, my brother Natchez told them to go. He said to them, "Our soldier-fathers will see that you are all right. They say you are to go back to the Malheur Agency."

Then Leggins said, "Reinhard is there yet. We ought not to

go there while he is there, for we shall die with hunger. We all know how we suffered while we were there."

Leggins said to me, "You, our mother, must talk to the soldier-fathers and have them send him away before we go back to the reservation. Tell them before we leave here that if we go there we will starve and then have another trouble."

I told the commanding officer what my people said about Reinhard. Then the commanding officer, Captain Wagener, got angry and said, "I don't want so much talk; if you don't go peacefully, I shall have to make you go. If we had not got orders from Washington, we would not say so. We are just like yourselves, we are ordered and we have to do our work. Tomorrow you must all get ready to go."

My poor people were in great trouble. They talked all night and then at last said, "We will go." Early the next morning, the horses were ready, and we were all ready to start. You should see how my people love each other. Old and young were crying at parting with each other. Brother Natchez went with us for two days. We got to Camp C. F. Smith. Here my brother left us to go back. In six days more we arrived at Camp Harney, and Leggins told the officers he and his people did not want to camp with the Bannocks and the rest of the wards.

Before we left Camp McDermitt, this man Leggins was appointed chief over them all by my brother and father. The commanding officer, Major Cochrane, told Leggins he could camp wherever he liked. At this I was very glad. So was he. The major is very humane, a very kind officer.

After we were at Camp Harney two weeks, my people were told to come to the commissary and soldiers' clothing would be issued to them. After they got their clothes, they looked so nice! But my heart ached for the women and children, for there was no clothing for them. There were no calicoes to be issued to them.

But it could not be helped. It was not as if they had it and would not issue it to them, as all the agents do. My people knew this, and they had nothing to say. All this time we were so happy. Leggins would often say or ask me, "When are we to go to the agency?"

I said, "I have not heard anything about it."

CHAPTER VIII

THE YAKIMA AFFAIR

ONE DAY the commanding officer sent for me. Oh, how my heart did jump! I said to Mattie, "There is bad news." Truly I had not felt like this since the night Egan was killed by the Umatillas. I got ready and went down to the office, trembling as if something fearful was waiting for me. I walked into the office.

Then the officer said to me, "Sarah, I have some news to tell you, and I want you to keep it still until we are sure if it will be true."

I then promised I would keep it still if it was not too awful bad news.

He said, "It is pretty bad." He looked at me and said, "Sarah, you look as if you were ready to die. It is nothing about you; it is about your people. Sarah, an order is issued that your people are to be taken to Yakima Reservation across the Columbia River."

I said, "All of my people?"

"No, not your father's, but all that are here."

I asked, "What for?"

He said he did not know.

I said, "Major, my people have not done anything, and why should they be sent away from their own country? If there are any to be sent away, let it be Oytes and his men, numbering about twenty-five men in all, and the few Bannocks that are with them. Oh, Major! If you knew what I have promised my people, you would leave nothing undone but what you would try not to have them sent away. Oh, Major! My people will never believe me again."

"Well, Sarah, I will do all I can. I will write to the president and see what he thinks about it. I will tell him all you have said about your people."

I was crying. He told me to keep up a good heart, and he would do all he could for me.

I went home and told Mattie all, and she said, "Well, sister, we cannot help it if the white people won't keep their word. We can't help it. We have to work for them, and if they get our people not to love us by telling what is not true to them, what can we do? It is they, not us."

I said, "Our people won't think so because they will never know that it was they who told the lie. Oh! I know all our people will say we are working against them and are getting money for all this."

In the evening Mattie and I took a walk down to their camp. There they were so happy; singing here, singing there and everywhere. I thought to myself, "My poor, poor people, you will be happy today; tomorrow or next week your happiness will be turned to weeping." Oh, how sad I was for them! I could not sleep at night, for the sad thing that had come.

At last one evening I was sent for by the commanding officer. Oh! How can I tell it? My poor heart stood still. I said to Mattie, "Mattie, I wish this was my last day in this cruel world." I came to myself and I said, "No, Mattie, I don't mean the world. I mean the cruel, yes, the cruel, wicked, white people, who are going to drive us to some foreign country away from our own. Mattie, I feel so badly I don't think I can walk down there!"

Mattie said, "I will go with you."

We then went down. Major Cochran met us at the door and said, "Sarah, are you sick? You look so badly."

I said, "No."

He then replied, "Sarah, I am heartily sorry for you, but we cannot help it. We are ordered to take your people to Yakima Reservation."

It was just a little before Christmas. My people were only given one week to get ready in.

I said, "What! In this cold winter and in all this snow, and my people have so many little children? Why, they will all die. Oh, what can the president be thinking about? Oh, tell me, what is he? Is he man or beast? Yes, he must be a beast; if he has no feeling for my people, surely he ought to have some for the soldiers. I have never seen a president in my life, and I want to know whether he is made of wood or rock, for I cannot for once think that he can be a human being. No human being would do such a thing as that, send people across a fearful mountain in midwinter."

I was told not to say anything till three days before starting. Every night I imagined I could see the thing called President. He had long ears, he had big eyes and long legs, and a head like a bullfrog or something like that. I could not think of anything that could be so inhuman as to do such a thing, send people across mountains with snow so deep. Mattie and I got all the furs we could; we had fur caps, fur gloves, and fur overshoes.

At last the time arrived. The commanding officer told me to tell Leggins to come to him. I did so. He came, and Major Cochrane told me to tell him that he wanted him to tell which of the Bannock men were the worst or which was the leader in the war. Leggins told him and counted out twelve men to him. After this talk, Major Cochrane asked me to go and tell these men to come up to the office. They were Oytes, Bannock Joe, Captain Bearskin, Paddy Cap, Boss, Big John, Eagle Eye, Charley, D. E. Johnson, Beads, and Oytes' son-in-law, called Surger. An officer was sent with me. I called out the men by their names. They all came out to me. I said to Oytes, "Your soldier-father wants you all to go up to see him." We went up, and Oytes asked me many things.

We had to go right by the guardhouse. Just as we got near it, the soldier on guard came out and headed us off and took the men and put them into the guardhouse. After they were put in there, the soldiers told me to tell them they must not try to get away, or they would be shot. "We put you in here for safekeeping," they said. "The citizens are coming over here from Canyon City to arrest you all, and we don't want them to take you; that is why we put you in here."

Ten soldiers were sent down to guard the whole encampment—not Leggins' band, only Oytes' and the Bannocks. I was then ordered to tell them to get ready to go to Yakima Reservation.

Oh, how sad they were! Women cried and blamed their husbands for going with the Bannocks, but Leggins and his band were told they were not going with the prisoners of war and that he was not going at all.

Then Leggins moved down the creek about two miles. At night some would get out and go off. Brother Lee and Leggins were sent out to bring them back again. One afternoon Mattie and I were sent out to get five women who got away during the night, and an officer was sent with us. We were riding very fast, and my sister Mattie's horse jumped on one side and threw her off and hurt her. The blood ran out of her mouth, and I thought she would die right off, but, poor dear, she went on, for an ambulance was at our command. She had great suffering during our journey.

Oh, for shame! You who are educated by a Christian govern-ment in the art of war, the practice of whose profession makes you natural enemies of the savages, so called by you. Yes, you, who call yourselves the great civilization, you who have knelt upon Plymouth Rock, covenanting with God to make this land the home of the free and the brave. Ah, then you rise from your bended knees and, seizing the welcoming hands of those who are the owners of this land, which you are not, your carbines rise upon the bleak shore, and your so-called civilization sweeps inland from the ocean wave, but, oh, my God! leaving its pathway marked by crimson lines of blood and strewed by the bones of two races, the inheritor and the invader. I am crying out to you for justice—yes, pleading for the far-off plains of the west, for the dusky mourner, whose tears of love are pleading for her husband, or for their chil-dren, who are sent far away from them. Your Christian minister will hold my people against their will; not because he loves them, no, far from it, but because it puts money in his pockets.

Now we were ready to start for Yakima. Fifty wagons were brought, and citizens were to take us there. Some of the wagons cost the government from ten dollars to fifteen dollars per day. We got to Canyon City, and while we camped there, Captain Winters got a telegram from Washington telling him he must take Leggins' band too. So we had to wait for them to overtake us. While we were waiting, our dear good father and mother, Mr. Charles W. Parrish, came with his wife and children to see us. My people threw their arms round him and his wife, crying, "Oh, our father and mother, if you had stayed with us we would not suffer this."

Poor Mrs. Parrish could not stop her tears at seeing the people who once loved her, the children whom she had taught—yes, the savage children who once called her their white lily mother, the children who used to bring her wild flowers with happy faces, now ragged, no clothes whatever. They all cried out to him and his wife, saying, "Oh, good father and mother, talk for us! Don't let them take us away; take us back to our home!" He told them he could do nothing for them. They asked him where his brother, Sam Parrish, was. He told them he was a long way off; and then they bade us good-bye, and that was the last they saw of him.

While we were waiting for Leggins, it snowed all the time. In two days the rest of my people overtook us. It was so very cold some of them had to be left on the road; but they came in later. That night an old man was left on the road in a wagon. The next morning they went back to get the wagon and found the old man frozen to death. The citizen who owned the wagon did not bring him to the camp but threw him out of his wagon and left him! I thought it was the most fearful thing I ever saw in my life.

Early the next morning, the captain sent me to tell Leggins that he wanted him to help the soldiers guard the prisoners and see that none of them got away. He said the Big Father in Washington wanted him to do this, and then he and his people could come back in the spring. I went to tell Leggins, but he would not speak to me, neither would my brother Lee. I told him all and went away. When I got back, the captain asked me what he said. I told him he would not speak to me.

"Did you tell him what I told you to?"

"I did."

"Go and tell the prisoners to be ready to march in half an hour."

We traveled all day. It snowed all day long. We camped, and that night a woman became a mother, and during the night the baby died and was put under the snow. The next morning the mother was put into the wagon. She was almost dead when we went into camp. That night she too was gone and left on the roadside, her poor body not even covered with the snow.

In five days three more children were frozen to death, and another woman became a mother. Her child lived three days, but the mother lived. We then crossed Columbia River.

All the time my poor dear little Mattie was dying little by little.

At last we arrived in Yakima on the last day of the month. Father Wilbur and the chief of the Yakima Indians came to meet us. We came into camp about thirty miles from where the agency buildings are and stayed at this place for ten days. Another one of my people died here, but oh, thanks be to the Good Father in the Spirit Land, he was buried as if he were a man.

At the end of the ten days, we were turned over to Father Wilbur and his civilized Indians, as he called them. Well, as I was saying, we were turned over to him as if we were so many horses or cattle. After he received us, he had some of his civilized Indians come with their wagons to take us up to Fort Simcoe. They did not come because they loved us or because they were Christians. No, they were just like all civilized people; they came to take us up there because they were to be paid for it. They had kind of a shed made to put us in. You know what kind of shed you make for your stock in winter time. It was of that kind. Oh, how we did suffer with cold. There was no wood, and the snow was waist deep, and many died off just as cattle or horses do after traveling so long in the cold.

All my people were dressed well in soldiers' clothes. Almost all the men had beautiful blue overcoats; they looked like a company of soldiers. But we had not been with these civilized people long before they had won all my people's clothes from them. Some would give them one buckskin for an overcoat and pants, and some of them got little ponies for their clothes, but the ponies would disappear and could not be found in the country afterward. Leggins had a great many good horses which were lost in the same way. My people would go and tell the agent, Wilbur, about the way his people were treating them and the loss of their horses, but he would tell them their horses were all right on the reservation somewhere, only we could not find them. My people would ask him to tell his people to tell us if they saw our horses so that we might go and get them. He told his Christian and civilized Indians, but none of them came to tell us where our horses were. The civilized Indians would tell my people not to go far away, for the white people would kill them; but my cousin, Frank Winnemucca, and his sister's son, who was named after our good agent, Samuel Parrish, were out hunting their horses. They were gone eight days. They traveled along the Yakima River and saw an island between Yakima City and the reservation. They swam across to it, and there they found their horses, and two of the Christian Yakima Indians watching them. They brought them back. After that it was worse than ever. All our best horses were gone, which we never did find. My Mericle was found three months afterwards. They were using my horse as a pack horse. It was so lean the back was sore. I took it to Mrs. Wilbur to show her what the Yakima Indians were doing to our horses. I asked her if I could turn the horse into their lot. She told me I could, but the horse was gone again, and I have never seen it since.

We had another talk with Father Wilbur about our horses, but he kindly told us he did not wish to be troubled by us about our horses. Then my people said, "We have lost all our clothes and our horses, and our father says he does not want to be troubled by us." My people said everything that was bad about these people.

Now came the working time. My people were set to work clearing land; both men and women went to work, and boys too. They cleared sixty acres of land for wheat. They had it all cleared in about ten days. Father Wilbur hired six civilized Indians to plough it for them; these Indians got three dollars a day for their work because they were civilized and Christian.

It was now about the last of April. I was told to tell my people that he had sent for clothes for them, and it was already at the Dalles. He was going to send seventeen wagons down and have them brought right off. I told my people what he said, and I assure you they were very glad indeed, for they were almost naked. No money, no, nothing. Now our clothing came; everything you could wish or think of came for my poor, dear people blankets of all kinds, shawls, woolen goods, calicoes, and everything beautiful.

Issuing day came. It was in May. Poor Mattie was so sick, I had to go by myself to issue to my people. Oh, such a heart-sickening issue! There were twenty-eight little shawls given out, and dress goods that you white people would sift flour through, from two to three yards to each woman. The largest issue was to a woman who had six children. It was six yards, and I was told to say to her she must make clothes for the children out of what was left after she had made her own! At this my people all laughed. Some of the men who worked hardest got blankets, some got nothing at all; a few of the hats were issued, and the good minister, Father Wilbur, told me to say he would issue again later in the fall, that is, blankets.

After the issue was over, my people talked and said, "Another Reinhard! Don't you see he is the same? He looks up into the sky and says something, just like Reinhard." They said, "All white people like that are bad." Every night some of them would come and take blankets off from sleeping men and women until all were gone. All this was told to the agent, but he would not help my poor people, and Father Wilbur's civilized Indians would say most shameful things about my people. They would tell him that they were knocking their doors in, and killing their horses for food, and stealing clothes.

At one time they said my people killed a little child. Their Indian minister, whose name was George Waters, told me one of my women had been seen killing the child. He said the child's head was cut to pieces. I said to brother Lee, "We will go and see the child."

I asked the white doctor to go with us to se it. I told him what had been said. They had him all wrapped up and said they did not want anybody to see him. George was there. I said, "We must see him. You said our people had killed him and that his head is cut in pieces." So the doctor took off all the blankets that were wound round him. There was no sign of anything on him. He had fallen into the river and had been drowned.

On May 29, my poor little sister Mattie died. Oh, how she did suffer before she died! And I was left all alone.

During this time, all the goods that were brought for us were sold to whoever had money. All the civilized Indians bought the best of everything.

Father Wilbur said to my people the very same thing that Reinhard did. He told them he would pay them one dollar a day. My people worked the same, and they were paid in clothes, and little money was paid to them. They were told not to go anywhere else to buy but to this store. At this my people asked him why he told them that the clothes were theirs. At this Mrs. Wilbur said they had to sell them in order to hold their position. This is the way all the agents issue clothing to the people. Every Indian on that reservation had to pay for everything.

For all the wagons they ever got, they were to pay one hundred and twenty-five dollars, if it took ten years to pay it. I know this is true, because the agent told me to tell my brother Lee so, and he told Leggins the same if he wanted wagons and that they could pay him little by little until they had paid it all.

We had the finest wheat that ever was raised on the reservation, for my people pulled out all the cockle and smut. The civilized Indians were so lazy they would not clean their field, and their wheat was so bad that after it was made into bread it was as black as dirt. I am sorry to say that Father Wilbur kept our wheat for his white friends and gave us the bad wheat, and the bad wheat was ground just as you would grind it for your hogs. The bad flour made us all sick. My poor people died off very fast. At first Father Wilbur and his Christian Indians told us we could bury our dead in their graveyard, but they soon got tired of us and said we could not bury them there any more.

Doctor Kuykendall could not cure any of my people, or he did not try. When I would go to him for medicine for them, he would say, "Well, Sarah, I will give you a little sugar and rice, or a little tea for him or her." He would say laughing, "Give them something good to eat before they die."

This is the way the agent treated us, and then they dare to say that they are doing all they can for my people. I say, my dear friends, the minister who is called agent says there will be or there is a time coming when everyone is going to give an account of all he does in this life. I am a little afraid the agent will have to give an account of himself and say, "I have filled my pockets with that worthless thing called money. I am not worthy to go to heaven." That is, if that book you civilized people call the Holy Bible is true. In that, it says he who steals and tells lies will go to hell. Well, I am afraid this book is true, as your agents say, and I am sure they will never see heaven, for I am sure there is hardly an agent but what steals a little, and they all know that if there is a God above us, they can't deny it before Him who is called God.

This was in July, 1879. We were now going to have a camp meeting, and some visitors were coming from the east. Bishop Haven and his son and daughter were coming. The agent told me to be sure and keep my people away, as they were very poorly dressed. I did not do as I was told. My poor people were almost as naked as they were born into the world, for the seventeen wagons of supplies were not issued to them.

When the time came, I came with all my people and camped near the agent's house, and during the meeting, I made them all come and sit down on the benches that Father Wilbur made for his civilized and Christian Indians. I wanted all to see how well we were treated by Christian people.

Day after day my people were begging me to go east and talk for them. I told them I had no money to go with just then, but I would as soon as I got some, for I had a little money coming to me from the military government.

The military authority is the only authority that ever paid me well for my interpreting. Their pay to interpreters is from sixty-five dollars to seventy-five dollars, and the lowest is sixty dollars per month. For this pay one could live. All the agents pay to interpreters is from thirty dollars to forty dollars. One has to live out of this money, and there is nothing left.

I always had to pay sixty dollars a month for my board (or fifteen dollars a week) when I was working for an agent. When I was working for the government, they gave me my rations, the same as they did to the soldiers. My last appointment was given me at Washington in 1879. It was to be very small pay. I wrote to the Secretary of the Interior, Mr. Schurz, telling him I could not pay my board with that, but he never answered my letter, and so it stands that way to this day, and I never got a cent of it. But their pet, Reinhard, without an Indian on the reservation, could be paid three or four years. I have worked all the time among my people and never been paid for my work. At last my military money came.

I told Father Wilbur I wanted to go back to see my people. At first he said I could not go; he stood a minute, and then said, "Well, Sarah, I can't keep you if you want to go. Who is to talk for your people?"

I said, "Brother Lee can talk well enough."

Then he said, "You can go after the camp meeting is over."

Now commenced our meetings every day. I went and got all the little children and came with them myself and sat down, and then went into the pulpit and interpreted the sermon to my people. Right here, my dear reader, you will see how much Father Wilbur's Indians are civilized and Christianized. He had to have interpreters. If they were so much civilized, why did he have interpreters to talk to them? In eighteen years could he not have taught them some English? I was there twelve months, and I never heard an Indian man or woman speak the English language except the three interpreters and some half-breeds. Could he not have had the young people taught in all that time? A great many white people came to see the Indians. Of course one who did not know them might think they were educated when they heard them sing English songs, but I assure you they did not know what they sang any more than I know about logarithms.

So I went away in November and stopped at Vancouver, Washington Territory, to see General O. O. Howard. I told him all that Father Wilbur was doing to my people and that I should try to go to Washington. Then he gave me a letter to some of his friends in Washington. I went straight from Vancouver to San Francisco. My brother Natchez and others met me there, and we stayed and talked about the agents, and none of them came forward to say, "Sarah is telling lies." If they ever do I shall say more.

I was lecturing in San Francisco when Reinhard tried so hard to get my brother Natchez to send some of our people to the Malheur Agency. Yes, he offered much money for each one he would bring to the reservation, but my brother told him he did not want his people to starve and he was never going to tell them to go there. When Reinhard could get no Indian to go there, he got the very man whose life my brother saved during the Bannock War. Because my brother had saved his life, he thought he had nothing to do but go and get all my people to go to the Malheur Reservation. He told them that Mr. Reinhard had everything for them on the agency.

My people told him to ask Reinhard why he did not give these good things to them before, then Oytes would not have gone with the Bannocks. This was just before I lectured in San Francisco.

I was lecturing one evening, and this very man came to me and said, "Sarah, I would like to have you help me get some of your people to go with me to the Malheur Agency. I will pay you well for it. Here are thirty dollars." He handed it to me.

I thought to myself, "The white people are better than I am. They make money any way and every way they can. Why not I? I have not any. I will take it." So I did, for which I have been sorry ever since, many times.

Well, while I was lecturing in San Francisco, a great deal was said about it through the western country. The papers said I was coming east to lecture. I was getting ready to come and was at Lovelocks, Nevada, with brother Natchez. There came a telegram to me there from a man named Hayworth, saying, "Sarah, the president wants you and your father and brother Natchez and any other chiefs, four in number, to go to Washington with me. I am sent to go with you."

I answered, "Come here, we wish to see you."

In two days he came, and we told him everything about the doings of the agent. Not only we told him, but the white people told him also. We asked him to go to Camp McDermitt and to the Pyramid Lake Reservation and down the Humboldt River that he might see for himself, and then he could help us tell the Big Father in Washington. He did so, and when we were ready, we started for Washington with him.

It took us one week to get to Washington. We stopped at the Fremont House. As soon as we got into the house, a doctor was sent to vaccinate us for fear we would take smallpox. We were told not to go out anywhere without the man who brought us.

The next day, at about ten o'clock, we were taken to the office of the Secretary of the Interior. As soon as we entered, the man there looked at me and said, "So you are on the lecturing tour, are you?"

I said, "Yes, sir."

"So you think you can make a great deal of money by it, do you?"

"No, sir; I do not wish to lecture for that."

"What, then? "

"I have come to plead for my poor people, who are dying off with broken hearts because they are separated from their children and husbands and wives and sons."

"But they are bad people. They have killed and scalped many innocent people."

"Not so; my people who are over there at Yakima did not do so any more than you have scalped people. There are only a few who went with the Bannocks who did wrong. I have given up those who were bad; the soldiers have them prisoners at Vancouver Barracks, Washington Territory. I have not come to plead for the bad ones. I have done my work faithfully. I told the officers if they would surrender, I would give up all the bad ones, which I did, and I ask you only to return to their home all that have helped the white people. Yes, sir; the very man who killed Buffalo Horn was sent to the Yakima Reservation."

The tears were running down my face while I was talking, and the heartless man began to laugh at me. He then said, "I don't think we can do anything about it."

Just at this moment Mr. Hayworth came in and said Secretary Schurz was ready to see us. "Sarah," he said to me, "you must not lecture here."

Secretary Schurz received us kindly, not like the man we had just left. Secretary Schurz said, "I want you to tell me from the first beginning of the Bannock War," which we did.

Then he told Mr. Hayworth to take us everywhere to see everything, to have a carriage and take us round. When we left him he said, "Come again tomorrow at the same hour."

We had a great many callers who wanted to see us, but the man Hayworth was with us every minute, for fear I would say something. We were taken somewhere every day only to come in and get our meals. Reporters would come and say, "We want you to tell us where you are going to lecture that we can put it into our papers." But Hayworth would not let us talk to them. The next day we were again taken to Secretary Schurz. My brother talked this time, and I interpreted for him.

My brother said, "You, Great Father of the Mighty Nation, my people have all heard of you. We think you are the mightiest father that lives, and to hear your own people talk, there is nothing you can't do if you wish to; therefore, we one and all pray of you to give us back what is of no value to you or your people. Oh, Good Father, it is not your gold, nor your silver, horses, cattle, lands, mountains we ask for. We beg of you to give us back our people, who are dying off like so many cattle or beasts at the Yakima Reservation. Oh, Good Father, have you wife or child? Do you love them? If you love them, think how you would feel if they were taken away from you where you could not go to see them, nor they come to you. For what are they to be kept there? When the Bannocks came to our people with their guns, my father and I said to them everything that we could, telling them not to fight. We had a talk three days, and only one man got up and said he would go with them. That was Oytes, with about twenty-five or thirty men. Oytes is a Harney Lake Paiute.

"We Paiutes never had much of anything. The Bannocks took everything we had from us. They were going to kill me, with three white men, who were living near by. I feared I could not get away, but thanks to Him who lives above us, I did get away with the three white men. They followed us about twenty miles as fast as their horses could run. My horse fell down and died. I cried out to Jack Scott, and he let me jump up behind him, but he left me and rode on. I ran a little way till I came to a creek, up which I ran, and in that manner I got away.

"So you see, good Father, we have always been good friends to your people. If you will return our people whom you sent away to Yakima Reservation, let them come to the Malheur Reservation and make the bad ones stay where they are. In time I and my people will go there too, to make us homes. And also send away Mr. Reinhard, whom we hate."

This is what my brother said to Secretary Schurz, and I am surprised to see that in their own report they say, "In the winter of 1878-9 a self-constituted delegation, consisting of the Chief Winnemucca and others of his band visited this city, and while here made an agreement, etc., to remove to Malheur, and receive allotments of one hundred and sixty acres to each head of a family, and each adult male; they were to cultivate the lands so allotted, and as soon as the law would enable it, patents therefore in fee-simple were to be issued to each allottee," etc.

I say we did not come on of ourselves; we were sent for, and neither my father or brother made any agreement to go to Malheur until those who belonged there could come back from Yakima and till Reinhard should be sent away.

I said one day I was going to lecture, as the people wanted me to, and try to get a little money to buy something for my father. Mr. Hayworth told what I said, and we were all sent for to go to the office of the Interior. We went in and sat down.

Secretary Schurz said to me, "Sarah, so you are bound to lecture."

I said, "People want me to."

"I don't think it will be right for you to lecture here after the government has sent for you, and your father and brother, and paid your way here. The government is going to do right by your people now. Don't lecture now; go home and get your people on the reservation get them located properly. And then, if you want to come back, write to us and tell us you want to come back and lecture, and we will pay your way here and back again."

He told me they would grant all I asked of them for my people, which they did; yes, in their minds, I mean in writing, promises which like the wind were heard no more. They asked where I was going to stop after I got home. "We want to know so that we can send you some canvas for tents for your people. You can issue it to them. Can you not?"

I said "Yes, if it comes."

"We will send enough to make your people one hundred tents. You can issue it and give the names of each head of the families and send them back here."

I said, "I shall be at Lovelock's in Nevada."

"We will send it as soon as you get home."

My poor father and brother said, "All right."

The secretary then told Mr. Hayworth to take us to the store and get father a suit of clothes, which father got; but brother and I did not get a pin's worth from any one. We never did get anything from the government or government officials. Poor father! He gave his clothes away after he got home, saying, "This is all I got from the Big Father in Washington. I am the only one who got anything; I don't care for them. If they had been given me by the good soldier-fathers, I would keep them."

On Saturday we were taken to the White House to see the president. We were shown all over the place before we saw him. A great many ladies were there to see us.

At last he walked in and shook hands with us, then he said, "Did you get all you want for your people?"

I said, "Yes, sir, as far as I know."

"That is well," he said and went out again. That is all we saw of him. That was President Hayes.

We went back to the hotel. In the afternoon Mr. Meacham came with a carriage to take us to the Soldiers' Home, but we did not go. My father and brother were feeling badly because I told them I was going to New York to lecture, and I would come home by and by. I only did this to make the man who was with us angry, because he was forever listening to what I was saying. The Soldiers' Home is the only place we did not see while we were in Washington.

Sunday evening we were to start for home. Mr. Meacham said to me the last minute, "Sarah, stop and give a lecture before you go. They can't stop you. This is a free country. If you stop, we will see you through."

Oh, if he had lived, I know I would have a good friend to help in my work, not like the one who has the charge of his work now. That is Dr. Bland.

"Well, if the government pets are to be the ones to condemn me, I have no fear whatever. I am not going into their private life, because I am not to condemn anyone. I am only telling what the agents are doing. I think it is better for the government to keep the money than to give it to agents."

We were now ready to start, and the man who brought us to Washington was going with us. I said to him, "I am not going as I came here."

"All right; you shall have a sleeping car."

We had been on the road two days when a lady joined us. She was going to Duck Valley Agency to her husband, who was an agent there. She had a Bible with her. Ah! ah! What do you think the Bible was? Why it was a pack of cards. She would sit every day and play cards with men, and every evening too. She was an Indian agent's wife.

Mr. Hayworth went as far as Omaha with us. He came to me there and said, "Sarah, I am going back."

I ran to the car where my father and brother were to tell them. He came in and bade them good-bye and gave brother three dollars to provide us all with eating on our way, more than a thousand miles.

This is a copy of the order Secretary Schurz gave me. I have the original in my possession now.

DEPARTMENT OF THE INTERIOR, WASHINGTON, D.C.

JULY 20, 1880

THE PI-UTES, heretofore entitled to live on the Malheur Reservation, their primeval home, are to have lands allotted to them in severalty, at the rate of one hundred and sixty acres to each head of a family, and each adult male. Such lands they are to cultivate for their own benefit. The allotment will be made under instructions of their agent. As soon as enabled by law to do so, this department is to give to the Indians patents for each tract of land conveying to each occupant the fee-simple in the lot he occupies.

Those of the Pi-Utes, who in consequence of the Bannock War, went to the Yakima Reservation, and whoever may desire to rejoin their relatives, are at liberty to do so, without expense to the government for transportation. Those who desire to stay upon the Yakima Reservation and become permanently settled there will not be disturbed.

None of the Pi-Utes now living among the whites, and earning wages by their own work will be compelled to go to the Malheur

Reservation. They are at perfect liberty to continue working for wages for their own benefit, as they are now doing.

It is well understood that those who settle on the Malheur Reservation will not be supported by the government in idleness. They will be aided in starting their farms and promoting their civilization, but the support given them by the government will, according to law, depend upon their intelligence and efficiency in working for themselves.

C. SCHURZ

SECRETARY OF THE INTERIOR

WHEN WE got home, we told our people to go to Lovelocks and be ready to receive some tents that were to be sent there for them. They came from far and near to hear of the wonderful father we had seen, how he looked and all about him. While we were waiting, we almost starved.

I wrote to the Secretary of the Interior for God's sake to send us something to eat. He answered my letter telling me to take my people to the Malheur Agency. Just think of my taking my people, who were already starving, to go three hundred miles through snow waist deep.

I told my people what the letter said. They all laughed and said, "We are not disappointed. We always said that the Big Father was just like all the white people."

What could we say? We were only ashamed because we came and told them lies which the white people had told us.

"You must make that up yourselves," they said, "for you have been to the white people's country, and all the white people say the Big Father at Washington never tells a lie."

My father rose and told his people he did not blame them for talking as they did. "I say, my dear children, every word we have told you was said to us. Yes, they have said or done more than this. They have given us a paper which your mother will tell you of." Then he called me and said, "Read the paper; your brother will interpret for you."

I did as I was told. I read very slowly. My brother did nicely, and after it was over my uncle, Captain John, rose and spoke, saying, "My dear people, I have lived many years with white people. Yes, it is over thirty years, and I know a great many of them. I have never known one of them do what they promised. I think they mean it just at the time, but I tell you they are very forgetful. It seems to me, sometimes, that their memory is not good, and since I have understood them, if they say they will do so and so for me, I would say to them, now or never, and if they don't, why, it is because they never meant to do but only to say so. These are your white brothers' ways, and they are a weak people."

Some of them said, "Oh, maybe he will send back our people." Others said, "Time will tell."

Just then my sister-in-law, brother Natchez's wife, said, "There comes a white man. Oh, it is Mr. Emory."

He came up and gave me a letter. It was my appointment to act as interpreter for my people at the Malheur Agency. After this, my people went away from Lovelocks.

Then I went from place to place, trying to get my people to go to the Malheur Agency, but they told me to go and get those who were at Yakima to come back there, then they would go.

So I took my sister and started for Yakima on the 1st of April. Just think how happy I was I to go for my poor, sick-hearted people. Yes, armed with a paper signed by Secretary Schurz. I thought I would not have anything to do but to go there and get them, because they told me at Washington that they would send a letter to Father Wilbur telling him what to do. I told them in

Washington that my people would be afraid to go back to Malheur alone. They told me that Father Wilbur would see that they were taken back all right. If he thought we should need an escort of soldiers, he would see to that.

So you see I never once thought I was going to have any trouble, and I traveled three days without seeing anyone. We had nothing to eat but hard bread. Our horses were better off than we were. That was better than all, for I would rather anytime have nothing to eat than have my horse go without anything.

We had traveled four days, it was very late in the evening, and we rode up to a house. The men all ran out to see us.

I said to sister, "I am afraid."

Sister said, "I know them. About one year ago, father and others camped here, and they were very kind to father. They killed beef for us, and we camped here a long time."

To my great joy there came up two of our people. One was my own cousin, Joe Winnemucca. Oh, how glad he was to see us.

"Is your father coming too?" he asked.

"No, we are all alone."

"What! You don't say you have come all the way from the reservation alone, have you?"

"That is just what I mean, and that is not all. We are going a long way."

"That can't be, you two women all alone."

"That is what we are going to do."

The white man came up to us and said, "Who are you? Where did you come from?"

I said, "Sir, I am Sarah Winnemucca, and this is my sister, and we came from Pyramid Lake Reservation."

"Oh, how do you do? I have heard of you so many times! Oh, how I wish my wife was here to welcome you. She would be glad to see you. But, however, you are welcome. Won't you come in?"

Then he called one of his men to come and get our horses and take them to the stable.

I said, "Sir, this man is my cousin, and I want to talk to him first."

I told my cousin where we were going and what for. How I was going to have our people back again at Malheur, and about the beautiful paper that the Big Father gave me, and what beautiful things they were going to do for us. Oh! How glad my poor cousin was, for his brother, Frank Winnemucca, was at Yakima.

Now the man came for us to go to supper. I told the white man the same after supper and showed him the beautiful letter that Secretary Schurz gave me,

He said, "I am so glad, for your people are good workers, and the government ought to do something for them. I have lived here over twenty years. I never lost anything by your people, and whenever they came, I always gave them something to eat. The last time your father was here, I killed beef for him and the few who were with him."

We stayed here three days because it snowed so hard we could not travel. At last it cleared off, and my cousin was going with us to the next place. He said there were very bad men there. Sometimes they would throw a rope over our women and do fearful things to them.

"Oh, my poor cousins," he said, "my heart aches for you, for I am afraid they will do something fearful to you. They do not care for anything. They do most terrible outrageous things to our women."

I thought within myself, "If such an outrageous thing is to happen to me, it will not be done by one man or two while there are two women with knives, for I know what an Indian woman can do. She can never be outraged by one man; but she may by two." It is something an Indian woman dare not say till she has been overcome by one man, for there is no man living that can do anything to a woman if she does not wish him to. My dear reader, I have not lived in this world for over thirty or forty years for nothing, and I know what I am talking about.

We did not get to the horrible place till the second day. We got there very late in the afternoon. As we rode up to the house, I heard one of the men say, "Why, there is Sarah Winnemucca!" Oh, how glad I was to hear my name spoken by someone that knew me. I knew I was all right. He came up to me and said, "Why, Sarah, what in the world are you doing away out here at this time of the year?"

He helped me off my horse. Sister jumped off hers, and he told my cousin to take our horses to the stable. I had known this man for some time. He used to live in Carson City, Nevada. His name is Crowles. I was glad to see him. We stayed all night and were treated beautifully. I offered to pay for our supper and breakfast, and for our horses too, but they would not take anything. So I thanked them, and we went on.

Cousin went a little ways with us and then said good-bye to us and went back. We had traveled about ten miles, when we looked back and saw three men coming after us as fast as they could ride. This Mr. Crowles had some Spanish boarders who were living near the house, and they saw us there. Well, we saw it was war then. I said, "Dear sister, we must ride for our dear lives."

Away we went, and they after us like wild men. We rode on till our horses seemed to drop from under us. At last we stopped, and I told sister what to do if the whole three of them overtook us. We could not do very much, but we must die fighting. If there were only two, we were all right; we would kill them. If only one, we would see what he would do. If he lassoed me, she was to jump off her horse and cut the rope, and if he lassoed her, I was to do the same. If he got off his horse and came at me, she was to cut him, and I would do the same for her. Now we were ready for our work.

They were a long way back yet. We kept looking back to see how far off they were. Every time we would get out of sight, we would rest our horses. At last, to our great joy, we only saw one coming. He would not dare to do us any harm. By and by he overtook us.

"How do you do?" he said.

We did not speak to him.

He said, "I know your brother Natchez well, and your father too."

I was so angry, I said to him, "Clear out, you mean, hateful man. We do not wish to talk."

He said again, "What made you run your horses so?"

I said, "What made you bad men run after us?"

We came to where there were two roads, one going to Camp C. F. Smith, and one to Camp Harney. We took the Camp Harney road. We could see a house across the valley, about five miles off.

He said, "Come with me to that place. I will give you fresh horses, for you have a long way to go."

I did not speak, nor did sister. When he saw we would not talk to him, he turned his horse and went across the valley toward the house. So we were once more left to ourselves. We rode about five miles, and stopped to rest our horses an hour or so, and went on again. At about two o'clock, we came to a warm spring and stopped and had a bath. Dear sister and I had a good time and were refreshed, and rode on till about five o'clock, when one of our horses gave out. We had quite a time getting the horse along, so it was very late when we got to the place where we were to go for the night. It was at Mr. James Beby's, who was married to one of my cousins on the south end of Stein's Mountains, and at last we got there. My cousin's wife was glad to see us, but he was not at home. We stopped there three days to see him. I knew if he was at home, we could get some horses to go on to the next place, where we could take the stage to Camp Harney.

I told my cousin we would go on. She said, "Dear, take fresh horses and leave them at Mr. Abbot's. He will go for them when he gets home."

I said, "No, dear, I am afraid he would not like it, and he may get angry with you. I think we can make it nicely today," which we did.

The next morning we were ready to go on with a man by the name of Smith, whose father was killed during the Bannock War. We left one of our horses there and rode in his wagon to Mr. Anderson's place. I knew everybody on that road. No white women on all the places where we stopped, all men, yet we were treated kindly by all of them so far. We did not know what kind of a place Mr. Anderson's place was now, but before the Bannock War none of my people would go there for years and years. But we had to go there now.

We got there about four o'clock in the afternoon. I had known Mr. Anderson for a number of years. He was a United States mail contractor and always had many cowboys at his place overnight. Sure enough, there were eight of them this night. There was only one room in the house with a fireplace. He was kind to us; I told him what I had told others.

After supper I felt like crying and said to sister, "What shall we do? Where shall we sleep? We have no blankets."

We could sleep out of doors, but there was snow on the ground. Oh, how badly I felt that night! It was hard to keep back the tears. At last they began to make their beds here, there, and everywhere on the floor.

Mr. Anderson said to the stage driver, "You and I must give up our bed to Miss Winnemucca tonight and go in with some of the boys."

Nothing more was said, and they went to bed with some of them, and by and by we lay down.

I said to sister, "Oh, how my heart jumps. Something is going to happen to us, dear."

"I feel that way too," sister said. We sat a long time, but it was very cold, and at last we lay down, and I soon fell asleep.

Someone laid a hand on me and said, "Sarah!"

I jumped up with fright and gave him such a blow right in the face. I said, "Go away, or I will cut you to pieces, you mean man!"

He ran out of the house, and Mr. Anderson got up and lighted a candle. There was blood on the side of the bed, and on my hands and the floor.

He said, "Oh, Sarah, what have you done? Did you cut him?"

"No, I did not cut him; I wish I had. I only struck him with my hand."

He said, "Well, a man who will do such a thing needs killing. Who was it?" He looked round, but the man was gone. Mr. Anderson did not blow out the light.

The man did not come in, but some of the men went out to look for him. When they came in, they said he was gone and had taken his horse. Some of them said they guessed he was ashamed and had gone off. Mr. Anderson said, "The big fool! He ought to be ashamed."

I never said a word more, and we did not sleep any more that night. Mr. Anderson got up a four o'clock breakfast, for we were to start at five. We had to make Camp Harney that day, sixty miles. I still took my horse with me.

We arrived at Camp Harney about six o'clock, and Captain Drury, then commanding officer, received us very kindly. There were only three ladies at the post. The captain's wife and the other officers' wives were kind to me while I stayed there. We stayed ten days, because we could not get over the Blue Mountains, the snow was so deep. I had no money, and I tried to sell my horse, but could not. I went and talked with Mr. Stevens, who was a storekeeper at Camp Harney for many years. I showed him my appointment as interpreter, and, thanks be to my Father in Spirit Land, this man gave me a hundred dollars. He thought I was good for it; that is, I would get paid for my work and pay him. So we got ready to go on with the government mail carrier. Captain Drury was so kind as to let me have a government horse to ride as far as Canyon City, and the mail carrier was to bring it back.

Oh, such a time as we had going over! The snow was soft; our horses would go down and up again. If we walked, we would go down too. It rained some during the day. It was ten o'clock before we got to a place called Soda Springs. The next morning it snowed, but we did not mind it, and we got to Canyon City at three o'clock in the afternoon, almost frozen to death. We had to swim our horses at one place. We stayed there three days, because the stage goes only twice a week and we had to wait for it. Here I tried again to sell my horse, but could not. I got a man named Mr. More to take him and put him on his farm until I should come back. The man sold him because I did not come, and that was the last of my horse.

Here I saw Mr. C. W. Parrish again. I showed him the papers which I got from Secretary Schurz for my people and told him of my visit to Washington. He was so glad, and said, "Sarah, your people will be happy to get back." I told him the girls and boys that used to love his wife and children were all dead. I told him the names of many of them so that he could tell his wife. She gave them all names when she had them at school.

A reporter also called on me, and I told all he asked me. He gave me his address and said he would help me, and put any thing into his paper that I wished him to. I thanked him for his kindness.

Mr. Parrish told me I had better see to my stage passage the first thing or someone might get ahead of me. It was not a stage but a little wagon called buckboard, and would carry only two persons besides the driver. So I went and paid my fare and my sister's, fifty dollars. It went at six o'clock in the evening, and it took two days and nights to go to the Dalles. We were to start that same evening. We had a very hard ride, arrived all right, found brother Lee waiting for us, stayed in Dalles two days, and hired horses from Father Wilbur's Christian Indians. It took us two days to get to Fort Simcoe, which we reached on the eighth of May.

Father Wilbur was glad to see me. I did not say anything for four days, but brother Lee went and told everything to our people. They came every day to see me. I told them about our people in Nevada, but did not say anything about our visit to Washington.

At last I went to see Father Wilbur, armed with my letters. I said, "Father, I have come to talk to you."

He said, "Come in."

I went in and sat down. I said, "Did you get a letter from Washington?"

He said, "No."

"Well, that is strange. They told me they would write."

"Who?"

"The Secretary of the Interior, Secretary Schurz."

"Why, what makes you think they would write to me?"

"Father, they told me they would write right off while I was there. It was about my people."

He said, "We have not heard from them."

"Father, I have a letter here, which Secretary Schurz gave me." I gave it to him to read. He read it and gave it back to me. I saw he was angry.

"Sarah," he said, "your people are doing well here, and I don't want you to tell them of this paper or to read it to them. They are the best workers I ever saw. If you will not tell them, I will give you fifty dollars, and I will write to Washington and see if they will keep you here as interpreter."

I said, "How is it that I am not paid for interpreting here so long? Was I not turned over to you as an interpreter for my people? I have worked at everything while I was here. I helped in the school-house and preached on Sundays for you—I mean I interpreted the sermons." I told him I thought he ought to pay me something.

He said he would if I would not tell my people about Schurz's letter. I did not promise and went away. I did not say anything for five or six days. At last my people came and demanded of me to come to them. Brother and I went to them.

Leggins got up and said to his people, "My dear children, you all see that we have no friend. You all see that our mother has sold us to Father Wilbur. You see that she does not want to let us know what our father Winnemucca has done for us. We are all told that she has a paper which has been given to her by the mighty Big Father in Washington, and she has burnt it or hid it so we won't know it. That way she has made her money, by selling us. She first sold us to the soldiers and had us brought here, and now she has sold us to this bad man to starve us. Oh, we shall never see our friends anymore! Our paper is all gone, there is nobody to talk for us, we are all alone, we shall never get back to our sweet country."

The tears ran down his face as he talked, and women cried.

Brother could not stand it any longer. He jumped up and cried aloud, saying, "For shame! What are you talking about? Are you mad? Why don't you ask before you talk?" I had told Lee what Father Wilbur had said to me. "Go and talk to Father Wilbur, not to my sister. It is he who has sold us, not sister. It is he who don't want us to go back."

Some of the women cried out, "That's what we told them last night when they were abusing our mother. We knew she would not do such a thing."

Some of them came and laid their hands on my head and cried, saying, "Oh, mother, forgive us for thinking badly of you. Oh tell us, can we hope we shall see our husbands, our children, our daughters?"

I got up and held up the paper over my head, and said, "My dear children, may the Great Father in the Spirit Land will it so that you may see your husbands, and your children, and your daughters. I have said everything I could in your behalf, so did father and brother. I have suffered everything but death to come here with this paper. I don't know whether it speaks truth or not. You can say what you like about me. You have a right to say I have sold you. It looks so. I have told you many things which are not my own words but the words of the agents and the soldiers. I know I have told you more lies than I have hair on my head. I tell you, my dear children, I have never told you my own words; they were the words of the white people, not mine. Of course, you don't know, and I don't blame you for thinking as you do. You will never know until you go to the Spirit Land. This which I hold in my hand is our only hope. It came right from the Big Father you hear so much of. We will see what his words are—if what the people say about him is truth. If it is truth, we will see our people in fifty days. It is not my own making up; it came right from him, and I will read it just as it is so that you can all judge for yourselves."

After I had read it through, they all forgot they were grown people. They jumped about and cried, "Oh, we shall be happy again." The little girls said, "We shall sing, we shall play in our own playground." Men and women were all like children running to me with outstretched hands, saying, "Mother, forgive us for thinking bad of you."

Leggins said, "Now, you have heard what our mother has told us. We will get ready to go at once, and all that want to can go with me, and all that want to can stay. Step aside, so I may know who are going with me, and then we can go and find our Father Wilbur so he can go with us or send for soldiers to go with us."

Everyone cried, "Why ask us? We are all dying off here. Who wants to stay here? We will all go; yes, we will all go, if we have to crawl on our hands and knees."

All but Oytes. He sat with his hands over his face, crying. Paddy said to Oytes, "Why do you hang your head? Have you turned into a woman? You were first on your horse when the Bannocks came. You got us all into trouble, and only for you, we had been in our own country. You are the cause of all our suffering. Now it is no time to cry. I felt like crying when you got up and said, 'Come, my men, get your arms, we will help the Bannocks.' At that time there was only one who got up and said, 'Men, what are you all thinking about? Don't you all hear your chief talking to you, telling you not to go with the Bannocks or you will all be killed? He is telling you good things, and you dare to cry war?'"

As Paddy talked, he pointed and said, "That old woman sits there who said these things. She knew what our Chief Natchez was saying to us. We had ears to hear and knew what was said was truth. If we had listened to what was said to us, then we would not have lost so many of our friends. Now they have done more for us than we deserved, yea, more than we would do for them. I am as bad as you have been. They went so far to talk in your behalf, and because our mother has come with good news from the Big Father, you have to cry. Stop your crying and tell us what you are going to do."

Oytes got up and said, "Dear brother," but broke down again and could not speak. He stood a little while. He looked up to me and said, "Mother, pity me. Give me your hand. Help me. I am just as Paddy says, 'I am a woman'; I shall be while I live." Then he cried out to Leggins, "Oh, brother, ask me to go with you to our dear Mother Earth, where we can lie alongside our father's bones. Just say, 'Come'; I will be only too glad to go with you."

I then said, "This paper says all that want to go can go. I say for one, Oytes, come, go with us, but all who want to can go."

Then Leggins said, "Oytes, I have no right to say to you, 'You have done wrong and you can't go to your own country.' No, I am only too glad to hear you talk as you do. We will all go back and be happy once more in our native land."

Then they all said, "We will all go. Why leave one here?"

Then the head men said to me and to brother Lee, "We will go and see Father Wilbur right off, and tell him to send for soldiers to go with us to keep the white men from killing us."

So we all started up to see our good Father Wilbur.

Our father did not want to talk to us. My people came every day to see him for four days. During the time there came some goods for my people. The storehouse was full of goods of all kinds. He came to me and said, "Sarah, I had some forty of your people working for me since you went away, some women too. I want you to tell them to come and I will pay them right off. I have to pay them in clothing."

I went and told them. My people said, "Now is the time to talk to him," but he did not want to talk to them.

Some got blankets, some calico for their wives. Some said, "I worked two months. Some three months. We ought to get more pay."

These words were not listened to by Father Wilbur. Eighteen men got paid and six women, and the doors were shut. My people tried to talk to him.

I went to him and said, "My people want to talk to you." He did not answer me.

I went back to them. They all began to laugh at me, saying, "Ah! ah! Your father talks every Sunday saying we must not get mad or do anything that is not right."

"Now, he is the first to get mad at me," said Leggins. They all laughed again and went to their camps.

The next morning the agent sent for me. I sent for Leggins and some of the head men and went to his home. He gave me a chair to sit down in. Dr. Kirkendorff and the head farmer, Mr. Fairchild, were there. My sister ran off and told them I was sent for and they had better go quickly.

Then he began on me by saying, "I am sorry you are putting the devil into your people's heads; they were all doing so well while you were away, and I was so pleased with them. You are talking against me all the time, and if you don't look out I will have you put in irons and in prison."

Here I jumped on my war horse. I mean I said, "Mr. Wilbur, you forget that you are a Christian when you can talk so to me. You have not got the first part of a Christian principle about you, or you would leave everything and see that my poor, brokenhearted people get home. You know how they are treated by your Christian Indians. You are welcome to put me in prison. You are starving my people here, and you are selling the clothes which were sent to them, and it is my money in your pocket. That is why you want to keep us here, not because you love us. I say, Mr. Wilbur, everybody in Yakima City knows what you are doing, and hell is full of just such Christians as you are."

"Stop talking, or I will have you locked up."

"I don't care how soon you have it done. My people are saying I have sold them to you and get money from you to keep them here. I am abused by you and by my own people too. You never were the man to give me anything for my work, and I have to pay for everything I have to eat. Mr. Wilbur, you will not get off as easily as you think you will. I will go to Yakima City and lecture. I will tell them all how you are selling my people the clothes which were sent here for them."

I had my say and got up and went away. He tried to keep me, but I walked away. That is the last I saw of Father Wilbur. I almost wished he would put me in prison, for that would have made my people see that I had not sold them. He sent the doctor to talk to me and to tell me if I wanted to go home, he would send his own team down with me to the Dalles. I told him to tell Wilbur I was going to Yakima City first.

"Oh, Sarah, you had better not. The Yakimas have been telling Father Wilbur lies about you through Oytes."

I said, "I have had my say."

We all talked the thing over, and they said I had better go to the Dalles and send a telegram to the Big Father in Washington, and then come for them. My brother Lee thought so too.

Later the doctor came again and said, "Lee, Father Wilbur wants to see you."

He did not want to go. "I am afraid he will put me in irons too."

"Don't be afraid; go and see what he wants with you." He again said to me, "Well, Sarah, do you want to go to the Dalles? I will take you down myself if you will say you will go."

I did not talk to him but got up and went away until brother came back. He came back laughing. At last he said, "Oh, sister, I am rich. I am going to have some land, and I am going to have a wagon, and I am going to have my own time to pay for it. It will only take one hundred and twenty-five years for me to pay for my wagon. He wants me to stay here, not to go away. Yes, I see myself staying here. Leggins, Oytes, Paddy, come and have supper with us."

Just as we sat down the doctor came and said, "Sarah, Mrs. Young is going down tomorrow."

"Doctor, I am not going till I get ready; not until then. When I want to have you take me down, I will let you know."

We had another talk, and then I promised my people that

I would work for them while there was life in my body. I told them I would telegraph to the Big Father in Washington as soon as I got to the Dalles. I then told Lee to go to the doctor and say I would go. He came over himself to see me. We got to Dalles the second day. I went to the telegraph office and sent the telegram, as I said I would.

The two army reports will go in this book, where my readers will see how many were against me. I then wrote to General Howard, telling him I was so poor I did not know what to do. I told him Father Wilbur never gave me a cent for the work I had done for him. I did not have money enough to go down to Vancouver, where General Howard was. Oh, thanks be to my Spirit Father, General Howard sent for me. They appointed me interpreter and teacher at that place. There were fifty Indians, called the Sheep-Eaters, and some others. I taught their children how to read, and they learned very fast because they knew what they were learning. During this time I received the five hundred dollars, which I dearly earned during the Bannock War, after working two years for it. I then paid Mr. Stevens what he had given me at Camp Harney.

While we were doing so well, there came an order that these Sheep-Eaters and Weisers must go to Fort Hill Reservation. Lieutenant Mills and I took them there, and I left them there. I paid thirty-five dollars which they ought to have paid for me. I wrote to General Howard about it, and he told me how to get it. I did as he told me to; but as in other cases, I never heard from it.

I wrote to my schoolchildren afterward. The head man, who called himself War Jack, got someone to write to me, saying my children had forgotten what they had learned as they were not going to school anymore. That is the last I heard from them, and my work at Vancouver for the military government may be my last work, as I am talking against the government officials, and I am assured I never shall get an appointment as interpreter. I do have a little hope if the army takes care of my people that they will give me a place, either as teacher or interpreter.

I tell you, my dear readers, the agents don't want anybody but their own brothers and sisters, or fathers and mothers, wives, cousins, or aunts. If they do have an interpreter, they get one that is so ignorant he does not know what is said. Yes, one that can't read, one that is always ready to sign any kind of letter that suits his own purpose. My people have been signing papers for the last twenty-three years. They don't know what they sign. The interpreter tells them it is for blankets, coats, pants, shoes, socks, woolen shirts, calicoes, unbleached muslin. So they put their names to it while it is only a report of the issues he has already made. He knows well enough that if they were told it was the report of an issue, they would not sign it. This kind of thing goes on, on all the reservations; and if any white man writes to Washington in our behalf, the agent goes to work with letters and gets his men and his aunts and cousins to help him, and they get any kind of Indians to sign the letters, and they are sent on to Washington. Yes, General Crook tells the truth about the agents stealing from the Indians, and whoever tells this truth is abused by the agent. He calls him nobody, and the agent is believed, because he is a Christian. So it goes on year after year. Oh, when will it stop? I pray of you, I implore of you, I beseech of you, hear our pitiful cry to you: sweep away the agency system. Give us homes to live in, for God's sake and for humanity's sake.

I left my poor people in despair; I knew I had so many against me. While I was in Vancouver, Mr. Chapman, the interpreter, was sent over to Yakima to see if he could help my people. He met with the same success I had had. He came back and told me my people were really starving. He said he never saw people in the condition they were in. He said he went into their tents to see if they had anything hidden away. He did not find anything, but he said he did it because Father Wilbur told him the people had plenty to eat. Sometimes they went four or five days without having a thing to eat, nor had they any clothes. Poor man! The tears ran down his cheeks as he told me, and of course I cried.

Just then Colonel Wilkinson came up and said, "Why, Sarah, what are you crying about? You are only an Indian woman. Why, Indian women never cry."

Ah, my dear friends, he is another one who makes people believe he is working for Indians. He is at Forest Grove. He is another one that started a school for the Indians, something like Hampton School, but people will not send to him because they have not confidence in him. He is the man that used to preach in the streets in Portland, Oregon.

I tell you the world is full of such people. I see that all who say they are working for Indians are against me. I know their feeling pretty well. They know if the Indians are turned over to the army, they will lose their living. In another sense they ought to be glad to have Indians (I mean all my people, who are Indian nations) under the military care, for then if we kill white people, the soldiers can just kill us right there and not have to go all over the country to find us! For shame! For shame! You dare to cry out liberty when you hold us in places against our will, driving us from place to place as if we were beasts. Ah, there is one thing you cannot say of the Indian. You call him savage, and everything that is bad but one; but, thanks be to God, I am so proud to say that my people have never outraged your women or have even insulted them by looks or words. Can you say the same of the negroes or the whites? They do commit some most horrible outrages on your women, but you do not drive them round like dogs. Oh, my dear readers, talk for us, and if the white people will treat us like human beings, we will behave like a people, but if we are treated by white savages as if we are savages, we are relentless and desperate yet no more so than any other badly treated people. Oh, dear friends, I am pleading for God and for humanity.

I sent the following letter to the Honorable Secretary of the Interior:

VANCOUVER BARRACKS

MARCH 28, 1881

DEAR SIR,

I take this matter in hand in behalf of the Indians who are prisoners here at this place. There are fifty-three (53) in all. Of this number thirteen are men, twenty-one women, eleven girls from three to fourteen years of age, and eight boys from three to sixteen. Twenty-three of the number belong to the Sheep-Eaters, thirteen belong to the Weisers' tribe, and seven from Boise. These belong to Fort Hall. This is the second winter they have been here, and they have been provided for entirely by the military here. They receive government rations. But the only way they have to provide for the women is by what they make out of selling the savings of some of their rations, and from what castaway clothing I can collect from employees here. I am employed here as an interpreter, and have been teaching them to read. I commenced last July. I have twelve girls and six boys in school. When I commenced to teach them they knew nothing, never had been to school. They are learning fast. They can all read pretty well, and are desirous to learn. What I want to ask is to have them stay here. They seem to be contented. Most of them would rather stay here than to go elsewhere, but in order to make them more contented and useful it would be well to help them. If they could have a place, or a bit of land given them to use for themselves, yes, a place for their own benefit, and where they could work for themselves, I would teach them habits of industry, and it would help much in supporting them; and it is necessary that there should be, at least for the present, some appropriation made for them, in order to provide clothing for the women and children, and a proper place to live in. At present they are living in tents. The men are working for the military here in improving the post, and they all have an interest in them for their work, and I think a little help from your department, as above mentioned, would be better for them than to turn them loose again to wander in idleness or learn evil, or go back to bad habits again. I think it would be the best that could be done for them in the way of enlightening and Christianizing them. They would all rather be under the military authority. They say they are not cheated here, and they can see that the officers are doing all they can for them. Hoping you will give this a careful consideration, I am, sir, very respectfully,

　　Your obedient servant,

　　SARAH WINNEMUCCA

I never had any answer to this letter, nor to any of the letters I wrote to Washington, and nothing was ever done to fulfill the promise of Secretary Schurz's paper, nor was any canvas ever sent for tents. General McDowell, in the last army report issued before he was retired from the service in California and which he sent to me after I arrived in Boston, wrote an urgent appeal to the government to do justice to these my suffering people who had been snatched from their homes against their wills.

Among the letters from the officers, in the army report, are two or three from Father Wilbur. He says he should be much relieved if the Paiutes were not on his reservation. They have been the cause of much labor and anxiety to him. Yet he does all he can to prevent their going away. What can be the meaning of this? Is it not plain that they are a source of riches to him? He starves them and sells their supplies. He does not say much against me, but he does say that if my influence was removed, my people would be contented there. This is as untrue as it was of Reinhard to say they would not stay on the Malheur Reservation.

While I was in Vancouver, President Hayes and his wife came there, and I went to see them. I spoke to him as I had done in Washington to the Secretary and said to him, "You are a husband and father, and you know how you would suffer to be separated from your wife and children by force, as my people still are, husbands from wives, parents from children, notwithstanding Secretary Schurz's order."

Mrs. Hayes cried all the time I was talking, and he said, "I will see about it." But nothing was ever done that I ever heard of.

Finding it impossible to do any thing for my people I did not return to Yakima, but after I left Vancouver Barracks I went to my sister in Montana. After my marriage to Mr. Hopkins, I visited my people once more at Pyramid Lake Reservation, and they urged me again to come to the east and talk for them, and so I have come.

APPENDIX A

The following petition was written by Sarah Winnemucca Hopkins and introduced in the US House of Representatives by Rep. Ambrose Ranney of Massachusetts on January 24, 1884, where it was referred to the Committee on Indian Affairs. The text of the document can be viewed on the website for the History, Art, and Archives of the House of Representatives. https://history. house.gov/Blog/2018/March/3-26-Winnemucca-Petition/

WHEREAS, THE tribe of Piute Indians that formerly occupied the greater part of Nevada, and now diminished by its sufferings and wrongs to one-third of its original number, has always kept its promise of peace and friendliness to the whites since they first entered their country, and has of late been deprived of the Malheur Reservation decreed to them by President Grant:

I, SARAH WINNEMUCCA HOPKINS, grand-daughter of Captain Truckee, who promised friendship for his tribe to General Fremont, whom he guided into California, and served through the Mexican war, together with the undersigned friends who sympathize in the cause of my people, do petition the Honorable Congress of the United States to restore to them said Malheur Reservation, which is well watered and timbered, and large enough to afford homes and support for them all, where they can enjoy lands in severalty without losing their tribal relations, so essential to their happiness and good character, and where their citizenship, implied in this distribution of land, will defend them from the encroachments of the white settlers, so detrimental to their interests and their virtues. And especially do we petition for the return of that portion of the tribe arbitrarily removed from the Malheur Reservation, after the Bannock War, to the Yakima Reservation on Columbia River, in which removal families were ruthlessly separated, and have never ceased to pine for husbands, wives, and children, which restoration was pledged to them by the Secretary of the Interior in 1880, but has not been fulfilled.

[SIGNATURES.]

APPENDIX B

OMAHA, NEBRASKA

APRIL 3, 1883

TO ALL WHOM IT MAY CONCERN.

This is to certify that Sarah Winnemucca, now Mrs. Hopkins, acted for my department and troops in the field as guide and interpreter during the Piute and Bannock War of 1878. Her conduct was always good, and she was especially compassionate to women and children who were brought in as prisoners. After this war she worked as interpreter and teacher for quite a time near Vancouver Barracks, Washington Territory. In this capacity she gave abundant satisfaction to all who were interested in Indian children. She always appeared to me to be a true friend to her own people, doing what she could for them.

Since my departure from Washington Territory and her marriage with Mr. Hopkins, I have had no further knowledge of her except from the public press; but she is probably endeavoring

241

to do something for the upbuilding of the Indians as well as earning her own living.

OLIVER O. HOWARD

BREVET MAJ.-GEN., U.S.A.

NEW YORK CITY

APRIL 5, 1883

THIS IS TO CERTIFY TO WHOM IT MAY CONCERN.

That Sarah Winnemucca was instrumental in bringing her father and his immediate band of Piute Indians out of the hostile Bannock camp near Juniper Lake, Oregon, in 1878; after which she remained with General Howard's command and rendered good service as scout, guide, and interpreter, and in inducing members of her tribe to come in and surrender themselves. She is intelligent, and appreciates the position of her people, and is not insensible to their destiny.

C. E. S. WOOD, U.S.A.

AIDE-DE-CAMP AND ADJUTANT GENERAL OF TROOPS IN THE FIELD

BANNOCK AND PIUTE CAMPAIGN, 878

OFFICE OF INSPECTOR OF CAVALRY, HEADQUARTERS MIL. DIV. OF THE MISSOURI

CHICAGO

MAY 31, 1838

TO MRS. SARAH HOPKINS (SARAH WINNEMUCCA), 74 TEMPLE

ST., BOSTON, MASS.

MADAM,

In acknowledging the receipt of your note of the twenty-sixth of April, it affords me much pleasure to state that I do not hesitate to concur with Gen. O. O. Howard in indorsing and commending you to the favor and consideration of the philanthropic people of the country.

Wishing you success in your present endeavor, I remain yours sincerely,

JAMES W. FORSYTH
LT.-COLONEL

1606 VAN NESS AVENUE, SAN FRANCISCO, CAL.

APRIL 19, 1883

MRS. SARAH HOPKINS (NEE SARAH WINNEMUCCA),

CARE OF FIRST LIEUT. C. E. S. WOOD, U.S.A., 61 CLINTON PLACE, NEW YORK, N.Y.

DEAR MADAM,

I duly received your note of the 7th inst., and do not know that I can better comply with your request than to send you, herewith, a copy of the official papers concerning yourself, kindly given me by the Assistant Adjutant General at Hd. Qu. Dis. Pacific; and by today's mail a copy of the printed copy of the report of the General of the Army of last year, containing my last annual report of Oct. 14, 1882. You will see that in my last official act before being retired, Oct. 15, I endeavored to have justice done your people in exile on the Yakima Reservation.

All the papers sent will, I think, show that the army have tried to be just to you and yours.

I am very truly your most obedient servant,

IRVIN MCDOWELL,

MAJOR-GENERAL RETIRED, LATE COMMANDER OF DIV. PACIFIC AND DEPT. CAL.

AUTHOR'S NOTE:

That Gen. McDowell did his best "to be just to" my people may be seen by the following extracts from the army reports he sent me with the above letter, with marginal notes in his own handwriting.

OCT. 14, 1882

Before relinquishing the command I now hold, I am constrained to ask the attention of the war and interior departments to the case of certain Piutes who were taken away from their tribes and homes in California, and carried to an Indian reservation among a strange people north of the Columbia River. Their case is fully set forth in the accompanying papers," and he says in a marginal note in his own handwriting, that these "accompanying papers he alludes to were left out of the printed report, no reason being given." He continues, "It will be seen, as it appears to me, that the reasons which caused the refusal of my application to have these innocent and suffering people sent back to their tribe and homes, have been mere questions of administration, of convenience and economy, while I submit their return is a matter of good faith and mercy. The Indians in question (and a list of them is herewith) were not hostile. They had done nothing meriting punishment. During the war they were carried away from their homes, because it was easier to move them during hostilities than to have a force to protect them at their homes. They are held in exile against their wills. They are kindred to Winnemucca and his children Natchez and Sarah, who periled their lives and were indefatigable in doing everything for the whites and the army. I am thus earnest, and may, perhaps, be thought importunate, in arguing this question, because it arose under my command and by officers acting under me, and those people and their families and friends look to me to see their wrongs redressed. I have had visits from Natchez and Sarah, and messages asking me to have these people sent home. They have no representative, no newspaper to speak for them, and, even if they could get their cases before the courts, are ignorant of the way to bring it there. I beg the proper officers may look again into this question, not as a matter of convenience to the service, but one of justice to unfortunate and innocent people.

AUTHOR'S NOTE:

On page 123 in this army report is a letter from James B. Wilbur, United States Indian agent of the Yakima Reservation, to which those 502 Indians had been sent against their will, in which he says: "Their atrocities, committed without the slightest provocation when they took up the hatchet, deserve no favor." To this Gen. McDowell writes a marginal note, saying: "The Indians whom it wished to send back to their home did not commit atrocities as stated."

Gen. Miles, commanding at the headquarters of the Columbia, Vancouver Barracks, Washington Territory, writes:

To the Assistant Adjutant General, Presidio: I am informed that the Piute Indians, who have for the last two years been resident on the Yakima Reservation, have recently moved southward to near the Dalles. They send word they wish to rejoin Winnemucca. This matter has been the subject of correspondence between the interior department and the military authorities for the last two years. I believe a portion of them will attempt to rejoin their friends in the south, even without permission. From all the information I have been able to gather upon the subject, I am satisfied the best disposition for these people will be to send them, under safe escort, to Winnemucca's reservation, and I request authority to make such disposition.

Under date of Jan. 7, 1882, he had already written to division headquarters, as follows:

Many of the Indians taken from Malheur agency by the military and placed on the Yakima Reservation, were always loyal to the government. Since they have been on that reservation they have been living in a wretched condition, with very insufficient food and clothing. I doubt the wisdom or loyalty of this course on the part of the government officials; and, as I understand their reservation has been, or is to be given up, it would, in my opinion, be an act of justice and good policy to promptly restore these peaceable Indians to their people, those known as the Winnemucca Indians near Camp Dermot, or to the Warm Spring Reservation, where they have friends. This action, if prompt, may prevent an outbreak in the spring. In this connection, I enclose a copy of a recent communication from the interior department on the subject.

AUTHOR'S NOTE:

Other officers express a similar opinion to that of Gen. McDowell. On page eighteen of the Army Report is a letter relating to the return of the Piutes from the Yakima Reservation to their home in Nevada, from Major A. M. Randol of the First Artillery, to the Assistant Adjutant General of the Headquarters M. D. P. D. C., Presidio of San Francisco, Cal.:

WINNEMUCCA, Nv., Aug. 15, 1882.
Sir,

I have the honor to report that I have just had an interview with Natchez, who, in reply to the questions contained in your communication of the 12th inst., says that about forty-three lodges had left the Yakima Reservation and crossed the Columbia, with the intention of returning to Fort McDennitt or Winnemucca, but that the agent had sent an Indian sheriff after them, who had taken them all back to the reservation, where they now are; that none of these non-hostile Piutes have returned to their old homes. He further says that he has received several letters complaining of their destitute condition, and requesting him to try to have them returned to their old homes. He gave me the last letter he received from Lewis, which I herewith enclose, and which he wishes retu ed to him when you shall have finished with it. This letter contains about all that Natchez knows about the condition of his people at the Yakima Reservation. He says that if it be decided to let them return. to their old homes, that he will go after them and select the good from the bad; that he would like to see Gen. McDowell, and hopes he will send for him to come to the Presidio as soon as possible, so that if his people are to return home they may do so before the weather grows cold, etc. He further says that Oytes and his six lodges (about one hundred people) are hostile, and should not be allowed to return.

Very respectfully, your obedient servant,

A. M. RANDOL

AUTHOR'S NOTE:

Here is Lewis's letter (corrected in orthography).

JULY 1, 1882

MY DEAR FRIEND NATCHEZ,

It is long time since you have written to me. I hope you did not forgotten us. Are you trying anything for my people towards going to their old home? The Piutes have nothing to eat at the Simcoe Reservation. My people there are willing to go to the old home in the fort, if the government should let them go, and will never to fight again. You try hard and come to see us right away; or do your people don't care for my people anymore? Legon (Leggins), the chief, is almost blind, and Oytes don't want to go home to Camp Harney. My people want go; about forty-three lodges, and Oytes six.

Yours truly,

J. J. LEWIS

HEADQUARTERS MIL, DIV, PACIFIC AND DEPT, OF CALIFORNIA, PRESIDIO, SAN FRANCISCO

AUG. 12, 1882

Official copy respectfully furnished to Maj. A. M. Randol, First Artillery, who will stop at Winnemucca or Wadsworth an Lovelock stations on the Central Pacific Railroad, at whichever place Natchez, an influential Piute, is; and read him this communication, and inquire if he knows anything about the movement of his people, who were not engaged in the Bannock War, southward from Yakima Reservation. If any, how many of these non-hostile Piutes have returned to their old homes; how many of these nonhostiles still remain north of the Columbia River, and their condition, etc., and report fully all the information furnished by Natchez. By command of Major-General McDowell.

    J. C. KELTON,
    ASSISTANT ADJUTANT GENERAL

WAR DEPARTMENT, WASHINGTON CITY

JULY 22, 1882

TO THE HON. SECRETARY OF THE INTERIOR
SIR,

I have the honor to invite your attention to the enclosed copy of a telegram from the Commanding General of the Military Division of the Pacific, dated the 19th inst., stating that he is informed by the Commanding General, Department of the Columbia, that the Piutes who have for the past two years been resident on the Yakima Reservation have moved southward, and have sent word they desire to return to Winnemucca.

    General McDowell concurs with the latter that the best disposition of these people would be to send them under escort to the Winnemucca Reservation, and requests authority to do so.

Very respectfully, your obedient servant,
WM. E. CHANDLER
ACTING SECRETARY OF WAR

DEPARTMENT OF THE INTERIOR, WASHINGTON

JULY 29, 1882

TO THE HON. THE SECRETARY OF WAR
SIR,

Acknowledging receipt of your letter of 22d inst., inclosing copy
of telegram from Gen. McDowell, to the effect that the Piutes,
residing for two years past at the Yakima Reservation, Washington
Territory, have moved southward en route to Winnemucca, and
requesting authority to send these Indians under escort to the
Winnemucca Reservation, as in his opinion the best thing to do.
I have the honor to invite your attention to the report of the
Commissioner of Indian Affairs, of the 28th inst., on the subject
(copy enclosed) setting forth the reasons why these Indians should
remain at the Yakima Reservation, in which I concur.
Very respectfully,
H. M. TELLER
SECRETARY

DEPARTMENT OP THE INTERIOR, OFFICE OF INDIAN
AFFAIRS

JULY 28, 1882

TO THE SECRETARY OF THE INTERIOR
SIR,

I have the honor to acknowledge the receipt, by your reference, of a communication from the Hon. Secretary of War, dated 22d inst., calling attention to a copy of telegram from the Commanding General of the Military Division of the Pacific (Major-Gen. McDowell), dated the 9th inst., stating that he is informed by the Commanding General of the Department of the Columbia, that the Piutes, who have for the last two years been resident on the Yakima Reservation, have moved southward, and have sent word they desire to return to Winnemucca.

Major-Gen. McDowell concurs with the latter, that the best disposition of these people would be to send them, under escort, to the Winnemucca Reservation, and requests authority to do so.

In reply, I have the honor to respectfully report that no supplies have been provided for those Indians at any other point than at Yakima, and that there are no funds to do so. The agent at Yakima has been authorized to purchase $2,000 worth of cattle for the Piutes of that place, and I am of the opinion that the best interests of the Indians will be subserved by keeping them there.

I have the honor to report that the following telegram was sent to agent Smith of the Warm Springs agency, Oregon, this day:

> If Piutes come to your reservation, you must send them back to Yakima, and if they refuse to return, you must not feed them.

Also the following to agent Wilbur, at the Yakima Agency:

> Do all you can to have the Piutes return to your agency. I have telegraphed agent at Warm Springs to aid you.

> Very respectfully, your obedient servant,
> H. PRICE
> COMMISSIONER

AUTHOR'S NOTE:

General McDowell's appeal, it will be observed, was written after the foregoing correspondence between the office of the interior and the various army officers who were acquainted with the subject, and Father Wilbur of the Yakima Reservation. The reasons for and against the people being sent back to their homes, and all the counsels upon the subject, were known to Gen. McDowell; and still, at the late date of October, 1882, he gives it as his opinion that the government can only do justice to the banished Paiutes by restoring them to their own country. He acknowledges the inconvenience, of doing justice to them, but still thinks it the duty of the government.

I know now, from the highest authority, that the government was deceived by the agent, Reinhard, who said the Indians would not stay at the Malheur Reservation. After being driven away by starvation, after having had every promise broken, falsehoods were told about them, and there was no one to take their part but a woman. Everyone knows what a woman must suffer who undertakes to act against bad men. My reputation has been assailed, and it is done so cunningly that I cannot prove it to be unjust. I can only protest that it is unjust and say that wherever I have been known, I have been believed and trusted.

Those who have maligned me have not known me. It is true that my people sometimes distrust me, but that is because words have been put into my mouth which have turned out to be nothing but idle wind. Promises have been made to me in high places that have not been kept, and I have had to suffer for this in the loss of my people's confidence. I have not spoken ill of others behind their backs and said fair words to their faces. I have been sincere with my own people when they have done wrong as well as with my white brothers. Alas, how truly our women prophesied when they told my dear old grandfather that his white brothers, whom he loved so much, had brought sorrow to his people. Their hearts told them the truth. My people are ignorant of worldly knowledge, but they know what love means and what truth means. They have seen their dear ones perish around them because their white brothers have given them neither love nor truth. Are not love and truth better than learning? My people have no learning. They do not know anything about the history of the world, but they can see the Spirit Father in everything. The beautiful world talks to them of their Spirit Father. They are innocent and simple, but they are brave and will not be imposed upon. They are patient, but they know black is not white.

FORT BOISE, IDAHO TER.

AUGUST 31, 1878

TO ALL WHOM IT MAY CONCERN,

This is to certify that Sarah Winnemucca has rendered most valuable services during the operations of this year against the hostile Bannock and Piute Indians. About the commencement of hostilities, she went for me from my camp to that of the hostiles, distant about a hundred miles, and returned bringing exceedingly valuable information concerning their number, location, intentions, etc., and she also succeeded in getting her father, the Piute Chief Winnemucca, with many of his band, to leave the enemy and go to Camp McDermitt, Nevada, where they remained during the summer campaign.

    R. F. BERNARD

    CAPTAIN FIRST CAVALRY, BREVET COL. U. S. ARMY.

CENTRAL PACIFIC RAILROAD CO.,

SUPT,'S OFFICE, SAN FRANCISCO

FEB. 13, 1878

MRS. SARAH WINNEMUCCA
DEAR MADAM,

Yours of the 12th to Mr. Towne received. Mr. Emmons, our agent
at Lovelock's, said that Natchez applied to him for passes for
himself and others (including you) from Ogden to San Francisco,
and I sent them to him a few days ago. You had better see Natchez
and get your pass, and if you will show this letter to our conductors, they will also allow your sister to ride to San Francisco with
you on the pass. If you should not be able to see Natchez and get
your pass, our conductors will let yourself and sister ride to San
Francisco, by showing them this letter. When here, and you want
to go back, call and see me.

    Yours, etc.,
    E. C. FELLOWS
    ASST. GEN. SUPT.

HEADQUARTERS BATTALION OF CAVALRY, CAMP ON
FAYETTE RIVER,

SEPT. 5, 1878

During the late campaign against the Bannock Indians Sarah
Winnemucca has been with the various commands in the field,
and has to my knowledge rendered very valuable service. She is
entirely trustworthy and reliable.

In my opinion she is deserving of great credit for her conduct during the campaign.

GEO. B. SANFORD
BREVET COL. CAL. MAJ. 1ST CAVALRY.

CAMP HARNEY, OREGON

OCTOBER 28, 1878

TO ALL WHOM IT MAY CONCERN.

During the campaign against the Bannock, Piute, and Weiser Indians this summer, Sarah Winnemucca has rendered the troops valuable assistance, from the beginning of June until the tenth day of October (when she brought one hundred and ninety-five Indians from Camp McDermitt to Camp Harney). She has been constantly in the field, enduring hardships that strong men succumbed under. Her efforts in the beginning of the campaign in getting her father and a large portion of the hostile Indians deserve great praise. She is now employed as interpreter at this post and fulfills her duties to the satisfaction of all parties.

THOS. M. GREGOR
CAPT. FIRST CAVALRY

VANCOUVER BARRACKS

NOV. 7, 1879

MRS. SARAH WINNEMUCCA,

I have promised to put in writing some opinion as to your capabilities, and it gives me great pleasure to state that during the

Bannock campaign of 1878, and also later, you have displayed an unusual intelligence and fearlessness, and loyalty to the whites in your capacities of scout, interpreter, and influential member of the Piute tribe of Indians. Probably very few will ever know how much credit is due you for a successful ending of the war in the surrender of the hostile members of your tribe, and their subsequent settlement on the Yakima Indian Reservation; but it is with sincerity I say that in my opinion you were of very great assistance to General Howard and Agent Wilbur.

I am very truly your obedient servant,

C. E. S. WOOD

VANCOUVER BARRACKS, WASH. TER.

NOVEMBER 7, 1872

TO GEN. B. WITTELSEY, INDIAN COMMISSIONER ROOMS, WASHINGTON, D.C.

DEAR GENERAL,

Please do what you can to assist Sarah Winnemucca to have a fair interview with Mr. Stickney and also with the Commissioner of Indian Affairs, should her people send her to Washington. She was of the greatest assistance to us during the campaign of 1878, and has since been working hard for her people. They are on the Yakima Reservation partly—partly on the Warm Spring Reservation, and the remainder in Nevada, near Fort McDermitt.

Sarah is going now to see the chief, her father, and then may go on to Washington with some propositions. Mr. Wilbur, the Yakima Indian agent, thinks Sarah is now a Christian, and wishes me to assist her to prosecute her journey to Nevada, which I have gladly done. Of course she knows but little of city life, and your advice and kindness will be invaluable to her.

Very truly yours,

O. O. HOWARD

BRIG. GEN. U. S. A., COLUMBIA DEPT.

OREANA, HUMBOLDT CO., NEVADA

DEC. 3, 1879

HON. WM. M. EVARTS, WASHINGTON, D.C.
DEAR SIR,

The bearer of this, Miss Sarah Winnemucca, leaves here for Washington in behalf of her people. I have lived among them in my mining pursuits for something over a year, and have found them industrious, painstaking, self-sustaining, and dignified in their daily life; quick to see and learn, and intelligent enough to see why they have been the victims of the convolutions of the reservation plan as managed by the agents here. The community do not desire to have them removed, and they seem to have passed the point of needing "reservation" care. While their story of right and wrong may be outside of your official responsibility, I know it is a matter near your heart. Miss Sarah can tell better than any one else why her kindred should be let alone. As a citizen, I can say they have shown by their daily conduct that they deserve to be. She deserves the attention of our best ears at Washington.

Respectfully yours,

ROGER SHERMAN DAY

(SON OF SHERMAN DAY OF NEW HAVEN, CONN.).

THIS LETTER IS UNSOLICITED.

WASHINGTON, D.C.

JAN. 24, 1880

At the request of Mr. J. M. Haworth, of the Interior Department, the following statement is made concerning the services rendered the government by Sarah Winnemucca during the Bannock campaign in 1878. About the 12th of June, 1878, Captain R. F. Bernard, 1st Cavalry, was encamped with his company on the Winnemucca road near Sheep Ranch, I. T. While there he was directed by General O. O. Howard, commander of the department of the Columbia, to send Sarah Winnemucca into the hostiles' camp to communicate with the Indians, and endeavor to bring in all or a portion of her tribe, offering her a reward should she succeed. Sarah Winnemucca accepted the offer and went into the Indian camp, and succeeded in bringing out Chief Winnemucca and a portion of her tribe. She also furnished valuable information concerning the number of Indians and the position of their camp.

The reward offered was $500 (five hundred dollars).

JOHN PITCHER

LIEUT. FIRST CAVALRY

OFFICE OF INDIAN AFFAIRS, WASHINGTON

MARCH 29, 1880

SARAH WINNEMUCCA, LOVELOCK'S, NEVADA.

MADAM,

By reference of the Honorable the Secretary of the Interior, I am in receipt of your letter dated the 21st ult., in which you request that your people be furnished with subsistence until such time as

they can be removed to the Malheur Reservation, Oregon, and
you are advised that this Department is powerless to grant your
request, no funds being at its command to meet such expenditure;
but here is a large quantity of subsistence supplies at said agency,
from which issues will be made at once upon the arrival of your
people at that point; therefore, it will be for their interest to
remove at as early a day as possible.

Very respectfully,

E. J. BROOKS

ACTING COMMISSIONER

WASHINGTON

JAN. 26, 1880

SARAH WINNEMUCCA, PRESENT,

You are hereby appointed Interpreter for the Piutes at the Malheur
agency, Oregon, at a compensation of $420 per annum, from this
date. The agent has this day been notified of your appointment.

Respectfully,

E. A. HOYT

COMMISSIONER

HEADQUARTERS OF THE COLUMBIA, VANCOUVER
BARRACKS, W.T.,

JUNE 17, 1881

TO ALL WHO MAY TAKE INTEREST IN THE BEARER OF THIS LETTER,

Sarah Winnemucca, I desire to say: During the outbreak known
as the "Bannock War," Sarah Winnemucca served with General

Howard as a scout and guide, and rendered valuable service, as I know from my personal experience. After the capture of "the hostiles" she devoted herself to the interests of her people, the "Piutes," going with them from Fort Harney, Oregon, to the Yakima Reservation, then to Washington City, ever intent on trying to accomplish something for their good. For the past year she has held a school for the Indian children, at Vancouver Barracks with marked success. I have known Sarah Winnemucca for a number of years, and have never known her to do or say a thing that was not perfectly upright and womanly. She is honest, true, faithful, and worthy the respect and esteem of all good people. I earnestly recommend her to the kindly regard of all who wish well to her race.

> EDWIN C. MASON
> LIEUT.-COL. OF 4TH INFANTRY, ASSISTANT ADJT.-GENERAL.

WEST POINT, N.Y.

AUG. 6, 1881

DEAR SARAH,

I enclose you a letter to the Chief Clerk, Indian Bureau, whom I know. I have your account for transportation made out in good shape, in duplicate, and send it with my letter to Mr. Stevens, and I guess you'll get a favorable reply.

I cannot help you in the tradership for your brother-in law. The agent on the Reserve must recommend him.

We are quite well, and Mrs. Howard will be glad to hear from you.

> Sincerely your friend,
> O. O. HOWARD

SARAH WINNEMUCCA, SALISBURY, MADISON CO.,
M.T.

WEST POINT

OCT. 1, 1881

My Dear Sarah,

What are you doing now, and how are you getting on? I write to
ask you as a favor to me to please to write me out a description of
the way the Indian young men and women do their "courting,"
and the marriage ceremony, and also the burial of the dead. You
told me at one time, but I have forgotten. If not too much trouble,
please also write me a description of that flower festival you say
the Piutes have in the spring-time. Please ask Mr. Symons to give
you the paper, pen and ink.

    All here are very well. Yours truly,

    C. E. S. Wood

PRESIDIO, SAN FRANCISCO, CALIFORNIA

OCT. 5, 1881

To the Commanding General, Department of Columbia,
Vancouver Barracks, W.T.
Sir,

The Piutes on the Yakima Reservation, who desire to return to
their people, have been given permission to do so by the Interior
Department; but Sarah Winnemucca represents that they are afraid
to travel through the white settlements, without the protection of

troops. The Division Commander, therefore, desires that when-ever the movement of a command is ordered from their neigh-borhood towards Fort Boise you notify these Indians, and that they be safely conducted there.

    Very respectfully,

    J. C. BRECKENRIDGE

    BY COMMAND OF MAJOR-GENERAL MCDOWELL

WEST POINT

JAN. 9, 1882

DEAR SARAH,

I congratulate you upon your marriage. I hope your husband will be very kind to you and make you happy, as I doubt not you will try to do for him. He will tell you where you can apply for the Montana matter. I do not know. When your history is done, I will gladly aid you all in my power, though I have not much time to spare here. With the best wishes from Mrs. Howard and myself, I remain

    Yours truly,

    O. O. HOWARD

APPENDIX C

Note from the editor of the 1883 edition:

The last pages of the Appendix will show that the friends of the agents she criticizes are active to discredit her; but it has been ascertained that every definite charge made to the Indian office has no better endorsement than the name of Reinhard, who is characterized, to my personal knowledge, by some of the army officers who have known of his proceedings, as "a thoroughly wicked and unscrupulous man."

MARY MANN

[EDITORIAL OF BOSTON TRANSCRIPT, JULY 6.]

A DASTARDLY ATTACK. Sarah Winnemucca (Mrs. Hopkins) has been made the object of a villainous attack (calling in question her private character) in a paper called the "Council Fire," whose obscurity would render the article harmless had not marked copies been circulated through the mails among the people to whom she is appealing for defense for her distressed people against the Indian-agency jobbers who have been robbing them. The elaboration and ingenuity of the means employed to break down her reputation indicate that the attack comes from persons accustomed to working upon public opinion. At once, upon the article in the "Council Fire" coming to her knowledge, Mrs. Hopkins wrote to US Judge Bonnifield of Nevada, and received the following reply:

WINNEMUCCA, NEV., JUNE 19, 1883

MRS. SARAH HOPKINS (NEE WINNEMUCCA),

Yours of 10th inst., with an article from the May number of the "Council Fire," is received. In reply, I take pleasure in saying that I have known you personally and by reputation ever since 1869. Your conduct has always been exemplary, so far as I know. I have never heard your veracity or hastily questioned in this community, I handed the article or editorial of the "Council Fire" to the editor of the "Silver State," and send you herein his reply. I also mail you a copy of the "Silver State."

Your people have just closed a week's "Fandango" at this place. Nearly all the captains were present, besides a number of Shoshones and Bannocks. There were present about four hundred in all. Hoping you may succeed in your war upon the corrupt Indian ring, I am yours, etc.,

M. S. BONNIFIELD

THE INDIAN BUREAU ALARMED. Sarah Winnemucca, the Piute princess, is lecturing in Boston on what she knows about Indian agents. She is throwing hot-shot into the camp of the "peace policy hypocrites," who plunder the red man while professing to be his best, truest, and only friend. She knows by practical experience, acquired at several Indian agencies, that the Indians, with the exception of the head men, are cheated out of their annuities, and not infrequently driven to the warpath by the inhuman treatment of those who are paid by the government to care for their corporeal as well as spiritual wants. She is aware that the Indians at the Malheur Reservation, many of them members of her own tribe, joined the hostile Bannocks in 1878, because they could get nothing to eat at the agency, and were starving when the hostiles, loaded with spoils, invited them to join them. She also realizes the fact that the only time that the Piutes received what .the government provided for them was when the military at Fort McDermitt were intrusted with its distribution. Now, because she states, before an audience in Boston, what the whites in Nevada and on the frontier generally know to be facts, the "Council Fire," the Washington organ of the Indian Bureau, roundly abuses her, and styles her the "Amazonian champion of the army." Without attempting to refute or disprove her assertions, which it undoubtedly knows would be futile, it endeavors to break their force by attacking her character. It adopts the tactics of the ring organs generally, and instead of showing wherein she has misrepresented the Indian agents, it contents itself with slandering her, ignoring the fact that it is the Indian Bureau system, not Sarah Winnemucca's character, that the people are interested in and that is under discussion. She was with General Howard during the Bannock War, and though he had an opportunity of knowing more about her reputation for truth and veracity than the "Council Fire," he approves her views of the Indian question, and countenances her expose of the hypocrites, who, while pretending to be the truest friends of the Indians, cheat, starve, and abuse them, and apply the appropriations made by the government for the care of the Indians to their own uses. What Sarah Winnemucca says of Indian agents in Boston she has asserted before large audiences on this coast, where the Indian policy of the government is thoroughly understood, yet no agent has had the hardihood to publicly deny her statements through the newspapers or before an audience west of the Rocky Mountains. As she states, the true peace policy in dealing with the Indians is to place them under the care of the military, who, so far as experience teaches, deal fairly with them, giving them all that the government appropriates for their use, and holding their chiefs responsible for their good behavior. The "Council Fire" ought to know that scandalous charges against this woman, based on false affidavits of rascally Indian agents and their paid tools, are not arguments, and are no answer to her indictment of these agents, the truth of which is not questioned by persons conversant with the Indian agencies.

www.ingramcontent.com/pod-product-compliance
Lightning Source LLC
Chambersburg PA
CBHW022118080426
42734CB00006B/177